~~HELL~~ HOPE ON WHEELS

a memoir

BY
LL O'BRIEN

CHRISTMAS LAKE PRESS

Published by Christmas Lake Press 2025

www.christmaslakecreative.com

Copyright © 2025 by LL O'Brien

ISBN 978-1-960865-27-4

This book is a memoir and, while based on true events, reflects the author's present recollections of experiences over time. Some names and characteristics have been changed, some events have been compressed, and some dialogue has been recreated.

Interior layout by Daiana Marchesi

~~Hell~~ Hope on Wheels

Dedication

Dedicated to my husband Bernie, who has helped me laugh at the absurdity of life. YNWA

Acknowledgments

Thank you to everyone who read and re-read my manuscript. Your input was essential in the crafting of this story. Thank you also to Christine Wolf and the team at Christmas Lake Press. A special thanks to Corby Ward, the teacher who shared his summer cycling adventures with his classes. Your slide shows were the inspiration for all our cycling adventures.

Epigraph

"But we also boast in our sufferings, knowing that suffering produces endurance, and endurance produces character, and character produces hope, and hope doesn't disappoint us."
— Romans, 5: 3-5

Contents

AND HOPE DOESN'T DISAPPOINT

ROMANS 5:5

At 5:48 Monday morning, February 21, 1984, my life changed.

I was asleep in my own bed for the first time in two weeks. I'd been staying with my friend Macy's family while my father had been lying in a coma at Providence Hospital in Portland, Oregon. At a mere forty-six years of age, he'd had to have triple bypass surgery. To this day, my mother claims he was a tragic victim of heart disease. Bullshit—this was karma. After decades of a daily diet of three quarts of Blitz beer, two packs of Lucky Strike cigarettes, and crappy food, his arteries were clogged. He went under the knife on February 7, and after complications arose, he never regained consciousness.

I was barely sixteen when I got the news of his passing—and I felt hope for the first time in my life. Hope that perhaps life could get better, that a ray of light would shine into the void of my family's dysfunctional chaos.

During our father's hospitalization, my eight siblings and I had been adrift in a sea of uncertainty. My four older brothers and sisters—Henry, Jr. (called Junior), twenty-two; Meg, twenty-one; Lindsey, twenty; and Nate, nineteen—sat vigil in the hospital with our mother the entire time. While I was at Macy's, my four younger brothers and sisters—Matthew, twelve; Marc, eleven; Myrtle, six; and Emily, two—had been divided between family friends. Being isolated from my family wasn't new to me. As the middle child, I had been pushed aside for years, but being totally out of the loop at such a critical moment felt personal, even if it was of my own choosing.

The previous evening, Sunday, February 20, my mother and older siblings had returned home from the hospital knowing that Dad didn't have much time left. After dropping Mom and the others off at our house in Willamette, my older brother Nate picked up my younger siblings and me from the various homes where we'd been staying. On the drive back to the house, Nate didn't come right out and say Dad was dying; he just told me I needed to help clean the house in preparation for visitors. Maybe he couldn't bring himself to say the words because he didn't want to be the one to tell the little kids that our dad would never come home.

The house, having been empty for the two weeks my father was in the hospital, was in need of a deep clean. In truth, it had been neglected for quite some time. The months leading up to our father's death had not been prosperous, and the winter had been unusually cold. The lack of funds prevented my parents from purchasing heating oil or firewood, resulting in the whole house freezing. After months of frigid temperatures, even the insides of the windows were covered in ice.

I didn't set eyes on my mother that night because she'd retired early. After we took care of the younger kids' needs, the older kids and I spent several very tense and anxious hours cleaning. It was well after midnight by the time I finally crawled into bed. Once tucked away in my own room, it took forever to fall asleep due to a combination of anxiety, cold, and exhaustion.

After only a few hours of sleep, Lindsey shook me awake, saying, "Laura. Laura. Wake up. Dad died."

Still half asleep, I tried to get my bearings as Lindsey sat down on the bed across from mine. Almost five years older than me, Lindsey had the same dark hair, angular features, and green eyes as our father. I could tell she'd been crying and was struggling to compose herself. I propped myself up on my pillow, wondering if I was still dreaming as I tried to get my bearings, waiting for her to speak.

Looking across the room at my sister, I could feel her profound grief. The pain etched on her face made me uncomfortable, so I turned my gaze towards the window. The problem was that I didn't share her feelings. I did not feel grief. I felt relief.

As we sat in silence, I did my best to appear upset. A few moments later, she pulled herself together and told me Mom and the older kids would soon be driving up to Portland to pick up Grandma Jacobson, our father's mother. From there, they would go to the hospital and then come home. Lindsey's parting words were, "You stay here and watch the little kids. Don't tell them Dad died. That's not your responsibility."

"Okay," was the only response I could think of, and then she got up and walked out.

Left alone, I lay in bed looking at the ice patterns on the windows. I don't know how long I spent looking for a sign in the intricate concentric stars, trying to receive some supernatural guidance on how to proceed without letting anyone know my true feelings. I didn't feel guilty about how I felt. I just didn't want to create more drama. I had never delved into the same depths of denial my family exhibited towards our father's alcoholism and abusive behavior. I'd experienced firsthand his cruel and sadistic nature and was incapable of seeing him as anything but the asshole that he was. The real trick over the next few hours, days, weeks, months, and years was how to hide my true feelings. I knew the harsh consequences of giving voice to my truth. It was only after I got older that I realized the damage I did to myself by keeping shtum. Hindsight can really suck at times.

When it became apparent the ice wasn't offering any divine secrets, I roused myself out of bed, threw on a sweatshirt, and waited. I didn't want to see my mother or older siblings before they left the house. For as long as I could remember, my relationship with my parents and older siblings had been full of conflict. My unwillingness to conform to the accepted gender norms set by my parents had been our household's single biggest cause of unrest.

My older sisters, Lindsey and Meg, had embraced our parents' conservative gender roles, which dictated the girls were to wear dresses, clean the house, and take care of the younger children, while the boys did nothing. I didn't look or behave like my older sisters. I was small for my age, and had short, dark, curly hair and big blue eyes. I was a mouthy tomboy who chose to defy my parents' expectations.

By the time of Dad's death, I was the oldest girl living at home and begrudgingly provided childcare and did household chores. The dresses? Well, they could shove the dresses up their proverbial asses. As punishment for my refusal to be a "normal girl," I had been labeled a dyke by my father from about the age of eight, a label that my older siblings latched onto. So, no, I did not want to see or speak to them before they drove off together. I had no desire to share in their collective pain.

To waste a little more time, I went over and opened the window and spent several moments looking out over the neighborhood. It was early, still dark, and unusually soundless. Normally, the buzz of the local lumber mill filled the air, but on this morning, all was quiet. Our neighbors' homes were dark and a light frost covered their rooftops. I envied the peacefulness within their houses. I could only assume they were still nestled in their beds all warm and cozy. The sound of my older siblings and mother getting into the car and driving away broke the solemnity of the moment. Once I knew they were gone, I made my way downstairs, went into the kitchen, fixed myself a cup of tea, and sat down at the dining room table.

The emptiness of the house weighed heavily. I was alone but trapped in the middle. As the older half of our family mourned together in a car headed to Portland, the four younger children were sound asleep, ignorant of all the chaos that would soon unfold around them. As I sipped my tea and took in my surroundings, under my breath I muttered, "Well, fuck it"—the best pep-talk I could come up with for myself.

During that time, I came to the conclusion that I would tell my little brothers that Dad had died. The more I thought about Lindsey's directive, the more pissed off I got. What a horrible position to be placed in. Her expectation was that I should just sit on this information and lie by omission. There was no way I was going to keep the truth from them. What Lindsey and the others didn't understand was that Matt and Marc were a hell of a lot stronger than they were given credit for.

Eleven months apart, Matt and Marc were known as "the little boys." Although they looked completely different, most people assumed they were twins. Matt, the older of the two, was a lanky, handsome boy with blond hair and blue eyes, while Marc had an impish quality with the same dark hair and green eyes as our father. It had been two years since the older kids had lived at home, and to them, "the little boys" were still two youngsters who ran around with towels tied around their necks playing Batman and Robin.

During the years of our older siblings' absence, a lot had changed in our household, and Matt and Marc were no longer young and naïve. The three of us had lived through the worst of our father's alcoholism and abuse. Plus, we had ringside seats to the chaos that was our parents' marriage. We had been through too much together, and I wasn't about to lie to them now.

About an hour later Matt and Marc emerged from the basement together. They didn't actually have a bedroom; they slept wherever they landed. Once they joined me at the dining room table, Matt asked, "Where is everyone?"

I replied, "Dad died early this morning and they've gone up to get Grandma and then go over to the hospital."

In resigned disbelief, Marc said, "So, he died, and no one bothered to wake us. They just left?"

"I was *instructed* to not say anything to you, but I thought that was bullshit."

The boys began to cry, and I wanted so badly to ask why they were crying. I didn't understand their grief. Instead, I chose to remove myself by going into the kitchen to make us all some tea. A hot, sweet cup of Lipton's and the space to cry was all I could offer.

I put the kettle on to boil and leaned back against the counter. That was when I noticed the cigarette burns on the countertop. Dad would rest his Lucky Strikes on the edge of the counter and forget about them, leaving marks all around the kitchen and any other flat surface in the house. The burn marks were a reminder that the scars he had inflicted would remain long after his death.

Once the water boiled, I made three cups of tea and brought them into the dining room. We drank our tea in silence. When their eyes were dry and our cups empty, the three of us decided it would be best if our mother broke the news to the little girls, Myrtle and Emily. We agreed they were too young to grasp the magnitude of the situation.

Later that morning, the little girls tumbled out of bed in their nightgowns, with tousled blonde hair and sleepy eyes. Neither asked any questions as they immediately went to the television and turned on their morning cartoon show. I had been their childcare provider during the summer and while my mother worked in the evenings. Therefore, it wasn't a surprise to them that I was the lone adult in the house. As the designated caregiver, I fixed us all a quick breakfast of cold cereal and juice, which we all ate in front of the television together, crunching on Corn Pops while watching Bugs Bunny and Daffy Duck. It was a perfect metaphor for a crazy day—*Looney Tunes.*

Our peaceful time together was shattered when our mother and the others returned home around noon. Mom went directly to her bedroom and shut the door. She clearly did not want to speak to anyone. I can only assume that she had Junior tell the four younger kids because she couldn't bring herself to do it. I always wondered what was discussed on that car ride that day. Some kind of decision must have been made about who would tell the little kids. Then again, maybe Junior just decided to take charge of the situation.

Junior spoke to the boys first. They played along and didn't tell him that they already knew. They could've won an Oscar for their performance. By this time, Matt, Marc, and I had been lying about so many things that deceit just came naturally.

After speaking to Matt and Marc, Junior took the little girls on a car ride to tell them that their dad was dead. While he was gone, the rest of us just went about our business. The little boys went down the street to shoot baskets. I hung out in the living room with Meg, Lindsey, Nate, and Grandma, but they weren't talking. The atmosphere in the room was thick with emotion. Feeling like I would suffocate if I sat there any longer, I went up to my room. I had just shut my door when I heard the front door open, little feet run through the house, and a door slam.

I went back downstairs and could hear Myrtle crying behind the closed door. I was shocked by the rawness of her emotions. She obviously grasped the concept of death and felt real grief. The only time I cried that day was while I was standing in the hallway listening to Myrtle because I felt so damn powerless. I knew that there was nothing I could do for her, and that she needed her mother, who had chosen to take the easy road of isolation. Just when I was beginning to get pissed off with Mom for abandoning her children, she moved past me and went in to comfort her little girl. It was the only time I saw my mother comfort any of her children that day. Or any day after.

Later that afternoon, Mom, Grandma, and the older kids went to the funeral home to make arrangements. Again, I was told to stay back and take care of the little kids. That was my designated role—stay out of the way and do what you're told. As the day wore on, my opinion of my older brothers and sisters did not improve. I had been the oldest child at home for years, but once they were on the scene it was like, "Fuck off, we're in charge." My deep-seated resentment of them was in full bloom, but there was very little I could do to fight back. I had never won a fight with any of them, and that day would be no different. I simply found it easier to follow their directions, regardless of my feelings.

When they returned an hour later, Lindsey told me the memorial service would be held at one o'clock that coming Friday. We had the better part of a week to plan a service and make arrangements for a reception afterwards. I wrongly assumed I would be included in the planning. The only time my mother said a word to me that day was to tell me that I was to go back up to Portland with Grandma Jacobson and stay with her until she was ready to return. I was being dismissed. She had been sending me away since I was nine, and each time she might as well have said, "Get the fuck out of my face."

From the moment I was sent to Portland, and for the next four years, my life became a race against my past. I ran from the Pacific Northwest, to New York, to Brazil, to Europe and just about every place in between. Every leg of the race brought me one step closer to liberation, but it wasn't easy. It didn't matter *where* I was running. I always had the same opponent—myself.

Chapter 1

MRS. FLOSSY'S WILD RIDE

An unattractive woman, Grandma Jacobson stood 4'10" and had a neck like a bullfrog. Her first name was Florence, and behind her back all of us kids called her Flossy the Frog, or just Flossy. Flossy wasn't exactly the warm, fuzzy, cookie-baking sort of grandma—quite the opposite. She viewed herself as the matriarch of the family and deemed it her responsibility to form her grandchildren into proper ladies and gentlemen. My unwillingness to conform to her expectations of femininity meant she was constantly on my case. From an early age she would deride my appearance with the added instruction, "You are a lady before you are a woman," to which I would respond, "What the hell are you talking about? How is that even possible?"

The idea of spending time alone with her on a normal day was bad enough, but to be sent away on the day of my father's death felt like a punishment. Not to mention that I had to be a passenger in her car, which was literally putting my life at risk.

Flossy was born in 1905, long before cars were a thing and back when the DMV didn't exist. In the 1920s she sent away for a driver's license, which she received in the mail. Therefore, she never actually took a driving test. If she had, she would have been a frequent user of mass transportation. She really needed driving lessons, but no one had the courage to tell her. Not to mention that her short stature prevented her from seeing over the steering wheel and her glaucoma compromised her vision. Her limited visibility caused her to "braille drive" on the freeway. My family called it braille driving because she would swerve into the other lanes, the tires would *thump thump thump* over the white reflectors, and then she'd sharply pull back into her lane. God, it was like driving with Mr. Magoo.

During the ninety-minute drive from Willamette to Portland, we barely spoke. Despite my frustration with my grandmother, I could only imagine the grief she was experiencing. My father was her only child, and her husband had died when Dad was eighteen. My mother and the nine of us kids were all the family she had left. There was so much that could have been discussed on that ride, but we chose silence. I spent most of the time staring out the passenger window of her '79 Dodge, praying we would reach her house safely and thinking about just how everything had gone wrong for my folks.

Even in their mid-forties, my parents appeared to be a young, successful, professional couple living the American dream. Our mother had the look and style of Julie Andrews, petite, with piercing blue-gray eyes, short, curly sandy blonde hair, and a perpetual mischievous expression on her face. Our father was on the shorter side, slight with dark hair. His mean, green eyes were the only sign of his true nature, which were well hidden behind horn-rimmed frames. The combination of his glasses, tweed jackets, button-down shirts, and khaki pants created the look of an intellectual. They had met in 1957 at one of Dad's fraternity parties during his third year at Washington State University, in Pullman. My mother, then a sophomore at University of Idaho, was studying education and belonged to the Kappa Alpha Theta sorority. They must have hit it off, because by September of 1959, they were married.

Within the first five years of their marriage, they had four children. During that time they moved to Willamette, Oregon, so Dad could attend law school in Salem. To support the family, Mom taught elementary school. Soon after Dad graduated, he was hired as the assistant district attorney for the county. With little debt and two incomes, they were able to purchase a large, four-bedroom, two-story home a block away from the courthouse. By the time I was born in 1968, Dad had been appointed the Willamette County District Attorney and Mom was the community's beloved fifth grade teacher. Between 1971 and 1981, they had four more children, securing my unenviable position as the official middle child of nine.

The dysfunction of our family was easily concealed. From the outside, we looked like the Kennedys of Willamette. We lived on the corner of a quiet street, which made it the perfect setting for a baseball diamond. On any given day there was a tribe of us kids out playing ball. The only requirements were a tennis ball, bat, and the desire for a game. Due to the critical mass of children in our own home, most of the neighborhood kids would soon join us. Unfortunately, the same youthful exuberance on display outside didn't carry into our home.

Behind closed doors, a whole different scenario unfolded. Our father had a cruel and vicious side, which he unleashed on his children. For instance, during bath time, Dad would hold our heads under the water just to watch us squirm. For fun, he encouraged bare-knuckle fights between the little boys in our living room.

When he was really bored, Dad pitted one child against another and provoked physical confrontations. After watching a fight break out, he "restored order" by holding court in the basement where the fighting parties were required to present their case to the judge (Dad) and jury (my older brothers and sisters). These trials were absolute bullshit.

Matt and I found ourselves facing trial a number of times. Although Matt was younger than me, he was stronger. The older kids encouraged him to goad me into a fight by either hitting or spitting on me. I'd retaliate with a roundhouse punch and all hell would break loose. Once the fight was broken up, we'd be ushered into court to face the biased jury.

The last time I appeared in basement court, I made my feelings known. Instead of presenting my case, I said, "You're a load of fuckers and this is all bullshit. Matt and I would get along fine if you'd just leave us alone. Fuck off!"

My boldness took everyone by surprise, and the judge ruled that I was in contempt of court for using foul language and sentenced me to an evening in my room. Perfect. I really didn't want to be around anyone.

I have no fond memories of my dad since he endlessly scared the crap out of me. In the silence of Flossy's car that day as we drove to Portland, I wondered why he'd been so damn mean. Was he always mean, or had it been the alcohol? As I sat in the front seat holding on for dear life, I wondered about my dad's childhood. I looked over at Flossy, who had just missed sideswiping a car by inches, and realized that she wasn't the type of person I could have an honest conversation with. I decided to let her focus on the road.

By my second year of high school, all that was left of my folks' American dream was a façade of success. Over the years, Dad had found himself in the middle of a number of political scandals, and by 1980, he'd lost his position as the district attorney. He joined a law firm in a neighboring town, but by 1984, he was a barely functioning alcoholic, incapable of managing his own affairs. As district attorney, he received his salary from the county, and his two competent secretaries kept him organized. In private practice, he found it difficult to keep track of his billing hours or send out invoices, which meant he wasn't bringing in money to the firm or our household.

Mom worked three jobs just to keep us afloat. Aside from teaching fifth grade, she taught GED classes two nights a week. During the summer she taught English as a second language classes at the local community college. The extra income wasn't enough to pay all the bills and support an alcoholic's lifestyle. By the time Dad died, we were so broke that we'd resorted to stealing our neighbor's firewood just to heat our home.

At this time, the four older kids were in college, paid for with their summer earnings from the local cannery, and miles from home, and my parents kept them in the dark concerning the realities of our economic straits. When the older kids returned for the holidays, my parents went to great lengths to plaster over ever-widening ruptures. To hide the severity of the situation, Mom purchased a hundred dollars' worth of heating oil and went grocery shopping so that for the few weeks everyone was home, the house was warm and the pantry full.

When the older kids returned to school, the austerity measures were put back into place. The heating oil would run dry and once again the only sources of heat were an open electric stove in the kitchen and whatever firewood Matt and Marc could steal, a skill that they would come to rely on later. Mom and Dad never outright told us to keep the truth from the older kids; we just instinctively knew to keep our mouths shut.

My parents' duplicity created a wealth of problems between my older siblings and me. The four older kids believed in the fairytale our parents created for them, and when they were around it was almost true. The problem was that I knew the truth and resented the whole situation. The number of times I watched my mother write checks for my older brother's fraternity dues was maddening. We were freezing our asses off half of the year because there wasn't enough money for firewood and heating oil—yet there was enough money for fraternity dues? Really?

With every one of their visits to our house in Willamette, I saw that my parents' pride took priority over those of us still living at home. I knew that one of the reasons Mom sent me to Flossy's that day was because my presence was a threat to the false narrative she wanted to create. I was aware of all of her secrets, and she couldn't risk me messing up her illusion.

When Flossy and I left Willamette, I was under the impression that we'd be returning the next day. It was only later that evening when I overheard one of her phone conversations that I discovered I'd be in Portland for three days. Hearing secondhand how long I'd be separated from my family was a punch in the gut. Mom, who'd been too distraught to speak to us that day, knew damn well what she was doing when she sent me to Portland. Any compassion I had for her that day went out the window. Lois may have looked like Mary Poppins, but she could be as cold as Nurse Ratched.

Flossy not only looked like a toad, but in her sleep, she croaked like one. Her snoring was so loud that the walls in the guest room, where I tried and failed to sleep, vibrated. I spent the time looking at the ceiling hoping for some kind of spiritual direction, but once again I was left hanging, wrestling with loneliness and the reality of Dad's death.

The last time I saw my dad was the afternoon before he left for the hospital. I hadn't realized that he was leaving that afternoon for his bypass procedure and had called him an asshole. He refused to give me a few dollars to purchase a folder for my sophomore science project. Before he could say anything, I went up to my room and slammed the door. A couple hours later I made my way back downstairs and discovered that Mom and Dad had left for the hospital. On the dining room table there was a new folder and a note from Mom instructing me to feed the younger kids dinner and to make sure they all got off to school in the morning. Almost as an afterthought, she added that my oldest sister, Meg, who lived in Salem, would help me with the little kids the next night.

The next day, everything went to plan until Dad didn't wake from his surgery. That evening when Meg joined me, she explained that Dad wasn't coming out of the anesthesia, and the doctors were worried. She went on to tell me that I wasn't to say anything to the younger kids. That evening we did our best to pretend that everything was fine while we prepared dinner and put the younger kids to bed. When Dad didn't wake up the following day, Meg and I found places for the younger kids and me to stay so she could go back up to the hospital. Two days later, my mother summoned me to the hospital through family friends, Phil and Mavis, who drove me to Portland.

I was not prepared for the scene that I found at the hospital. Mom, Grandma, the older kids, and a few of the older kids' friends had been camped out in the ICU waiting room for days. It was like walking into some kind of exclusive vigil. Mom, sitting on a sofa between Junior and Nate, looked up at me and said, "I am so glad you came." It was like she was speaking to a family friend and not her daughter.

While I tried to come to terms with Mom's detachment, and the chaos of the waiting room, Lindsey walked in and said, "There still isn't any change."

It dawned on me she must be talking about Dad. I wanted to see him so I could get some idea of what was going on, but when I asked my mother if I could go into his room, she looked at me and said, "No. I don't think that would be a good idea." I knew Mom too well, and once she said no, there really wasn't any arguing. At that point, I did the one thing that I really didn't want to do in front of everyone. I cried.

Lindsey thought that my tears were for Dad and led me to the hospital chapel so she could comfort me. I didn't want to go to the fucking chapel, and I didn't want Lindsey's sympathy. I wanted to go home. Instead, I found myself sitting on a hard bench in a small, dark room with an altar and a huge crucifix. Lindsey droned on about how Dad was suffering like Jesus on the cross.

I looked at her and realized, not for the first time, that she was fucking delusional. We were not a religious family, but I had a slim understanding of Jesus. If Dad and Jesus were two peas in a pod, then Jesus could go to hell.

I turned my attention to the suffering Jesus and felt nothing. There he was, hanging from the cross, bloody, beaten, and dead. He looked powerless, and I wondered what some guy's death on a cross thousands of years ago had to do with the crap that had gone down in my family over the years. Where was suffering Jesus when Dad tortured us? I couldn't adopt Lindsey's reconstruction of our father into some kind of suffering servant, so I left the chapel.

I spent the rest of the day watching other people, both family and friends, go back to my father's room, and that's when the real reason I'd been summoned dawned on me—my staying in Willamette wasn't a good look. What if people in town began to wonder why I wasn't with the family? I wasn't brought here to give and receive support during this difficult time; I was here to help Mom save face. Once I put two and two together, I caught a ride back to Willamette and never went back to the hospital. I couldn't give a damn what people in town thought. I wasn't going to sit in a waiting room with a group of people who didn't want me there in the first place.

Lying awake in Flossy's guest room with her snores as background noise, I had never felt more alone. I wondered if my family back in Willamette even realized I was gone. I sincerely doubted it.

The day before the funeral, I survived Mrs. Toad's wild ride back to Willamette. I walked into my home and found it full of family and friends. A large group sat around the dining room table, so I pulled up a chair and joined them, and that was when I discovered that, in my absence, my family had been hanging out sharing stories. One of the ladies sitting next to me turned to me and said, "Last night I was here while the family sat around talking about your father. It was such an honor. Where were you last night?" I told her I had been in Portland with our grandmother. Then I got up and went into the kitchen.

The resentment that I had towards my mother was turning into pure anger. In the kitchen, I found a number of liquor bottles lined up behind the burn marks on the counter, so I poured myself a rum and Coke.

I'd been drinking for years, but in that moment, I began to abuse alcohol. The relationship between my family and me was like the burns on the countertop, the wounds of those relationships scorched deep into my soul. I was discovering that Dad's death would not be the miracle healing salve that I had hoped for. I did not experience the great wave of peace and forgiveness I'd hoped to feel. Instead, I felt rage. All was not well, and the only thing that numbed my pain was alcohol.

Unlike my father, I wasn't a mean drunk. Alcohol allowed me to create an alter ego where I became a person who could just go with the flow. I became a person that could easily laugh at myself and at the absurdity of life instead of getting angry. Booze made me more engaging and entertaining, and created a safe façade behind which the "real" me could hide. That is, until it no longer works and the weight of reality destroys the illusion.

Chapter 2

A TALE OF TWO HENRYS

The night before the service, my older siblings and I drank too much and stayed up too late. Drinking with my siblings wasn't unusual for me. The older kids would forget just how much younger I was than they were, and I had been taking advantage of their lapse in memory to acquire alcohol since I was twelve.

In junior high school, I discovered it was easier to be around the older kids if I had a good buzz on. That night, with my anger and resentment right under the surface, I used alcohol to keep my feelings at bay, which meant that the morning of the service I was hungover.

There were twelve people staying in our home, and most of us were feeling pretty rough that morning. The house felt like the inside of a pinball machine. We were bouncing off of one another, getting in each other's way and on each other's nerves. Flossy barking orders at us didn't help. Somehow, we managed to get our shit together before the service began without a major argument erupting. A small miracle.

We only had two cars at our disposal that day, so there wasn't enough room for everyone to drive to the church. To make room for others, Nate, Lindsey, and I walked the six blocks to the First Presbyterian Church on Hayter Street. I used that time to clear my head.

Our journey took us past the ivy-covered courthouse with its clocktower, then through the middle of town. All the familiar landmarks seemed so bleak. There had been a time in the '70s when Willamette was a thriving mill town. The main street had two women's dress shops, a shoe store, jewelers, drug stores, JC Penney's, and numerous cafés. By 1984, most of the businesses had closed and were replaced with thrift stores. The town had acquired an aroma of musty old clothes.

On the way to First Presbyterian, I asked Lindsey and Nate if they found it ironic that Dad was having a church service.

Aghast, Lindsey looked at me. "Where else would his service be?"

Nate gave me a look that said, *Shut up.*

So, I dropped it. Still, I was amazed that his service was being held in a church. On a good day, it may have been safe to call my dad an agnostic. I knew of his belief system from listening in on his conversations with my older siblings during their holiday breaks. All the older kids were studying political science, and at times, they would delve into the deism of our Founding Fathers. I came to understand that Dad subscribed to the belief that God was like a giant watchmaker who put the universe into motion and then stood back and watched life play out. It was during these conversations that I caught an inkling of what my father had once been. Those moments revealed a well-read, intelligent man who was interested in his children. I craved that kind of relationship with my father, but it would never be. Whereas my older siblings knew a father who could be attentive, and perhaps at times abusive, I knew a man whose addictions destroyed his life and twisted him beyond repair.

At the church, Nate, Lindsey, and I were sent to the basement to wait with the rest of the family. Years before, my mother had been a member. She even had all of us kids baptized. I had a vague memory of going to Sunday school in the musty basement where they served Oreo cookies and Hawaiian Punch. I could picture Matt and Marc sneaking around the cookie table, pocketing extra Oreos.

With only a tentative connection to the church, I really didn't feel comfortable in the building. It possessed a coldness that permeated everyone and everything. Even when friends snuck into the basement to share their condolences, their quick embraces felt like ice. I just wanted to get on with the service and get the hell out of there.

At one o'clock, the pastor escorted us to the sanctuary, which overflowed with people from the community, including Mom's friends and colleagues, most of the attorneys in town and their wives, and many of our school friends. An usher led us to the front two pews. Mom sat with Flossy and all the boys. The girls sat in the second row, which seemed about right—we always took a backseat to the boys.

Upon taking my seat, I took in our physical surroundings. The inside of the sanctuary was even colder than the basement. The pews and floors were all hardwood. The only sign of light came through the stained-glass windows that lined both sides of the building, but the blues and reds of the glass only made the space feel colder. Just like in the chapel at Providence Hospital, I had no sense of God in this space. What I felt were hundreds of eyes watching our every move.

I turned to Lindsey and said, "God. I can't believe how many people are here."

"Well, what did you expect?" she replied. "He was a much-loved member of the community."

Again, it dawned on me that Lindsey was nuts.

Dad was not a much-loved member of the community. If he was so loved, why had he lost the election to remain district attorney? If he was so well-loved, why were people so intimidated by him? Love was not what brought people to the church that day. It was the drama of the situation that gathered us all together. Dad had left a forty-five-year-old widow with nine children, which made Mom the town martyr. Sure, some people came to pay their respects, but I felt others just came to gawk.

My attention soon turned to the people sitting in the pews near us. There was a sniffle here and there and plenty of talking in whispers. All of a sudden, someone behind us began sobbing. Lindsey heard it too, because she poked me and said, "Check that woman out."

I turned around to look and my stomach sank. I recognized the woman. I had seen her once before. One afternoon on a school day when I should have been in class, I had decided to go home. When I walked up to the front door of our house, I saw her through the window, sitting on the couch with Dad. They didn't see me at first, and then the woman noticed I was standing there. Dad turned around to look, and I figured there was no turning back, so I walked in. No introductions were made, and I said, "Um. I'm not feeling well. I'm going to lie down."

Dad made some kind of reply and I went up to my room. A few minutes later, I heard them leave and I went back downstairs. I knew something was going on but kept the whole thing a secret. By this time, I was keeping so many secrets from so many people, I figured what was one more?

Now, that same woman was making a scene. As she progressed from sobbing to outright hysterics, two attorneys escorted her out of the church before the service even began. "Man, she's really upset," said Lindsey.

"She sure seems to be," I replied, and left it at that. I wasn't about to share my secret with anyone that day, but inside I wanted to shout, "Pull your head out of your ass, Lindsey. Why do you think she's so upset?"

The hypocrisy of Dad's memorial service made me nauseous. Judge Franklin, a close friend of my parents', gave the eulogy. He was a handsome, distinguished man and actually well respected in the community. He spoke of Dad's honesty and integrity by sharing anecdotes of Dad in his courtroom. Like everyone else in the sanctuary, I knew that Dad had faced disbarment twice for fraud. I found Judge Franklin's words disingenuous. What I really wanted to do was stand up and shout, "Objection! You, sir, are full of crap," and then ask, "Oh, by the way. Who the hell was that woman who just left, and why was she in hysterics?" I happened to know that Judge Franklin himself was well acquainted with infidelity, as he kept an apartment in the clocktower of the courthouse.

Honesty and integrity, my ass.

Lindsey was the only one of us kids who spoke that day. She had the audacity to say what a wonderful and caring father he was and how he loved all of his children. She then went on to talk about how he loved nature and could see amazing things in driftwood. What the hell? Driftwood? I fought the urge to burst out laughing and a strong desire to puke.

Looking over at my family, who were all crying, I felt like a total bitch. *Can't I just mourn this man? Can't I just cry like the rest of them?* But I didn't have a lot of tears to shed for Dad. When he wasn't sitting in the basement watching television and getting drunk, he'd be brutalizing his children. He'd belittle his daughters and call them bitches. He provoked confrontations between all his kids just to watch us beat the crap out of each other. He was not an honorable and honest man. Just because a judge said it in a eulogy, didn't make it true.

The service ended with the congregation singing "How Great Thou Art." Everyone in the sanctuary raised their voices in song.

"Then sings my soul, My Savior God, to Thee, how great Thou art. How great Thou art."

Looking around the cold sanctuary, I thought to myself, *Who is so great? God? Prove it!* I'd been looking for God for a long time, and to my eyes, he was nowhere to be seen.

After the service, mourners poured into our house, and most of them brought some form of alcohol to share. The hodgepodge gathering included Nate and Junior's fraternity brothers, the attorneys in town, a number of schoolteachers, and quite a few of our school friends. The house was packed, but our mother was nowhere to be seen. Once again, she chose to hide out in her room, leaving others to deal with the guests.

Throughout the day, adults kept taking me aside and telling me that I needed to become more responsible and take care of my younger siblings. These people all sang the same refrain: "You'll be the oldest one home and you need to take care of your younger brothers and sisters because your mother is stuck with all you kids."

They must have bought Lindsey's line of crap and thought that Dad had been this wonderful parent who pulled his weight. I wasn't going to shatter my parents' façade, but I really wanted to say, "Fuck, man, I've been taking care of the kids since I was eleven while Dad buried his head in beer and cigarettes." Instead, I just nodded my head.

The real revelation that day was when Meg introduced me to her boyfriend, Jake. She explained that she had dropped out of school and had been living with Jake for the last six months.

I asked, "Why have you kept your relationship a secret?"

"I didn't want Jake to meet Dad. I didn't trust Dad. I figured he'd be a jerk to Jake, and I didn't want to take that risk," she explained.

At that moment I knew Meg and I were on the same page. Maybe not all of my older siblings were delusional.

During the reception, Jake took the time to talk to me and spend time with Matt and Marc. While all the other adults in the house were either getting hammered or instructing me on how to fulfill my new responsibilities, Jake seemed genuinely concerned for the younger kids. He looked like Steve Perry from Journey and he radiated kindness. That afternoon, I decided I would love to have Jake as an older brother.

Predictably, the evening ended in chaos. The older kids departed to go bar hopping, and Nate's behavior became so out of control that he and a friend ended up getting arrested for criminal mischief. After being chased out of a bar, they broke a neighbor's window with a can of beer.

At around 10:30 that night, while I was sitting at the dining room table with some family friends, the two came sauntering in through the front door, smiling. Nate plopped down a citation on the table stating they had both been arrested. The police had called Judge Franklin, and he had released them from jail. Meanwhile, Junior, his fraternity brothers, and Lindsey were still hanging out at the local bars. God only knows when they returned home that night. I went to bed, hoping that things would settle down by morning.

Our home, which had been so dominated and controlled by our father, had erupted into anarchy. I didn't want to go back to the way it had been when Dad was alive, but I did wonder if order would ever arise.

The chaos of winter came and went, and the school year came to an end. The soft spring rains had produced the vibrant colors of early summer. Mom's roses were in full bloom, the fragrance of the lilac trees hung in the air, and the fruit trees of the Willamette valley were presenting their fruit. All around was the revelation that winter's death always gives way to new life.

That summer would bring about everlasting change. Meg and Jake were engaged, and their wedding would be the first of September. However, something even bigger was in the mix. A seed would be sown that would change the course of our family's story. The idea of a bike ride would blossom into a plan and, within a year, come to fruition.

Chapter 3

GREEN BEANS AND PIPE DREAMS

Summer. God, I loved summer.

After months of overcast drizzle, the clouds would disappear and the sun would shine for the next four months. I spent my afternoons hanging out with friends at the local swimming hole, jumping off of rocks into mountain streams, and riding my friend Orville's minibikes in a field down by the creek. I ended the days running around with neighborhood friends, playing hide and seek late into the night. In so many ways, our summers were like a modern day Norman Rockwell painting.

I also hated summer. More specifically, I hated my summer job, which had been thrust upon me at the age of eleven. I babysat my younger brothers and sisters five days a week. When I was eleven, that included Matt (eight), Marc (seven), and Myrtle (two). Emily was born in June of the year I turned thirteen, adding an infant to my responsibilities.

Mom taught ESL classes at the community college in Salem and left for work at six in the morning. Dad worked in the neighboring town and left at around eight. The older kids worked the graveyard shift at the local cannery during the summer. They returned home at 7:30 and slept until around three in the afternoon. While my parents worked, I was to care for and entertain the four little kids *and* keep the house clean. All this was to be done quietly so we didn't disturb the older kids.

The only positive aspect of my job was that Mom paid me $150 a month for my services. Granted, the money had to go towards school supplies and clothes, but it meant I always had some cash on hand. After Dad's death, Social Security benefits greatly improved our financial situation and made it possible for Mom to quit her evening and summer jobs, which left me unemployed.

The summer after Dad's death, Mom decided it was time for me to join the older kids at the cannery. There was only one problem with this plan—the cannery only hired people eighteen and older, and I'd just turned sixteen. When I told Mom I was too young and the cannery wouldn't hire me, she said, "Oh, Laura, just put on one of Lindsey's college sweatshirts, lie about your age, and you should be fine."

"Mom," I replied, "I barely look twelve! There's no way in hell the cannery's gonna think I'm eighteen."

"Well, you don't really have a choice. You're going to apply tonight with Lindsey and Junior, so don't blow it. Just do what your brother and sister tell you to do, and you'll be fine."

That night, I followed Mom's advice, put on Lindsey's orange and black Oregon State sweatshirt, and headed out the door to spend the evening waiting in line with Lindsey and Henry. The cannery's hiring process was based on a first-come, first-served basis, and people would wait all night outside the plant's main office to get a good spot in the hiring line.

On the way to the cannery, we stopped at a market and got a couple bottles of Mad Dog 20/20 and 7 UP. The four of us spent the night camped outside the cannery's main office, drinking the nasty concoction with other college-aged kids. Buzzed on disgusting booze, I decided that maybe the cannery wouldn't be such a horrible place to hang out for the summer.

At around 3 a.m., one of Junior's friends looked at me and said, "There is no way you're eighteen."

"No," I replied, "I'm eighteen, and I'll be starting my first year at OSU in the fall. Do you really think Henry and Lindsey would let me drink this crap if I weren't at least eighteen?"

He thought about this for a second and then asked, "Okay, then what are you going to study?"

I'd spent enough time around my older siblings to know their college lingo. "Oh, my first year I think I'll just fulfill my basic requirements and then pick a major a little later on. I don't want to flit from one major to another. Right now, I'm thinking about a history and political science degree."

Obviously, I was full of shit, but it got the guy off of my back.

At 7 a.m., the cannery office opened their doors and began leading people in ten at a time to fill out applications. I was sure they would take one look at me and tell me to leave, but they just gave me the application to fill out and said "Next." About a week later we all got a call telling us to show up for work at eleven o'clock that night.

Walking into the cavernous main plant for the first time, the sweet smell of green beans made me nauseated. There were conveyor belts running every which way and metal platforms crisscrossing each other. The plant hummed with the sound of never-ending moving parts. While I was still reeling from the odor, a woman in a hardhat and hairnet led me into a room where I was given my own hardhat, hairnet, and earplugs. These wonderful accessories of blue-collar work would be the first of many that I'd collect over the years.

Once I was properly dressed, I was led into another room, where I was introduced to Betty, my supervisor.

Betty was a large woman who dressed like Rosie the Riveter but looked like a battle ax. She never actually introduced herself; she just barked, "Follow me," and led me to a conveyor belt in the main plant. Shouting her instructions over the noise of all the machinery, she told me to pick the bad beans and any other debris off the belt and throw them into a nearby bucket.

Working the belt was the smelliest, slimiest, and most monotonous job imaginable. The only thing that kept me from falling asleep was the sporadic green bean thrown by Betty that would bounce off my hardhat.

Betty would walk up and down the belt lines, and if she saw someone picking rotten beans with only one hand, she would throw beans at your head and shout, "Two hands! Two hands!"

Between the hypnotic flow of the conveyor belt and Betty's sporadic projectiles, I had eight hours to think about an academic plan that I'd implemented in junior high school, and the wisdom of that plan.

I'd never been a good student, and always struggled academically. For example, in junior high school my grade point average was a whopping 1.54. All Ds, and one A in physical education. The only time it crept higher was during basketball season, when I needed a C average to play ball. When the season ended, my grades plummeted back down to Ds. At the end of every grading period, my parents would ground me, and Mrs. Johnson, my guidance counselor, would summon me to her office.

Mrs. Johnson was the perfect specimen of professionalism, and I couldn't stand her. She was a tall, distinguished woman with a sharp bob who wore business suits and had been on my case since seventh grade. She'd sit me down across from her and say, "Laura, for most of the year you're ineligible for sports, and at this rate you'll never graduate from high school."

I would reply with what she wanted to hear: "You're right, Mrs. Johnson. I should try harder. I will do better."

The truth was that during these "counseling sessions," I developed a desire to show her that at *my* rate, I'd graduate, but just barely. However, it wasn't until the end of the eighth grade that I saw a clear path to achieving this goal.

In 1982, at the end of junior high school, Mrs. Johnson held an assembly for the incoming freshmen. All 350 soon-to-be freshmen gathered in the gym, where Mrs. Johnson instructed us on the challenges we'd face in high school. Dressed in her best tweed suit and sensible shoes, she asked us to look at the person on our left and on our right. She then told us that one of the three of us wouldn't be there on graduation day.

I turned to my friend Tami, who was sitting on my right, and said, "I think you'll make it."

Tami said, "Yeah. You'll *just* make it."

I turned to my friend Macy, who was sitting on the other side of me, and said, "I guess you're screwed."

All three of us began to giggle. Mrs. Johnson gave us a look, and we settled down.

Mrs. Johnson proceeded to lay out how many credits we needed to graduate, and that's when she made a huge mistake.

She said, "You can only receive four Fs throughout all four years of high school. If you receive more than four Fs, you will not be able to graduate on time."

This was said as a warning, but what I heard was, "You can flunk four classes and still graduate!" That was music to my ears. From that moment, I began to plan which classes I would fail. I also began to plan just how often I would attend school. If I was going to maintain a D average and flunk four classes, I only needed to be at school a couple of days a week.

By the time of Dad's death, my plan was in full swing. I was still eligible for basketball during the winter, but the rest of the time, I was barely passing any of my classes. The spring after Dad died, I discovered that none of my teachers would outright flunk me because they felt sorry for my mother. How could they flunk the daughter of the town's martyr? The combination of my apathy and my teachers' sympathy put me on course to graduate—barely.

I didn't really despise school. The truth was, I was afraid of trying. What if I really did try and still failed? I just didn't have any confidence. It would take an incredibly fortunate set of circumstances in 1988 to change my mind. In the end, I would receive a bachelor's degree in history from George Washington University, and a master's in theology. Until then, I was content with being an embarrassment to my family. However, during the eight hours I spent watching green beans pass by, I wondered if my future would look a lot like Betty's, throwing beans at people's heads for a living.

After my shift, I'd get home at around half past seven in the morning and sleep until one in the afternoon. When I wasn't working or sleeping, I was helping Mom get the house ready for Meg's wedding reception. Mom's focus on Meg's wedding appeared to lift her spirits. She wanted the back patio remodeled, so the two of us spent the better part of a month laying paver stones over what had been concrete. During our time together, we talked more than we had in years. Unfortunately, most of our conversations were about Dad. Where she came up with some of the things she talked about baffled me.

One afternoon, she said, "Your father always told me the thing he was proudest of was you nine kids."

I think she wanted a response, but I couldn't think of anything positive. "Uh-huh."

She must have taken my response as affirmation of her narrative, and as we loaded more sand into the wheelbarrow, she began talking about how Dad had been a victim of political attacks and that those attacks had destroyed him. I knew that this was just a half-truth and could feel resentment building within me. Instead of continuing in this vein, I decided to change the subject with a story about my theater teacher, Mr. Ford.

We were on our knees, spreading sand with a trowel and using a level to make sure the stones would lie flat, when I told her about Mr. Ford and his summer bicycle trips.

Mr. Ford was a small, wiry man who looked like a cross between Woody Allen and Groucho Marx. He wore wire-rimmed glasses and 1930s-style men's clothes with tennis shoes. His style and demeanor flew in the face of Willamette conservatism, and I absolutely adored him. His theater classes were the only ones I refused to skip.

His classes met in the theater, which felt like a world apart from the rest of the school. The entrance was an inconspicuous door in the middle of 2nd hall that opened onto the stage with steps leading down to the theater seats. We'd sit in the seats while Mr. Ford taught from the stage. The curriculum changed every semester, which meant students could take theater over and over. One semester we would study Shakespeare and another we would focus on improvisation.

What I really loved about his class was his method of teaching. Mr. Ford spoke to us as equals and challenged us to think outside the box. Almost all topics of discussion were on the table in his class, from art to politics and music to pop culture.

Whereas Mrs. Johnson's lectures left me feeling caged, Mr. Ford's class empowered me to believe that the world was just waiting to be explored.

His slideshows of his summer bicycle adventures caught my attention. I was enraptured by the idea that a bicycle could carry me as far away from Willamette as I wanted to pedal. I used to fantasize about riding off into the sunset with only the bare necessities long before I ever shared his stories with my mom.

In the middle of laying a row of paving stones, I said, "You know, Mom, last year Mr. Ford bicycled from Oregon to the Mexican border. You should see the pictures he has of the Redwoods and the California coast."

Mom looked up at me. "Really? How long did it take him?"

I had to think about it for a bit. "I'm not sure, maybe a month."

After we got another wheelbarrow of sand and some more paver stones, Mom said, "Wouldn't it be great if we just took off on bikes, too?"

I leveled out more sand. "Where would we go?"

"Because there are so many of us, we couldn't go far. How about Crater Lake? It's in Oregon, and we've never been."

"That would be kind of cool. I wonder how long it would take us."

"I think at least a couple of weeks."

As we continued to work and talk, Mom's demeanor changed. Briefly, her blue eyes brightened, almost sparkling, and for the first time she seemed interested in something other than her dead husband. We spent the rest of the afternoon working on the patio and planning a bicycle trip to Crater Lake that I knew would never happen. I thought that the discussion was just a good way to keep Mom's focus on the future instead of dwelling on the past. I'd no inkling the idea of a bicycle trip would become Mom's ultimate means of coping with her grief.

By the time of Meg and Jake's wedding, my season at the cannery was over, the patio was paved, and everyone seemed to be in a good place.

The wedding was held in the Presbyterian Church, and on this warm late summer day, the atmosphere couldn't have been more different from the day of Dad's service. We were all in a festive mood.

Junior walked Meg down the aisle. My other brothers were all groomsmen. Myrtle and Emily were flower girls, and Lindsey and I were bridesmaids. I had to wear a godawful tea-length peach satin dress that my mother had made herself. I've never felt more out of place in my life. Meg and Jake looked like Barbie and Ken dolls as they sweetly exchanged their vows. They could have been their own wedding cake toppers.

In the photos, we all appear so young, healthy, and hopeful. Even Mom looks happy. The problem with photos is they don't tell the whole story, because Mom wasn't in a good place. Once the wedding was over and everyone went back to school, she slid back into depression, and all hell broke loose.

The weekends weren't a problem because Mom kept us busy. Most weekends, the older kids would come home. When they weren't around, Mom would drive us up to Flossy's house to spend the weekend with her. Usually, Lindsey would join us on these trips to Portland. It was the weekdays that were the real problem.

With the older kids gone, the house felt empty. In their absence, an unbalanced, disjointed feeling crept in. Mom's moods became unpredictable. Some days she'd be great. She would wake up, get everyone dressed and out the door. On other days, she could barely get herself ready. I just had to go with whatever each day brought. I really thought her change had to do with the wedding being over and having nothing to focus on. What I soon learned was Mom's chaos served as a distraction to avoid dealing with the reality of Dad's death. For example, she had not picked up Dad's ashes from the funeral home. So really, she hadn't moved past square one in the grief department.

I was sixteen years old and had no idea that when someone was cremated, they were put in an urn to then be disposed of by the family. For me, Dad was there one day and then just gone the next. By early October, I came to find out that the funeral home had contacted Mom several times over the last seven months, requesting that she pick up Dad's remains. Her way of dealing with the stress of the situation was to pick up the ashes and disappear.

I realized this at five o'clock one afternoon, when I walked through the front door and found the four younger kids sitting in the living room waiting for me. I knew something was wrong the moment I crossed the threshold, because those four were never just sitting. Matt and Marc were always doing something outside, and the little girls were never static.

I turned to Matt and asked, "What's going on?"

"I don't know," he replied. "Mom wasn't here when we got here."

"How did the little girls get home?"

"The sitter dropped them off about twenty minutes ago," said Marc. "She said Mom told her to bring them to the house."

I wondered, *What if no one was here?*

Looking at the four of them sitting there so lost and confused, I felt powerless. The only thing I could think of doing was to call Mom's good friends Frank and Mavis to see if she'd gone to their house.

Mavis said they hadn't seen her. I asked them to call me if she turned up there, and they promised they would.

I didn't know what to do, so I did what came naturally. I made dinner, cleaned the house, put the girls to bed, reassuring them that Mom would be home soon, then waited with Matt and Marc on the living room couch. The night progressed slowly, and with each passing hour, we grew increasingly worried. Every time a car drove by, the headlights lit up the living room, and we hoped it was her, but as the lights moved past and we realized it wasn't, our anxiety seemed to collectively rise.

Matt asked, "Should we call one of the older kids and let them know she's missing?"

"No," I replied. "What good would it do? They can't do anything at this point." To bolster our mood, I said, "You guys, she'll come home. She can't have gone that far."

The boys looked at me like I was full of shit. We all knew she was struggling, and we really didn't have any idea what she was capable of doing.

I may have said she'd be back, but in the back of my mind I was wondering if—and maybe hoping—she had left for good. I had conflicting feelings about this possibility. I could picture her getting in the car, without packing a suitcase, and just driving away. The few short weeks I'd been back to being the oldest child at home had been incredibly difficult. While I was thinking through the pros and cons of her disappearing for good, the phone rang. It was Mavis, calling to tell me Mom was at their house.

Mavis said Mom was slightly drunk, and that she would drive her home later. I asked where she had gone, and Mavis replied that Mom had gone out to our local swimming hole, where we used to picnic, to dispose of Dad's ashes. I shared this information with Matt and Marc.

Matt looked at me. "Dad's ashes?"

Marc added, "Why would she do that on her own?"

"I have no idea," I replied. "She's safe. It's okay. Let's just go to bed."

That night was warm, and once I entered my room I opened my window, climbed through, and sat on the outside ledge, looking up into the clear night sky. There were so many stars, too many to count in a million lifetimes, which made me feel incredibly small. An overwhelming sense of powerlessness and loss swept over me, and I began to weep. I had held it all together until I just couldn't anymore. My tears weren't for the death of my father, but for the conflicted feelings I had towards my mother. Despite all of the times she rejected me, I *needed* her. Before Dad died, Mom was the one who kept the family together, and now she was crumbling. In my heart, I knew that

I didn't have enough love or compassion for her to be of any help. In the midst of this realization, my gaze switched from the stars to the two streetlights below. The streetlights that Matt, Marc, and I used as goalposts for touch football. Where the light of the stars left me empty, the streetlights illuminated one simple truth. I loved my little brothers and sisters, and I knew I could keep my shit together for them. I just didn't know for how long.

After the disposal of Dad's ashes, Mom's mood swings only got worse. Matt, Marc, and I were constantly on guard. If Mom was happy, just give it a few minutes, and she'd be crying. At this point, the days were devolving into a pattern. In the morning, Mom would be in tears, by the afternoon she'd be tired and irritated, and come evening, she'd be so depressed that she'd just go to bed. Trying to stay one step ahead of her was exhausting.

After Thanksgiving, during one of our car rides to Flossy's, everything changed when I told Lindsey and Mom about Mr. Ford's latest adventure. He and his new wife had spent the summer bicycling from Florida to Canada. This time, both Lindsey and Mom began discussing taking a bicycle trip with me and the little boys and little girls. Mom was still thinking of cycling to Crater Lake, but over time the trip grew incrementally, from Crater Lake to Yellowstone National Park, to Mount Rushmore, and, ultimately—to New York City.

I loved these conversations because they gave Mom something to focus on other than our father. Still, I never really believed we'd go on a bicycle trip. Not to Crater Lake, and definitely not to New York, because as we discussed what we needed for a successful cycling trip, there were clearly just too many obstacles. We didn't have bicycles. We'd never camped in our lives, and two of our group would only be eight and four years old. Therefore, we needed a car to carry the little girls and all our supplies, which was a huge problem. Our car was a two-door Ford Escort.

My parents had been notoriously hard on our family cars. Right before Dad's death, our only vehicle, a 1978 Cougar, had crapped out, and they'd had to buy a new one. Since they were broke, the only car they could afford was an Escort, the most impractical car for a family our size. If there were more than five of us in the car, the others had to ride in the hatchback. Therefore, during our rides to Flossy's, Matt and Marc were wedged in the trunk, unaware of our discussions. In my mind, all the talk of a cycling trip was just a pipe dream to keep Mom occupied. I soon discovered that sometimes, even pipe dreams come true.

Chapter 4

WHAT WERE WE SMOKING?

I began to wonder just what Mom was smoking in her metaphorical pipe, because despite all the impracticalities of a cycling trip across the country with six children, she fully threw herself into the dream. From December of '84 throughout the following spring, all Mom could talk about was the trip. I thought it was just talk, even when she purchased Peugeot 12-speed bicycles for me, Lindsey, Matt, Marc, and herself. Mom's idea was that the little girls would ride in the car. I still couldn't see her really going through with it, especially considering the way Lindsey and Mom were making plans, which was ludicrous. They could only see the big picture of cycling across the country and ignored most of the details. Their lack of vision became blatantly obvious in January when Mom purchased a *Rand McNally US Road Atlas* to plot our course.

Mom gathered all the would-be cyclists around the dining room table and opened the atlas to the map of the United

States. Even Myrtle and Emily were invited to throw out ideas, but they spent most of the time under the table playing with their Care Bears.

The smart thing would've been to draw a straight line from Willamette to New York City and circle destinations along that route. Instead, Mom and Lindsey began with the destinations and made our route that way.

With her old sparkle back, Mom went first, saying, "We have to go to Yellowstone."

Because she was so adamant about going there, I asked why.

"I went there when I was a little girl and I've always wanted to go back," she responded.

With a shrug, I said, "Sounds like a good enough reason," and she drew a circle around Yellowstone. I accepted her answer, because she was always a bit—well, more than a bit—of a mystery.

Lindsey wanted to see both the Tetons in Wyoming and Mammoth Caves in Kentucky and circled both national parks.

Matt wanted to see Mount Rushmore, so we made a circle in South Dakota.

Marc wanted to see Lincoln's tomb in Illinois, so we made a circle around Springfield, Illinois.

For reasons that I would learn about later, Mom wanted to go to Independence and Hannibal, Missouri, so we circled them.

Spying Washington, D.C. on the map, I said, "Well, we have to go to Washington, D.C. It's no good crossing the country and bypassing the capital." So, we circled Washington, D.C.

Almost as an afterthought, Mom circled New York City. She then drew a line to each of our circles on the map, creating a giant zigzag across the country—at which point we should've rethought our route. Unfortunately, all Mom and Lindsey saw was America the Beautiful and an opportunity to see it up close. What I saw was a lot of unnecessary cycling, which brought us to our next set of problems. The first being that none of us had ever cycled more than twenty miles at a time.

Our sole preparation for the trip that spring? Mom led us on one cycling trip to a neighboring town ten miles away. We stopped at an old-fashioned soda fountain, had a soda, and cycled back. The route was flat and took us about two and a half hours in total. Looking at the map and the connect-the-dots route Mom and Lindsay had created, the distances they wanted us to cycle each day were crazy—we'd have to at least triple that.

Accommodations were another big hurdle. To save money, it was decided that we'd camp the whole way. Mom told us that every day we'd bike from campground to campground despite never having camped before. So between our tiny car, minimal cycling experience, lack of camping skills, and ignorance of the terrain we'd traverse, it seemed that we might actually make this trip. What made the whole idea even more ludicrous was how young we all were: Lindsey was twenty-two, Matt was fourteen, Marc thirteen, Myrtle eight, Emily four, and I was seventeen.

It was a warm spring day in the middle of April when Matt, Marc, and I found ourselves alone at the house while Lindsey and Mom were out shopping with the little girls. While they were gone, the three of us sat on the front steps, chatting and throwing a tennis ball back and forth. At one point I asked them, "Do you think this whole bicycle trip thing will ever happen?"

"Probably not," said Marc. "I just don't see how it can work. Maybe we'll take off, but we won't get too far."

"Biking across the country sounds kind of cool, but I agree with Marc. It won't work," Matt said.

"Why did she buy the bikes then?" I asked.

Marc tossed Matt the ball and said, "God. Who knows why? Why is she doing anything right now?"

I thought over all the preparations Mom had made. "I have a sneaky feeling we just might go."

Matt's eyes widened as he tossed the ball to me. "Well, if we do, I hope Mom and Lindsey have a better plan in place. Have you looked at the places they've circled on the map? They have us going in every direction but straight."

As I threw the ball back to Matt, I said, "I know. I think they're just looking at all their options. If we go, we won't go to every place they want to go because it'll take too long."

"I just can't see us actually doing it."

I thought about this for a second. "I guess we'll just have to wait and see."

Mom and Lindsey pulled up in the car and our conversation ended, leaving us with a lot of questions and no answers.

Maybe we'd go on a cross-country bicycle trip, and then again maybe we wouldn't.

In early May, Mom announced she planned on us cycling out of town on the 17th of June. At this point, I thought we'd probably just cycle across the Willamette Valley.

Later that month, she purchased five one-way plane tickets from New York City to Portland, Oregon for August 15.

Confused, I asked Mom why she only purchased five tickets. "Because Lindsey and you are driving the car back, and I'll fly back with the four youngest kids."

This was the first time I'd heard this. "What? Just the two of us?"

"Well, I'm going to ask Jake to fly out and drive home with you two. The car needs to get back, and it's the only way that'll work."

What she told me made sense, but I wished she'd have at least discussed it with me first.

Even with all this information, I continued to think our summer vacation would be a car trip. When Mom made arrangements with the school district to deposit her checks directly into her checking account, I still assumed we'd be driving.

A few days before we left, she added my older brother Nate to her checking account so he could deposit the monthly Social Security checks and pay all the household bills while she was gone. Nate, who had zero desire to cycle with us, would be staying home. He told me that he thought the whole idea was crazy. But he was probably looking forward to all of us being gone—it would be the first time in his life he had the whole house to himself.

With all her finances in order, Mom then turned her attention towards gathering the supplies we would need for an eight-week road trip.

Lindsey and Mom went shopping and purchased a couple weeks' supply of food. They bought Bisquick, syrup, bread, peanut butter, jelly, hotdogs, buns, and condiments. They also picked up a whole bunch of tea, Kool-Aid, and powdered Gatorade. From the looks of things, we'd be eating a lot of crap for the first couple of weeks, but at least we'd be well hydrated.

With the food taken care of, Mom then began to acquire camping supplies. She borrowed a ten-person tent and six sleeping bags, a camp stove, and some cooking utensils. Upon seeing all of these things assembled, I was resigned to the fact that we'd be leaving soon. It wasn't until the day before we left that I knew for sure we would be leaving by bike.

On the morning of June 16, Mom woke me up, handed me a pillowcase, and told me I needed to start packing for the trip. "How?" I asked without hiding my shock. "Am I to use this pillowcase to hold my things?"

"We each get one pillowcase, so pack wisely," she said, and left the room.

One pillowcase? Looking around my bedroom, which was a mess, I didn't know where to start. All of my clothes were scattered around and dirty. The whole concept of packing everything I'd wear for an entire summer into one pillowcase seemed impractical.

A few minutes later, Lindsey came into the room. "Throw all your dirty laundry together so we can wash it and then figure out what you want to take. We also need to pack for Myrtle and Emily, so hurry up."

When she left the room carrying a pile of dirty clothes, I wanted to tell her to fuck off. Instead, I lay back in my bed and looked out the window. It was a beautiful summer morning and all I really wanted to do was go back to sleep. Just when I began to shut my eyes again, Mom yelled up the stairs, "Laura, get up!"

Under my breath I said, "Mom. Fuck off," and got up.

I went downstairs in the clothes I'd slept in. "Why are you in such a hurry?"

Mom was holding a pile of dirty laundry. "Because we're leaving tomorrow morning and we have a ton of things to do. We need to get everyone's clothes washed, dried, and put in their bags. We need to figure out how to pack the car, and we're going to Jake's parents' house tonight because they're going to install a bike rack onto our car."

Her mania was too much for me to handle, so I went into the kitchen to make a cup of tea, where I found Matt and Marc eating breakfast. I said to both of them, "So, one pillowcase?" Matt and Marc both gave me a look that said, *don't go there.*

With my cup of tea in hand, I found Mom in the living room and asked her how we were supposed to pack for Myrtle and Emily. "The little girls are in their bedroom getting their things together," she said.

"Mom, they're eight and four! They will only pack their Care Bears."

"Don't be daft. Lindsey's in there helping them."

Better Lindsey than me, I thought, and went outside to finish my tea on the front porch, where I found Nate sitting on the steps.

Nate and I sat in silence for a few minutes. Then he turned to me. "So, you guys are really going?"

"Right now it looks that way."

We didn't say anything for a few more minutes, and then he asked, "How far do you think you'll get?"

He asked this with such concern in his voice that I was kind of taken aback. I thought about his question. "Nate, I really don't think we'll get very far. Maybe across the state. I think Mom just wants to go on a trip and see how far she can get."

It was the first time that Nate and I ever really spoke to one another as equals. The fact that he was asking me these questions and not Lindsey or my mother meant everything to me.

Mom began the day by stacking all of our supplies in the middle of the living room. When my clothes were laundered, I threw some shorts, a pair of jeans, a few t-shirts, and underwear into my pillowcase and added it to the pile. By mid-afternoon, the pile had become a small mountain consisting of seven sleeping bags, a ten-person tent, a cooler, a box of food, a box of dishes and cooking utensils, seven pillowcases full of clothes, a toolkit, and a small box with bicycle repair supplies, such as inner tubes and a bicycle pump. The only thing missing was bicycle helmets. It was 1985 and no one wore helmets, let alone cycled across the United States.

Somehow, we needed to get all of our supplies and up to four people into our two-door Ford Escort, a job that Mom assigned to Matt and me. Matt looked at me and said, "What the fuck? This is impossible."

"You're right, it is. Let's just clean the car first and then see what we can do."

As we walked outside, Matt stopped and stared at the car. "This is stupid."

"You're right, it is stupid."

The two of us spent two determined hours trying to figure out how to make everything fit. Finally, we realized that the only way it'd work was if we unrolled the sleeping bags and laid five of them flat along the backseat and draped the other two over the front seats. Then we wedged the pillowcases into the leg areas of all the seats except the driver's. We consolidated the boxes so there were only a couple, and we were able to get the rest of the stuff in the trunk. It wasn't pretty, but it worked. Unfortunately, we then had to unpack everything because we had to go over to my brother-in-law's parents' house for a bon voyage spaghetti dinner and to pick up a bike rack.

Jake's dad fancied himself as an inventor. One of his creations was a bicycle rack which held six bikes that he attached to the bumper of our car. This contraption was both massive and convoluted. The rack was a semi-circle that allowed the bikes to stand straight up and was held in place by bungee cords. While we were being shown how to attach the bikes, I kept thinking there was no way our car would be able to hold all the weight and hoped we'd never have to attach all the bikes at once. The thought of seven people, six bikes, and all of our gear stowed in this little car just defied the laws of physics.

At some point in her planning, Mom decided I would be the bicycle mechanic. However, she only informed me of my new position after dinner that evening. She said, "Go with Jake, he's going to show you how to fix bicycles."

"What? Why me?" I knew a little about bicycle repairs, but not much.

Mom looked at me. "Because you know how to fix a flat tire."

"So I'm the mechanic?!" I responded.

Jake said, "Laura, it's not that hard. I'll just show you how to do a few things."

"I guess I don't really have a choice," I said, and followed Jake out to his parents' garage, which was all kitted out as his dad's workshop. Every tool had its place on the pegboard.

Jake had set up an old bike to practice on, and he showed me how to tighten loose brakes and straighten bent tire rims.

In the middle of his tutorial, he said, "You'll mostly have to fix tires. If you keep the tires full of air, you probably won't have to fix too many of those."

"God, I hope not. Your dad's bike rack is confusing enough. Shit, Jake, between trying to figure out how to pack the car, load the bike rack, and do repairs, I don't know if I can keep it all straight."

"I think you'll all have a lot of fun. I can't wait until I fly out to New York in August to catch up with you and Lindsey and drive back home."

"I'm glad you're driving back with us."

"You know, the only ones I'm worried about are the little girls. I wish they'd stay back with Meg and me, but there's no way your mom would agree. Right?"

"Probably not. They'll be with all of us, so they'll be okay. Plus, they'll travel in the car the whole time, so I wouldn't worry about them."

I only gave Jake's concerns for Myrtle and Emily's safety a passing thought. The little girls were always around, and they always seemed to be fine. I just couldn't see how our cross-country trip could be dangerous for any of us.

When we returned home, Matt and I showed Lindsey and Mom how to pack the car. Then Mom gathered us around the dining room table and told us how the next day would unfold. Pointing to the map, Lindsey and Mom showed us how we'd bicycle to Blue River, Oregon and spend the night at a campground nearby. This was the first I'd heard that we were biking to Blue

River, which is in the Cascade Mountains, east of Eugene and around 120 miles from Willamette.

I was shocked. "You've got to be fucking kidding me!"

"It's not that far," said Lindsey. "We can do it. Mom's gonna drive with the little girls to Eugene and then she and I will switch places. She'll bicycle with you guys to Blue River."

Taken aback, I asked, "Oh, right. So, Matt, Marc, and I are expected to bike the whole way?"

Mom blew past my question. "We're going to Blue River because your dad's aunt used to live there, and I want to go there."

Looking bewildered, Matt said, "Isn't Dad's aunt dead?"

"Why are we going south to go east?" Marc chimed in. "Why aren't we just going straight east?"

Mom ignored both of their questions, too, and said in her typical dismissive tone, "We're biking to Blue River and that's that. Now, go to bed. We're leaving at six in the morning, so I'll be waking you all up at five."

Realizing that Mom wouldn't change her mind, we all marched off to bed clueless about our fate. That night I lay awake, conflicted. I wanted to be away from Willamette but was terrified by our lack of planning. The conversation before bed only reaffirmed my belief that there must have been some weed in Mom's pipe because there was no way we'd survive the first day. If by some miracle we made it to Blue River, there was no way we'd survive the following week. In the end, I decided not to give the situation any more thought and went to sleep. Five o'clock was coming around real soon.

Chapter 5

AND WE'RE OFF

Lindsey shook me awake before dawn the next morning, telling me to get dressed and ready to go. I could hear people talking and moving around downstairs and wondered if I really wanted to join them. I thought about it for a few seconds and came to the conclusion that cycling was better than spending another summer working at the cannery, so I got up.

I put on a John Mellencamp concert t-shirt, shorts, and a pair of pink canvas Sperry topsiders. At that point I hadn't realized that I forgot to pack an extra pair of shoes and that the topsiders would be my footwear for the whole trip. Actually, I would wear pretty much the same outfit for the next eight weeks. Hell, I only had a pillowcase! What was I supposed to pack?

When I made it downstairs, I found Myrtle and Emily sitting on the couch still in their nightgowns. Myrtle held her Grumpy Care Bear. Emily, clutching her Strawberry Shortcake baby quilt, sucked her two fingers. The two of them looked scared and confused. Even though we'd been discussing the bicycle trip for almost a year, I don't think they ever really grasped what we were talking about. *They're Mom's problem,* I thought, and went into the kitchen, where Mom and the others were eating some donuts she had bought the night before. Mom handed me a frosted donut. "Eat up. We're taking off soon."

I grabbed it and began eating. With my mouth full, I asked, "So, how's this going to work?"

"Didn't you pay attention at all last night?" Lindsey asked. "We're riding over to 99W, biking south through Monmouth, then Corvallis, and on to Eugene. Mom's meeting us in Eugene, and then you guys will bike to Blue River."

"When are we leaving?" I asked.

"As soon as you eat that donut and you guys get on your bikes," said Mom.

I shoved the rest of the maple bar in my mouth and mumbled, "Fine. Let's go."

Mom bundled up Myrtle and Emily and took them out to the car. Lindsey, Matt, Marc, and I went outside and got on our bikes. Mom drove off while we were still getting ready, which was when Nate appeared on the front porch. He didn't say anything; he just sat down on the front step and watched as we biked away. We didn't wave goodbye. We just left him there with a confused expression on his face.

As we pedaled out of town, the four of us barely spoke. A few miles later, we reached Highway 99W. By that time, Matt and Marc had pulled way ahead of Lindsey and me. A short time later, I pulled ahead of Lindsey. Without speaking, we found it easier to let people ride at their own pace, which also gave everyone some space. Riding alone meant I didn't have to make small talk with anyone, and I was free to think and experience the ride.

As I biked into the neighboring town of Monmouth, I wondered how long it would be before I saw Willamette again. Would it be a few days, weeks, or even months before we made it back home? Once I passed the Monmouth City Limits sign, it dawned on me I was beginning to bike further than I ever had before, and I found that kind of thrilling. Every green milepost marker I cycled by was a new record, and I felt like I could bike forever.

My feeling of invincibility probably had more to do with the fact that we were cycling through the Willamette Valley, which would be the flattest part of the whole trip. Because the ride was so easy, I was able to enjoy the richness of the valley. The weather was warm, the fields were green and fragrant. The softness of the valley lulled me into believing the whole trip would be this easy.

About ten miles south of Corvallis, I saw Matt and Marc standing next to our car under a cloudless blue sky. Mom had pulled over to see if we needed a drink or something to eat. When I pulled up next to them, Mom gave me an earful about not riding in a group.

"Laura, you guys need to ride together. What if something were to happen to one of you, how would we find out?"

I was confused by her sudden outpouring of concern. "I don't know. But Matt and Marc are a lot stronger riders than Lindsey and me. We can't keep up with them. Matt and Marc, do you guys want to ride slower?"

"Don't drag me into this," said Matt.

"Why not? You guys pulled away."

"Laura, you pulled away from Lindsey!" said Marc.

Mom interrupted us before we could get into a huge argument. "There's Lindsey. Ask her how it feels to be biking behind everyone."

Lindsey cycled up to us with her long brown hair flying behind her, wearing a huge smile. As she pulled closer, she asked, "Why are we stopped? I thought we were meeting in Eugene?"

"You're okay with this riding situation?" Mom asked her.

"Yes. This way if someone gets hurt, I'm behind them and will find them."

That cracked me up because she was worried about us and didn't stop to think what would happen if she got hurt. How would we know if we were in front of her?

"If you're okay with this setup, fine," said Mom. "I don't feel good about it, but if it works for you, then so be it."

While Mom was talking, I looked in the backseat of the car and saw that Myrtle and Emily were fast asleep. Then Mom said, "Where should I meet you guys in Eugene?"

We looked at the map and decided we'd meet her where 99 meets Highway 126. Mom would pull over somewhere and switch places with Lindsey. From the looks of things, we still had about twenty-five miles, or an hour and a half, to bike before we made the switch.

In Eugene, Mom had pulled into a rest area to wait for us. As I cycled up to her, I saw Matt and Marc sitting at a picnic table with Mom, eating sandwiches and drinking Coca-Colas as the little girls played nearby. As I got closer to them I was struck by how relaxed they all looked. Mom's curly hair was a bit messy, and even from a distance I could see her blue eyes sparkling with excitement. The little boys were stretched out on the picnic benches just chatting away.

I jumped off my bike and joined them at the table. Mom gave me a soda and told me to make a sandwich. A few minutes later, Lindsey arrived.

I hadn't realized how hungry and thirsty I was until I began drinking my Coke and eating the cheap white bread baloney sandwich. I really don't recommend cycling seventy miles on a maple bar and some water. While we ate our lunches, Mom and Lindsey looked at the map and decided we'd camp at Blue River Reservoir. Lindsey would drive ahead with the little girls and find a campsite. Those of us biking would get there eventually. A few minutes later Mom, Matt, Marc, and I hopped on our bikes and began cycling east towards the Cascade Mountains and Blue River.

At first, Mom insisted that all four of us cycle together in a group, but it didn't take long for her to figure out why we'd decided to let everyone go at their own pace. Matt and Marc didn't cycle as slowly as her, and they bitched about it for the first five miles. Finally, Mom said, "Please go ahead of me. I'm not enjoying this at all."

Matt and Marc pulled forward and were out of sight within about ten minutes. I chose to cycle with Mom because it didn't feel right to just leave her on her own. We didn't really talk much on our ride because the scenery was just too beautiful. Our route took us along the McKenzie River and into the foothills of the Cascades. Between the rippling of the water and the terrain changing from meadows to forests, I thought, *This cycling thing is pretty cool.*

When Mom and I reached the campground, we were both pretty shot. As we pulled up to our campsite, Mom puffed up her cheeks and blew out her breath with pursed lips and a "Phew." This would become her sign-off at the end of every ride indicating she was exhausted. She really didn't need sound effects to reveal her physical state. She had just cycled over fifty miles and was a sweaty, disheveled mess—but I think a happy mess.

I had cycled 120 miles and was more than ready to stop for the day. I know what you're thinking—how could someone who had never cycled more than twenty miles go that far in one day? I was seventeen years old and in good shape. Plus, all but the last twenty miles had been flat, and the wind was at our backs.

The Blue River Reservoir was the perfect ending to our first full day of biking. Matt and Marc were already swimming by the time we arrived. Lindsey was sitting on the picnic table with the little girls, waiting for us. Without a word, I jumped off my bicycle, ran down to the water, kicked off my shoes, and joined the boys. A few minutes later, we were joined by Mom, Lindsey, and the little girls. We spent the next couple of hours swimming and enjoying the moment.

The reservoir was surrounded by evergreen trees, and the smell of fir mixed with fresh water was invigorating. The cold water cleansed our bodies of all the road grime, which we would later learn would become a never-ending battle. The perfection of our first day lured me into believing that the rest of the trip would be just as wonderful.

We'd tackled our first hurdle—cycling long distances. Next, we had to figure out how to assemble the tent, a huge White Stag beast that slept ten people. None of us had ever assembled as much as a pup tent before. We had no clue where to even begin.

Mom and I unrolled it, laid out all the pieces, then tried to figure out how it all went together. I can only compare the experience to trying to assemble a piece of IKEA furniture without the crappy illustrated instructions. Our flat pack tent had numerous aluminum poles that slotted together, and ropes that needed to be attached to pegs.

Assembling the tent began as a group project, but within minutes, the group dwindled down to just Mom and me. Everyone else went back to the reservoir to swim. This was a sign of just how incredibly difficult it would be for all seven of us to work together. Eventually, the tent did get assembled, but like self-assembly furniture, we had leftover parts and it didn't look quite right. It sagged in the middle and stayed up more by grace than anything else.

Our next challenge was cooking. Our borrowed camp stove lacked the attachment for gas, rendering it useless. We'd have to cook over an open fire. That night we ate hotdogs and beans. After cycling 120 miles, we were starving. Mom had bought two packs of hotdogs, and since Myrtle and Emily only ate one each, that meant the rest of us could eat three. Not the most nutritious of meals, but it did the trick.

After dinner, we all went swimming one more time, and then gathered around the fire to roast some more marshmallows. As we stuffed our faces, Mom and Lindsey took another look at the map.

"Right," said Mom to Matt, Marc, and me. "Tomorrow morning Lindsey will be cycling with you guys to Sisters. In Sisters, Lindsey and I will switch, and then we'll cycle to Prineville."

"How far is that?" Matt asked.

"I don't know. A few inches on the map."

Marc rolled his eyes. "Okay. Whatever."

"What time are we leaving?" I asked.

"I want to leave at around six in the morning," said Lindsey.

"Why so early?"

"Because I want an early start."

Myrtle chimed in, "I want another marshmallow," and the subject was dropped. We'd be leaving at six. End of discussion.

We all climbed into our tent at around ten o'clock that evening. Though it was large, there were seven of us, and space felt limited. The little girls snuggled around Mom, and the rest of us tried to create some personal space.

As we were lying there, Matt asked the question that was probably on most of our minds: "Will this thing stay up all night?"

"Let's hope so," Mom replied.

Just when I was beginning to wonder what would happen if the tent collapsed on all of us in the night, Lindsey turned on a flashlight. "I brought a whole bunch of paperback mysteries. How about we choose a book and read a chapter a night?"

"That's a great idea," said Mom. "What did you bring?"

Lindsey opened a paper bag and began pulling out books. "We have a few Ed McBains, a few Fletch mysteries, some Dick Francis, and Agatha Christies. What do you want to read?"

We discussed it for a few minutes and decided to begin with the first Fletch mystery. Lindsey wedged the flashlight between two pillowcases stuffed with clothes and began reading: *What's your name? Fletch. What's your full name? Fletcher. What's your first name? Irwin What?*

I got comfortable in my sleeping bag, lay back, and listened to how Fletch got entangled in a murder-for-hire scheme. Before Lindsey finished the chapter, I was fast asleep.

Chapter 6

HARD LESSONS

With what felt like only a few minutes of sleep, I could hear someone moving around the tent. It was Lindsey shaking Matt and Marc awake. "It's six. You need to get moving." I got up before she could get to me.

Matt and Marc rolled out of the tent in the clothes they slept in, while I tried to quietly change before joining them. All three were already on their bikes waiting for me when Lindsey said, "Hurry up. Let's get going."

Still half-asleep, I mumbled, "All right. Gimme a second. I need to pee before we go."

"We'll stop off at the restrooms on the way out," said Lindsey.

I climbed on my bike and mindlessly pedaled towards the restrooms, where we all went in to relieve ourselves. A few minutes later, we were all back on our bikes and began cycling east towards the town of Sisters, which is on the other side of the Cascades.

Our ride began in the gorgeous Willamette National Forest, where the shade of the fir trees protected us from the sun. About an hour in, I reached down and grabbed my water bottle only to discover it was empty. "Shit," I said out loud. In my early morning brain fog I'd forgotten to fill it. In the hope that either Matt or Marc had water, I pushed ahead and caught up to them.

I pedaled next to Marc. "Do you have any water?"

"No. We forgot to fill our bottles. We're going to cycle into the next campground and see if they have some."

The next campground was about a mile ahead, and when we pulled in the first thing we saw was a sign saying, "No Water."

"Fuck me," I said to no one in particular.

We cycled back out to the highway and waited for Lindsey. She arrived about fifteen minutes later and the first thing she asked was, "Do you guys have any water? I forgot to fill my bottle."

"No," I said. "We just went into that campground looking for some and they don't have any. I guess we go to the next campground and see if they have water."

"Well, Mom should pass us soon and we'll wave her down. Maybe she can find us something to drink."

The next three campgrounds didn't have water either, but we figured we'd survive until Mom caught up with us, so we kept biking.

A few miles later, we entered the first ring of hell as we began to really climb. The cool green forest gave way to lava beds and scorching heat. The road narrowed and rose into what appeared to be never-ending switchbacks. Around every turn, I was sure we'd reach the summit sign, but each turn revealed the road climbing even higher through more lava beds. A thick layer of film was beginning to coat my mouth, and I had quit sweating. The only thing keeping me going was the hope that Mom would appear soon and save us. That glimmer of hope was squashed about an hour later.

When Mom and the little girls caught up with us, she didn't stop. We did everything we could think of to flag her down. We waved our arms, shouting "Stop!" But instead of stopping she rolled down her window and shouted back, "I'll meet you in Sisters!" and sped away.

As the Escort disappeared around the next bend, I said, "That bitch!" It was then that I realized that we wouldn't make it without water. I looked over at Lindsey and the boys and said, "Fuck this. I'm done," laid down my bicycle, and began trying to hitchhike.

Matt and Marc seemed to agree because they laid their bikes down and stuck their thumbs out too. Lindsey thought about it for a second and joined us. A few minutes later an older couple in a pickup pulling a camper stopped and asked where we were going.

Through chapped lips, Lindsey croaked, "We just need to get to Sisters."

"We're headed to Bend," the man said. "Throw your bikes and yourselves in the back and we'll drop you off in Sisters."

I didn't believe in angels, but looking back, I realize that this older couple were the first of many angels that we would encounter on our travels.

After we threw our bikes in the bed of the truck and climbed in, the man opened a cooler and handed us each a Coke, saying, "This'll clear the dust in your throats." I could have cried. That was the best fucking Coke I had ever tasted.

As we passed the summit sign, Lindsey said, "What have we learned from this fiasco?"

I couldn't believe she was lecturing us. I was just beginning to feel revived by the Coke and she wanted to play the adult. Frustrated with the whole situation, I said, "That Mom is an inconsiderate bitch!"

"Well, that, but what else?" she replied.

"Don't be a bitch yourself, Lindsey," said Marc. "I think we now know to fill our water bottles."

Forty minutes later, the driver pulled up at a little drive-thru restaurant on the edge of Sisters and let us out. We thanked him and his wife, then cycled through town to find Mom and the girls.

Mom and the little girls were waiting for us at a picnic table in the city park. Mom looked relaxed and well-hydrated with a soda in front of her. As we pulled up next to them, she asked, "How did you guys get here so fast?"

Proud of our problem-solving skills, I said, "We hitched a ride."

Instead of asking why we felt the need to hitchhike, she blew up. "What? First you guys won't ride in a group, and now you're hitching?"

I lost it. She had no idea what she'd done when she blew past us. So, before she could really get going, I interrupted her mid-sip and yelled back, "What the hell were we supposed to do? We tried to wave you down because we were out of water and dying. Did you stop? NO! You kept going. We couldn't keep going! It's the fucking Cascades, Mom!" I had rarely stood up to my mother, but I was so angry that I was shaking.

Lindsey stood right by me while I went toe to toe with Mom. The boys quietly slinked off to avoid the conflict.

By the look on Mom's face, I could tell she was shocked by my outburst, but I was pissed. When I was done, I noticed that her jaw was set, so I dropped it. She didn't apologize, and neither did I. I grabbed some food and went off to be by myself. Thirty minutes later, Mom told us to fill our water bottles because we were leaving soon.

Lindsey stayed behind with the little girls and Mom began riding with the boys and me. We continued to bike along Highway 126 towards Prineville. At this point, I decided Mom could ride by herself. I didn't feel like chatting with her for the next few hours.

The ride between Sisters and Prineville was hot and dry and nothing like the Willamette Valley. The smell of Douglas fir trees had given way to sagebrush and ponderosa pine. The snow peak of Mount Jefferson stood majestically behind me as I cycled towards the hazy outline of the next mountain range. As I followed the white line of Highway 126, all I could think about was why I had responded to Mom the way I did. I realized that when she flew past us, it stirred up feelings I had spent years trying to ignore. Feelings I was about to face head on as I kept pedaling in the scorching sun.

When I was nine years old, my mother removed me from the household for more than two years. She sent me away to spend my evenings and mornings with an elderly neighbor, Mrs. Hall. According to Mom, I didn't actually *live* with her. I just spent my afternoons, evenings, and mornings there. Mom said it was my responsibility to keep her company because Mrs. Hall's husband had died and she was lonely. My mother was able to make the distinction between keeping an old lady company day and night and *living* there. Because Mom couched it as *my responsibility* to keep Mrs. Hall company, I felt it was my *duty* to stay at Mrs. Hall's.

This was right after Myrtle's birth and during our father's first disciplinary hearing with the Oregon Bar Association. It was also when my older siblings began tormenting me about being a tomboy. They would call me a dyke and refer to me as Larry or Lawrence, all because I refused to conform. So maybe my mother was trying to protect me, but what I felt was rejection. Either way, she didn't want me there.

The nights I spent at Mrs. Hall's house were lonely. She lived in a small, two-bedroom bungalow filled with hoarder's gold. It smelled like an antique store—a potent combination of Pledge, varnish, and dust. She was in her late seventies, bird-thin, and suffering from dementia. We didn't really talk much during our time together. She never asked if I needed to study or do homework. She simply went about her business while I hung out.

I spent most of my time watching television. *Carol Burnett* reruns and Merv Griffin became my solace. I used to daydream that one day I would be on stage with Harvey Korman, Tim Conway, and Carol, busting up in the middle of a skit. Or maybe being interviewed by Mr. Griffin.

In the early evening, Mrs. Hall would fix us a small dinner, which we'd eat in her kitchen. Afterwards I'd hand-wash the dishes. She would go to bed around 7:30 and I'd make up the sofa bed in the living room. I had no personal objects, such as a stuffed animal, there to make me feel connected to home, since in my family we didn't have things like that. Crappy '70s sitcoms kept me company. Eventually I'd fall asleep after *The Tonight Show* with Johnny Carson.

In the morning, Mrs. Hall would wake me up, fix me breakfast, and give me a couple dollars for my trouble. Then I'd run home, change my clothes, go to school, and do it all over again.

My parents presented this living situation to my family in such a way that it appeared normal. My brothers and sisters didn't seem to think it was strange, and my teachers had no idea I wasn't spending my nights at home.

That was my life until the summer when I was eleven. Mrs. Hall moved to Minneapolis to live with her daughter, and Mom needed me to watch the little kids. Looking back, this was always about my mother's needs, not mine.

As an adult, I've even asked my older sisters about why I lived with Mrs. Hall. They each responded with some form of: "You didn't *live* there. You just spent the nights there." Mom did an effective job of framing the situation in such a way that even loving, rational adults *still* don't see a problem with sending a nine-year-old away.

In the solitude of the bike ride that day, I struggled to shake my feelings of neglect and abandonment. I'd spent years pretending that the time at Mrs. Hall's had never happened. Mom's complete disregard for our safety that morning stirred everything up.

God, I hated having sad feelings because they made me feel vulnerable. I despised being vulnerable because it made me feel weak. By the time I reached the campground outside of Prineville, I slid back into what I knew best—detachment and denial. At the time, it was just so much easier to dwell in the land of make-believe than deal with the reality of the past.

That night we camped at Ochoco Reservoir. I cycled into the campground looking for our site and was pleased to see that the tent had already been assembled. Lindsey and Matt were sitting at the picnic table, chatting. Matt and Lindsey looked relaxed, but when I pulled up near them, their demeanor changed. They were probably wondering if I was still angry.

To let them know I was in a better place, I asked, "Who put the tent together?"

"Me," replied Matt. "I spent the whole night last night worried it would come crashing down on us, so I put it together."

"It only took him about fifteen minutes," Lindsey said.

"Well, if it stays up that will be fifteen minutes well spent," I replied.

I then asked where the others were. "The little girls are playing in the tent and Marc is down at the reservoir, swimming," said Lindsey.

"I think I'll join him."

Matt wanted to go swimming too, so we both headed for the reservoir, where we found Marc dangling his feet in the murky water. Matt and I sat down on either side of him. For a few moments the three of us didn't speak. I took this time to take in our new surroundings. The landscape was dry and arid. The lushness of the previous night was gone. Scraggly pines and sagebrush bordered the reservoir. Marc looked tired and small. His short, dark hair was windblown, and he was a bit sunburned. Matt, though taller and blond, was sporting the same look.

To start up a conversation, I asked Marc, "How are you doing?"

Marc looked at me. "Did you have to yell at Mom? I hate it when you start yelling because it's embarrassing."

Before I could say anything, Matt said, "Yeah, Laura. Your voice carries and everyone could hear you."

Looking at the two of them, I could tell that they were angry with me, so I said, "I'm sorry. I was just really pissed off."

Marc tossed a rock in the water. "So were we, but we didn't let the whole world know it."

I hadn't really thought of their feelings in the moment. "Okay. I'll try not to yell anymore. I was just really pissed."

A few minutes later, Mom, Lindsey, and the little girls joined us, and we changed the subject. For the next hour we all cooled off in the water and pretended the argument between Mom and me had never happened. Detachment and denial works every time.

That night, Mom held a group meeting. "In the future, make sure you have enough water with you."

No shit! I thought, and began to say something, but Mom cut me off: "And whoever is driving in the morning *will* stop and check to see if the riders need anything. Agreed?"

We all nodded in agreement. Mom continued, "Now, let's look at the map and decide where we're biking to tomorrow. I'll be biking first, and Lindsey will tear down the camp. We need to pick our final destination for the day and a midway point for Lindsey and me to switch."

Lindsey laid the map on the picnic table so we could all get a good look. We followed her finger as it traced Highway 26. It was decided that we'd cross the Blue Mountains and finish in the town of John Day.

With the next day planned, Mom said, "I need you guys to gather firewood so we can eat."

Between the seven of us, we collected enough wood for a week, and the boys built a raging fire. For a second night in a row, we ate hotdogs and baked beans. I was getting a little tired of processed meat and beans but thought it wouldn't be wise to complain.

When we crawled into the tent after cleaning up the dinner dishes, I was even more exhausted than the night before and was sound asleep before learning anything more about Fletch's adventures.

Mom woke Matt, Marc, and me up at around six the next morning. As I climbed out of the tent, the first thing I noticed was that it was freezing-ass cold. Then I spied Mom, Matt, and Marc standing around a little fire Mom must have built. When I went over to join them, Mom handed me a bowl of oatmeal and a cup of tea.

"Thanks," I said, and scarfed the food down. It seemed Mom was trying to make up for yesterday's mishaps.

When we finished our breakfast, Mom told us to put our dishes on the picnic table and Lindsey would clean them up later. Then she got on her bike and said cheerfully, "Okay. We're off."

I climbed on my bike and looked down to see that Mom must've filled my water bottle. I thought to myself, *Well that's progress.*

Our campground was at the base of the Blue Mountains, which meant we were climbing. It was so cold that morning I could see my breath, and the clothes we wore didn't help. We were all in shorts and t-shirts. Cycling warmed us up some, but our hands were bitterly cold.

"This is a stupid idea," said Matt, "but what if we put our socks on our hands?"

"It sounds like a brilliant idea," I said. We pulled over and turned our socks into gloves.

As I struggled up the Blues, I looked down at my socked hands and realized just how ill prepared we were for this trip. We were clueless about the terrain and the weather east of the Cascades. Growing up in the Willamette Valley, we'd only experienced fairly mild summer temperatures. Eastern Oregon felt like a completely different planet.

Oregon history is taught in the fourth grade, and I really didn't pay too much attention. If I had, maybe I would've known that Eastern Oregon consists of two mountain ranges: the Blue Mountains and the Strawberry Mountains. The valley between the ranges is high desert, which means the nights and early mornings are freezing cold, and the late mornings and afternoons are hotter than hell. That being said, our mother had taught this shit for years. She should've known.

That morning we began with our socks on our hands to keep warm. By the time Lindsey met up with us in Mitchell, the temperature had risen by fifty degrees, and the socks were off. It began to dawn on me why so many people died in the Oregon Trail video game. This part of the state sucked.

In Mitchell, we ate lunch, then Mom and Lindsey switched places. I asked Mom for a few dollars just in case we passed a gas station, where we could get some sodas.

"I don't know if there'll be anything, but here's five dollars."

I took the cash. "Thanks."

We refilled our water bottles and then took off. The town of John Day was another seventy miles east, and we wanted to get there before six.

The four of us fell back into cycling at our own pace and didn't see one another for a couple of hours when Matt and Marc stopped for a Coke. The time alone on the bike was both a blessing and a curse. I liked being alone and going at my own pace, but I hated where my mind would take me. Mom wasn't the only one who was a master of denial. I too had my own worries that I didn't want to face.

We'd left home just a few days after the end of school, and before my grades arrived in the mail. I'd barely passed all of my classes and wondered if I'd received enough credits to graduate on time next spring. My academic plan was working, but by this time I was beginning to realize that it wasn't working *for me*. In the fall I'd be starting my senior year, and I had no idea if I'd graduate, or what I'd do after graduation. Just thinking about school was giving me anxiety, and I decided to forget about it until we returned to Willamette in August.

I found the boys sitting on a bench in the shade of an old convenience store and gas station. The store was made of wood planks with flaking white paint. The gas pumps were so old that they looked like they originally filled Model-Ts.

As I joined them, Marc said, "Give us the five Mom gave you so we can get some Cokes."

I dug in my pocket and handed him the money, instructing him to get one for each of us. Lindsey pulled in while Marc was in the store and asked what we were doing.

"Marc's getting some Cokes."

"Oh, good idea," she said as she got off her bike.

Marc returned with four cans of pop and joined us on the bench. We downed our drinks and started biking. We still had about another hour and a half to bike.

We actually rode the last leg together. We spent the time laughing about our experiences thus far and talking about what we thought the next few days would bring. It was the first time since beginning the trip that we'd all enjoyed each other's company.

The campground in John Day was along the John Day River, and we found our campsite near the water. Before we arrived, Mom had shopped at a local grocery store and bought ice, hamburger, buns, watermelon, and potato salad. When we rode into the site at around five, Mom had even made us Kool-Aid.

"I'm sick of hotdogs," Mom said. "So I got stuff for burgers."

"We're *all* sick of hotdogs," said Matt, and he began setting up the tent.

Marc, Lindsey, and I collected firewood while Mom started on dinner. While I was walking around picking up twigs and breaking down branches, I saw Myrtle and Emily playing together. I hadn't really given the little girls a lot of thought over the last few days. I only really saw them when Mom and Lindsey switched places, and in the evenings. They looked like they were having fun, but I thought they must be bored to death being in the car most of the day.

While we were eating, Mom opened up our trusty map and said, "All right. Tomorrow we're going to Vale. I've made arrangements to stay with my friend Isla for the night. We'll do our laundry there, and then we'll head out for Idaho the next day."

Isla was a friend of Mom's who used to live in Willamette. Mom had called her before we left and asked if we could camp out at her place for a night.

"How far is it from here to Vale?" Lindsey asked.

Mom squinted at the map. "It's a long way. We have to climb the Strawberry Mountains tomorrow. It'll take us all day. How about we switch places in Unity?"

With the plan for the next day settled, we cleaned up our dishes, put out the fire, and went to bed early wondering why they were called the Strawberry Mountains. To this day I still don't know.

Over the last few nights, each of us had laid claim to our own spots in the tent and had already set up our sleeping bags. In no time at all, we were settled in and listening to chapter four of Fletch. Fletch had agreed to kill Alan Stanwyk for $50,000, but it was all a con. Now we just needed to learn what the con was. If I could just stay awake for a whole chapter, maybe I would have had a better idea of the plot, but I was fast asleep by about the second page.

Mom woke us at six the next morning. I tumbled out of the tent, slipped on my shoes, which still looked pretty good after three days and almost 400 miles, and tried to get my bearings. Once again, Mom had made us a small breakfast of oatmeal and tea.

I was beginning to like cycling with Mom in the morning. The temperature during the early portion of our ride was in the mid-thirties. We wore sweatshirts that morning and slipped our socks back on our hands. Once the sun was up over the horizon, we took the socks and sweatshirts off and continued on our way. Lindsey and the girls caught up with us at around ten o'clock. She slowed down and asked if we were okay, then sped off.

The mountain range we were cycling through, while not as densely forested as the Cascades, did provide us shade as we cycled. There was very little traffic on the road, and we were able to ride at our leisure.

A few hours later we found Lindsey and the girls parked outside a small post office in Unity. She said, "There's really not a lot here. Where should we go and eat?"

Mom's demeanor changed, and she asked tersely, "Is there a park or even a little pull-in where we could make some sandwiches?"

Lindsey shot back, "I don't know. I didn't look."

Sensing the tone between the two of them was a little testy, I wondered if a fight was in the making.

Mom got off her bike and dropped it. "I'll tell you what. Take your bike off the rack. Put my bike back on and I'll drive through town and see where we can eat."

"You do that!" said Lindsey.

At that point I knew there was a fight brewing. I couldn't figure out where the tension was coming from. The ride that morning had been serene. Mom's behavior changed so quickly that I was left kind of numb as I watched Lindsey switch the bicycles, jump on hers, and start cycling through town. As Matt, Marc, and I stood looking at each other, I heard Mom slam the car door and watched her drive away.

Marc looked at us. "Well, this should be interesting," he said, and all three of us followed them.

We found Mom waiting for us at a small rest area right outside of town. She'd pulled out the cooler and was making sandwiches for us while the little girls were off doing their thing. Lindsey was sitting under a tree by herself drinking a soda. The rest of us ate our lunch in silence. A little while later, Lindsey jumped on her bike and pedaled off before the boys and I were done. As I watched her go, I thought, *Wow! This is going to be a fun afternoon.*

It took us another four hours of cycling before we made it to Vale. Mom was waiting for us at the city limits, ready to tell us how to get to Isla's house. I was relieved that we'd be staying with other people. That way Mom and Lindsey would *have* to put their differences aside—at least for the night.

We only spent two nights at Isla's, but it gave us time to do laundry, restock our food supply, and get some much-needed rest. Plus, it was just nice to talk to someone new. Eastern Oregon is an isolated area, and we really hadn't met many people.

The best thing about Isla's house was her bathroom. In the shower I was able to wash away three days' worth of road grime. It's impossible to explain what it's like to actually feel clean after something like that. A close second to the shower was sitting in an actual chair. If I wasn't sitting on my skinny bicycle seat, I was sitting at a picnic table or on a log by the fire. To sit in a chair was pure luxury.

During our mini break, I was feeling pretty good about our accomplishments. Each day, we were becoming stronger cyclists. We were getting the hang of camping. Thanks to Matt, I was no longer afraid that the tent would come crashing down on us. Granted, during our second day in the lava beds when I felt like I was going to die, I'd had my doubts. But now that we were almost to Idaho, I thought we might actually make it—to Montana.

It was hotter than hell the day we cycled the seventy miles between Vale and Boise, Idaho. The original plan was to cycle to Boise and find a nearby campground. When Mom drove ahead, all she could find was a KOA campground in the town of Meridian, a few miles outside of Boise.

Mom paid for a site and unloaded the car. Once that had been done, she and the little girls drove back and found the four of us cycling outside of Boise. She told us how to get to Meridian and the KOA camp. Why she didn't let us load up our bikes and drive us to the campground, I'll never know. When we finally did make it to the KOA, we were surprised to discover that it had a pool.

Matt looked over at me. "What is this? Luxury camping?"

"I have no idea. What even is a KOA?"

"Who cares!" said Marc. "There's a fucking pool! Maybe they even have showers."

After finding our site, Mom informed us that there were showers and even a laundromat. My thoughts were only on the pool, and the others felt the same, because we all changed into swimsuits and went swimming. We spent the rest of the afternoon lounging poolside.

I still don't know what a KOA is, but over the course of the trip we'd stay at quite a few of them. They'd be the closest we'd get to staying in an actual motel.

Later that night, we decided the next day we'd bicycle towards Mountain Home and stay the night in Bruneau Dunes. It would be a hot ride, but only seventy miles. Lindsey would ride the first shift and switch places with Mom in a town called Regina. The whole ride would only take us about six hours. A very hot six hours.

The thirty-five miles our mother cycled from Regina to Bruneau Dunes were hard on her. We were riding through desert; the whole area was like something out of *Lawrence of Arabia*. When we finally made it to the campground, she sat in the shade of the tent and drank buckets of water. While she was recovering, I took the younger kids for a walk around the park while Lindsey stayed with Mom.

The only other people staying there were paleontology students from the University of Idaho. The students were there searching for dinosaur bones and other fossils, which I found ironic. While they were trying to uncover prehistoric remains, we were just trying to ignore our past and figure out who we were as a family now. At least the students knew what they were looking for. We had no clue what we were doing.

We returned to our campsite to find Lindsey and Mom sitting in the shade together, looking at the map.

"Hey, you guys, come over here," said Mom.

The five of us ambled over and joined them. "Listen," she said. "We've been looking at the map, and we don't think it's a good idea to cycle the next section."

Matt asked why. "We'd be riding through the Craters of the Moon wilderness area, which is more than 100 miles of lava, sagebrush, and no facilities," said Lindsey.

"I really can't take this heat," said Mom. "In Oregon we at least had small towns, rivers, and lakes to head to. Not here. I just can't do it."

I looked at the map, and it was obvious that the next section would be torture. I was relieved that Mom felt the same way, but couldn't help but wonder how we'd get all of us from point A to point B, so I asked, "What are we going to do?"

"We're going to drive across the state. We'll load up our things, put the bikes on the rack, and drive."

That was exactly what I was worried she'd say. I looked at the Escort, thinking, *This definitely won't work.*

That night, a windstorm blew through the camp—an omen of things to come. As the wind howled, I thought for sure that the tent and all of us in it would be blown away. By some miracle, our tent stayed up.

Crawling out of the tent in the morning, I saw that all the students' tents and camping gear had been strewn all over the place. Some of their tents had blown into the sagebrush, and papers were scattered about. But thanks to Matt's tent-building skills, we were all okay.

Admiring his handiwork, Matt shook a tent pole. "Man, I can't believe this thing stayed up all night."

Mom, who was shaking out a sleeping bag, said, "Let's not press our luck. Start packing your things so we can get moving."

Matt and I looked at each other, realizing that it would be up to us to make everything, and everyone, fit in the Escort.

Matt mouthed, "*How?*"

In response I just shrugged my shoulders and began moving our gear near the car. We attacked the problem like a puzzle and began loading up the car like a Tetris board. Back in Willamette we had discovered the trick of laying the sleeping bags across the seats. We then stuffed as much stuff as we could into the trunk and under the front seats of the car. In the end there was just enough space for everyone if the little girls sat on people's laps. Emily sat in the front on Lindsey's lap, and Myrtle sat in the back with the boys and me. The big question was whether or not the bicycle rack could really hold all of our bikes.

Matt and I loaded the bikes and secured them with bungee cords. They looked stable on the rack, but was the rack fully secured to the bumper? That was the real question.

When we were done, Matt said, "God, I don't know. Laura, what do you think?"

"Well, they're on there now," I said. "Maybe we'll be okay." Then we all climbed in the car and began heading down the road.

Not long after we left the campground, Mom hit a bump in the road, the car bounced, and there was a huge crash. Mom hit the brakes and Marc jumped out of the car, asking, "What the hell was that?"

As I climbed out too, I saw Marc chasing a bike tire down the road. It was so comical I started laughing, and only stopped when I realized the rack had fallen off the bumper.

The whole situation was absurd. We were in the middle of the Idaho desert, in this teeny tiny car, crammed with seven people and six bikes, and the damn rack falls off. All Mom could do was stand there scratching her head while Matt and Marc pulled the rack to the side of the road. Fortunately, an older guy in a truck stopped and asked if we needed any help. Another angel?

"Oh, thank God you stopped," said Mom. "Our rack fell off the car and I don't know what to do."

The man looked at the car, then the rack, and then at all of us kids and said, "I'll tell you what. I know a guy in Mountain Home who may be able to help you. Why don't you throw the bikes and rack in the back of my truck and follow me?"

A look of relief swept across Mom's face. "Would you do that? Oh, thank you."

Grateful for the offer, Lindsey and Marc took the bikes off the rack. Before Matt and I put them in the man's truck, we checked the bikes for damage. Miraculously, they were still in good shape. With the bikes sorted out, Matt heaved the rack on top of the bikes.

The man asked, "Do any of you want to ride with me?"

Matt, Marc, and I jumped at the chance, so he told us to climb in the front. Then he turned to Mom and said, "Follow me."

When he got in the truck, we all introduced ourselves and he told us his name was Luther. The first thing I noticed about him was his manner. He had a gentle way about him. As we were driving, he asked, "What the hell are you guys doing out in the middle of nowhere with all those bikes, anyway?"

"We're cycling across the country," said Marc.

Luther gave us a sideways look. "Really? That's crazy."

With no hesitation, Matt replied, "Yes, it is."

As we drove along, Luther asked us where we were from and where we were cycling to.

"We're from Oregon," I said, "and we're headed to New York."

Luther let out a belly laugh. "Well, I'll be damned."

As he pulled into a rundown garage outside of Mountain Home, he said, "This fella is a good guy, but he's a little different. Let me go talk to him."

Mom had pulled in right behind him and got out of the car. Matt, Marc, and I jumped out of Luther's truck to join her. A few minutes later, Luther returned with a man he introduced as Hoot.

Hoot appeared to be in his mid-thirties, was of medium height, and skinny. His hair was long, pulled back into a ponytail, and he wore a red bandana as a headband. He had on torn, faded Levi's, a white T-shirt with a pack of cigarettes rolled up in his sleeve, and had at least two tattoos—one on each forearm. He looked at Mom and said, "What's the problem?"

Mom explained that the rack had fallen off the car and we needed to get it back on.

"Pull it into the garage and I'll see what I can do."

Luther looked at us. "Well. I need to go. You kids help me get the bikes off the back of the truck." With the bikes and rack unloaded, he chuckled and said, "New York? Good luck, you guys," and he jumped back in his truck and drove away.

With the Escort parked in his garage, Hoot asked, "Now. What the hell are you guys doing out here in Idaho in the first place?"

Mom explained what we were doing. When she was done talking, Hoot looked at her and said, "Lady. Are you fucking nuts or something?"

Matt, Marc, and I busted up laughing because the whole situation *was* nuts. Hoot didn't wait for Mom's reply and just said, "Well, let's see what I can do for ya."

Hoot's solution was to weld the bottom section of the rack onto the bumper. When he was done, he said, "The bumper will come off before this rack ever falls off again."

Mom thanked him and offered to pay for his services. Hoot refused. "Lady, keep your money. You need all the help you can get."

Chapter 7

THIS SUCKS

Mom backed the car out of Hoot's garage, and we put all the bicycles back on the rack. Once that was done, we all climbed back into the car and headed east towards Wyoming.

Lindsey was sitting in the front with Emily on her lap while I was squeezed between Matt and Marc with Myrtle on my lap. The car was hot, and our body odor could have killed a large elephant. I asked Mom and Lindsey to roll down their windows so we could get some fresh air, which didn't help that much. As for Myrtle's bony bottom digging into my thighs, there really wasn't much that could be done.

As we left Mountain Home, I asked Mom, "How long are we going today?"

Lindsey answered, "We're stopping before the Wyoming state line at Island Park Reservoir. It's over three hundred miles."

"So about *five* hours?" I whined. "Can we at least stop along the way? I don't know how long I can ride like this."

Mom looked back at me through the rearview mirror. "Well, we have a full tank, and I don't think we'll have to stop for gas. I'd really like to just drive straight there."

Adjusting Myrtle's bony butt again, I asked, "Could you maybe think about stopping when we're halfway? Let us get a soda or something?"

Perched in the front seat like Mom's lady in waiting, Lindsey said, "Laura, don't be a baby. Let's just get there, okay?"

Easy for you to say, Lindsey, I thought. *You try sitting back here between Stinky One and Two with a bony-ass girl on your lap for a while and see how you like it.*

As if the smell and cramped conditions weren't bad enough, the Escort only had an AM radio that rarely picked up any stations. To pass the time, Matt and Marc were each silently reading one of the mysteries that Lindsey had packed. With Myrtle on my lap, I could barely move, let alone read, and resigned myself to listening in on Mom and Lindsey's conversations. All they seemed to talk about was how Dad would have loved going on this trip.

About the time Lindsey said, "This trip would've been right up Dad's alley. He was such a student of history and an outdoorsman," I'd had it. Once again, Mom and Lindsey were rewriting history, creating their own fantasy. I felt like a hostage fighting against Stockholm Syndrome. To fight off their offensive, I thought about the reality of our father's health in the last years of his life. Dad's drinking, smoking, and diet deteriorated his body to the point that he couldn't walk up the stairs in our house without getting winded. The mere idea that he could've cycled around the block was ludicrous. In an attempt to tune them out, I leaned my head back and shut my eyes. As the two of them droned on about how amazing our dad was, a memory of Mom and Dad helping me write an essay for Mr. Ford's class sophomore year floated into my consciousness.

Mr. Ford had assigned us the task of writing a description of where we saw ourselves in ten years. I couldn't see where I'd be in one week's time, let alone ten years, so I asked my mother for help. Mom took my notebook and my parents wrote the essay for me. When Mom handed *their* essay back, I was given a glimpse of my parents' perception of me. In a nutshell, it said that I was a pseudo lesbian but would have a house full of children from various partners. My home would be filthy, with dirty diapers piling up while the kids crawled all around me. I would spend my time smoking cigarettes and watching television while I lived off of welfare. I never got the essay back from Mr. Ford and always wondered what he thought.

Quite honestly, my parents' image of me was the only future I could visualize for myself. My life would amount to nothing, and any hope for a prosperous future seemed futile. Ironically, it would take divine intervention to change the course of my life. However, as a teenager, I didn't have a lot of hope in the divine. Thankfully, God's intervention isn't dependent on my hope or faith.

I must've fallen asleep, because the next thing I knew, Mom was pulling into a service station. "Okay, guys," she said. "We have about another hundred miles to go before we get to the campground. I'm going inside to pay for gas, and I'll get us something to eat and drink. Matt, you pump the gas, and the rest of you guys get out and walk around."

As I waited for Matt and Marc to get out of the car, I quickly calculated that we had about an hour and a half to go. With the little break, and some fresh air, I figured I could tough it out.

We probably looked pretty strange as all seven of us tumbled out of the Escort. But we were in the middle of nowhere, Idaho, and the only person who saw us was the clerk in the service station.

As Matt finished pumping the gas, I took in our dry, bleak surroundings and asked Lindsey where we were. "Mud Lake," she said, not looking up from the map.

"Great name for such a godawful place," I said as I stretched my legs.

"At least we can see where the Rockies start from here," Marc said. "Maybe where we're camping will be better."

Looking east, I realized Marc was right. From 150 miles away, the outline of the Rockies appeared as a hazy beacon of hope. "Well," I said, "it can't be worse than here."

At that point Mom arrived with a bag of potato chips and a six pack of Coca-Cola. She handed each of us a soda and told Myrtle and Emily to share a can. With our sodas in hand, we all climbed back into our designated spots and continued on our way.

We hadn't eaten since breakfast and because we were starving, we practically inhaled the chips and sodas. The combination of salt and sugar on an empty stomach plus a stinky car made me nauseated. I thought for sure I was going to hurl before we reached our destination. The only thing that stopped me was the fear of mixing vomit with all the other odors. To cope with the discomfort, I leaned back, closed my eyes, and prayed we'd be stopping for the night soon.

Before sunset, we were out of the desert and camping in the foothills of the Rockies near a mountain stream. We jumped out of the car and headed for the water to cool off and wash away the stink. Between the rack falling off, Hoot, and the five-hour ride, it had been a hell of a day. I was now surrounded by trees, breathing fresh air, and swimming in cool water. I felt mercifully free of family drama, at least for now.

In the tent that night, as we lay in our sleeping bags, Marc said, "I can't believe we're here. I really didn't think we'd get out of Mountain Home."

I looked over at him. "Man, you should've seen yourself chasing that tire down the road. That was funny."

We all began laughing, and then Mom said, "Sometimes I think someone is watching over us."

"Well, whoever it is," I said, "I hope they're getting a good laugh."

"Who wants to read tonight?" Lindsey asked.

"I finished Fletch," said Marc.

Matt added, "Yeah I finished it the other day. Can we read something else?"

I was kind of irritated. "You jerks. I haven't read it yet. I thought we were reading it out loud?"

"I read it a long time ago," said Lindsey. "How about we read *Carioca Fletch*?"

"Just as long as I can finish the first book," I said. Lindsey handed me the first Fletch book, and then she began to read aloud the exploits of I.M. Fletcher in Rio de Janeiro.

The next morning, I woke to the smell of a campfire and to Lindsey and Mom talking quietly. I slipped on my shoes and climbed out of the tent. Mom was making pancakes and Lindsey was boiling water for tea. When I sat down at the picnic table, the map was open, so I asked if they had a plan.

"Mom and I decided that we're going to drive up to Yellowstone National Park today, and camp in Cody tonight," Lindsey said.

"Why?"

"I don't think it's a good idea to try to cycle over the pass," Mom said. "The elevation is almost eight thousand feet. We struggled in both the Cascades and the Blue Mountains, which was half that elevation."

I could see her point. "I really hate riding in the car, but you're right. Plus, we don't have enough socks to keep our hands warm."

Mom laughed. "I really didn't put a lot of thought into climbing mountain ranges, did I?"

"Well, Mom," I said, "if we'd thought this trip through, we wouldn't have left." For a moment, I wondered if my honesty would be met with the usual resistance.

Instead, she chuckled. "Could you tell the others that breakfast will be soon? I'd like to reach Yellowstone Lodge before noon today."

I poked my head into the tent and told the boys and little girls to get up and that there were pancakes for breakfast.

Looking back, I think this was the point when I began to feel more confident in myself. I began to voice my own quirky opinions without fear. It didn't bring my mother and I closer as mother and daughter. Rather, I began to differentiate myself from her perception of me.

Yellowstone Lodge was only fifty miles from our campground, and in no time at all we were standing by Old Faithful, waiting for her to blow. It felt like being in a *Mutual of Omaha's Wild Kingdom* episode. All that was missing was Marlin Perkins narrating the whole experience. When it did finally blow, I thought, *That's pretty cool; can we go now?* Unfortunately, Mom wanted to spend most of the day walking around looking at hot springs, mud pots, and other geysers. The truth is, once you've seen one mud pot, you've kind of seen them all.

The best part of the day was the cafeteria in the main lodge. Aside from that morning's pancakes, our meals had consisted of oatmeal for breakfast, peanut butter and jelly sandwiches for lunch, and hotdogs or hamburgers for dinner. Being able to order food, sit down in a chair, and eat something different was more exciting than all the natural wonders we'd seen that day. The side of fries with ketchup tasted like the eighth wonder of the world to me.

When we finally got back in the car and headed for Cody, I was more than ready to get going. I wish I could tell you how beautiful the scenery of Yellowstone was, but all I saw were the tops of trees. My view was obscured by Matt's armpit on the left and Marc's head on the right. The little bit I could glimpse was through a small gap between Myrtle, who was on my lap, and Emily's head, who was riding up front with Lindsey.

Outside of Cody, Mom pulled over at Buffalo Bill's hunting lodge in Pahaska Tepee. She and Lindsey wanted to consult the map, and she told me to take the younger kids to look at the lodge.

The lodge was an old, rustic, two-story log cabin with a wrap-around porch. The five of us climbed the stairs to the front door and discovered that it was closed. I took Myrtle and Emily by the hand and we walked around the porch, looking in through the windows. Matt joined us while we peered into the living room, where there was a fireplace and bear skin rug.

I said to him, "It's weird. I never really think of Buffalo Bill as being a real person. He seems more like a legend."

After days of sitting squished together in the back of the car, I must've been getting on his nerves, because he turned to me and said, "Laura, sometimes you're a fucking idiot. Of course he was a real person. Don't you read?"

The only thing I hated more than being called a dyke was being called an idiot. "Go to hell, Matt! I know he's a real person. Jackass."

"Would you guys knock it off and just look at the damn house?" said Marc.

Just when I was going to say something back, Mom and Lindsey showed up. Mom told us to get back in the car and informed us that we would be staying at a KOA camp outside of town.

I asked if I could ride in the front for a change, and Lindsey said, "No way."

Mom looked at Lindsey. "Switch places with Laura."

I thought Lindsey was going to throw a fit, but she just got in the back. As Myrtle was climbing in, I said, "She has a bony butt. Enjoy."

"Emily does too, so suck it," said Lindsey.

Emily's butt was bony, but at least I wasn't wedged between two stinky boys.

It was about four in the afternoon when we drove into the KOA. After setting up camp, Lindsey took the younger kids to the swimming pool while Mom went off to do laundry. I stayed at the campsite, giving myself some time and space away from everyone. Between listening to Mom and Lindsey's conversations about how wonderful our father was and my altercation with Matt, I could feel a growing sense of irritation. My chest became tight, and my ears were buzzing. I needed to get my mind off of my family. To calm myself down, I finished the first Fletch book and finally discovered how I.M. Fletcher solved the mystery.

Between chapters, I realized how much I missed cycling and longed for the rhythm of our days in Oregon. The freedom of biking on my own at my own pace was liberating. Sitting in the car felt like torture. My biggest fear was that our mother had lost her nerve and we'd drive the rest of the way. Just the thought of spending that much time in the car made me anxious.

A couple of hours later, Mom returned with the laundry and began folding the clothes on the picnic table. I began to help her and asked, "Mom, are we going to cycle tomorrow?"

Mom kept her head down. "I don't think so. We still have to go over the Tetons. I think we'll drive to Sheridan, where a college friend of mine said we could stay for a couple of nights."

"Why can't we drive over the Tetons and then bike to Sheridan from there?"

I waited for an answer, but Mom just kept folding the clothes. Giving up, I grabbed a clean towel from the pile. "I'm going to take a shower."

The showers in KOAs are awesome. Each shower was in its own little room with a personal changing area. That day I took my sweet time getting clean. In the steamy confines of my shower, I began to wonder what Mom's goal was for this trip. Was it to just get out of Willamette for the summer? Was she trying to prove something to herself? Was she on some kind of a quest that maybe even she wasn't aware of?

While I got dressed, I looked in the mirror. I hadn't looked at myself for days, and I noticed how tan I was, and how skinny I was getting. I looked into my own blue eyes and said out loud, "What do *you* want out of this whole thing?" Hell, I couldn't even answer that question.

That night after dinner, Mom told everyone else her plans for the next few days. Matt, who was a few inches taller than me, asked, "Can you at least let us all take a turn sitting in the front seat? It's hell back there."

"Fine," said Mom. "Lindsey goes first, then you can ride up front next, Matt."

Marc asked how long we would be in Sheridan, and if she still planned on going to Mount Rushmore. Mom said, "We'll be at Mount Rushmore for the Fourth, I promise you."

Her promise seemed to mollify the boys, and they didn't ask any more questions.

"Will we cycle after Sheridan?" I asked.

Lindsey said, "I don't see why not."

Mom didn't say anything. She was the only one with any real authority, and I just hoped that after visiting her friend, she'd get her nerve back.

The next morning, Mom roused all of us out of the tent to get an early start. I waited for Lindsey and the boys to climb out first and then forced myself to get up. I took a seat at the picnic table, where Mom had a breakfast of fruit and cereal waiting for us. Just as I was getting ready to eat my first bite of Corn Pops, I heard a sound like a wounded animal. I turned around to see Myrtle wandering around the camp half-asleep, groaning, "Uhhhh. Uhhh." As Mom went to guide her to the table, I asked, "Is she always this bad in the morning?"

"Myrtle's not really a morning person," said Lindsey. "She's fine when we let her sleep in, but otherwise she's a mess."

While I was watching Myrtle's early morning suffering, Emily had crawled out of the tent and was sitting across from me, sucking her two fingers and clutching her Strawberry Shortcake quilt. I poured her a bowl of cereal and said, "Emily seems to be okay with mornings."

"Yeah, but I don't think she's really awake," said Lindsey.

By this time, Mom had settled Myrtle down at the table between Matt and Marc and poured her a bowl of cereal too. With everyone in place, Mom joined us. "Okay. We're staying with my friend Jane for the next couple of days. She's expecting us later this afternoon. So, I want you guys to pack up everything while I get the girls ready."

"How long will it take us to get there?" asked Matt.

"About four hours. We're going to take our time, though, and make some stops along the way. We'll be crossing the Tetons, so I'm sure there're places we can get out and walk."

When we all got back in the car, I felt like the little bit of separation from one another the day before had helped. Matt and I weren't on each other's last nerve, and the thought of staying in an actual home and seeing other people seemed to ease the tension.

What I could see of the Tetons was spectacular. The grand peaks looked like something out of *The Sound of Music*, which prompted Lindsey to begin singing, *The hills are alive...*

When our mother, who can't carry a tune in a bucket, joined in, I said, "Please, God, make it stop."

To add to the cacophony, Matt and Marc began singing at the top of their lungs. From there they proceeded to sing all the *Sound of Music* songs they could remember. To tune them out I put my fingers in my ears and said, "Na na na, I can't hear you."

When they finished with *The Sound of Music*, they moved on to Simon and Garfunkel songs, which was only marginally better.

We were actually all enjoying each other's company that day, but that ended when Mom pulled into a McDonald's on the outskirts of Sheridan.

She parked the car. "Okay. You guys, we're going to eat here before we go to Jane's house. I don't want us arriving at her home starving to death. So, let's go in, order our food, and then I'll call her to let her know we're on the way."

When she was done talking, we all got out of the car, which is when we noticed that the other customers were staring at us. We *were* a strange sight. It's not every day that you see seven people scramble out of a two-door Ford Escort—originally white but now somewhere between brown and gray—with six bikes hanging off the bumper.

Matt was the most embarrassed by all the attention. "We look like circus freaks. Everyone's gawking at us."

Matt had a tendency to get embarrassed, and it could drive me a bit crazy. One minute he'd be fine, but if he noticed someone looking at us, he'd get upset. I just couldn't figure out why he cared what complete strangers thought of him.

Mom echoed my thoughts: "Matt, who cares? You'll never see these people again."

"I care. This is humiliating." He crossed his arms and glared at us.

"Let's just go inside," Mom said. "If it'll make you feel better, you can order whatever you want."

Without answering, Matt walked into the restaurant and got in line to order food. We lined up behind him, got our food, and found a place to sit. Matt took his meal and went and sat in a corner by himself to pout. I looked over at him eating his Quarter Pounder and thought, *Quit being such a dick.*

While we were eating, Mom used a payphone to call her friend Jane to let her know we'd be there in an hour or so. When we finished our meals, Mom said to Matt, "If it makes you less embarrassed, sit in the front seat."

"It helps," said Matt, "but it's still embarrassing."

Jane was a college friend of our mom's; they'd shared a dorm room their freshman year at the University of Idaho. Over the years, they'd exchanged Christmas cards but hadn't really kept in touch. Prior to leaving Oregon, Mom had contacted her to see if we could spend the night at her house when we traveled through Wyoming. Jane said that she had more than enough room for all of us and that she'd love to have us.

Jane's split-level home was in a nice part of town. When we knocked on her door, a tall, lean woman opened it and gave Mom a hug. "Lois, it's been too long. Bring your tribe in and let's get you settled."

"I am really happy you said we could stay," said Mom. "I think we could all use a break right about now."

Jane introduced us to her husband, Bob, and their two teenage sons, Danny and John. Then she showed all of us where we'd be sleeping. There were two guest rooms on the main floor where Lindsey, Mom, and the little girls would sleep. Matt, Marc, and I were to camp out downstairs in the family room, where there was a large screen television and a pool table.

It didn't take long for everyone to go in separate directions. Matt and Marc disappeared with Danny and John. Lindsey took advantage of having a room to herself and went to lie down. Mom, Jane, and Bob went into the living room with the little girls to talk. I found myself alone in the basement, so I flopped down on the couch and watched MTV for the rest of the afternoon. It was bliss.

That night, Jane ordered pizza and we all gathered around the kitchen table. Since leaving Isla's a week prior, we hadn't really talked to anyone outside of our group. It was nice talking to outsiders again. Bob, an engineer for the Wyoming Department of Transportation, asked us about the route we'd taken and where we planned on going next. Mom told him about cycling through Oregon and then Marc told him about our adventures with Hoot in Mountain Home.

Midway through the dinner, Jane looked at Mom and asked, "So, Lois, how many more kids do you have at home?"

"I have three more children at home."

Jane looked at all of us kids. "So, you have nine kids?"

Mom put her slice down and stared at Jane. "Yes. Four boys and five girls."

"Damn, most people drink when they're stressed. You and Henry must've used sex."

Lindsey and I locked eyes, and Matt and Marc looked shocked. I'd always wondered why Mom and Dad had nine kids, but never in a million years would've asked. I also didn't know how my mom would respond to Jane's question. It was a relief when Mom began laughing and picked up her pizza slice. She took a big bite. "I guess that's one way to look at it."

It was good to see Mom relax and laugh at herself. Maybe seeing Jane reminded her that there was a time before she was married, and she could thrive now that she was a widow.

The break did us all good. But up until the night before we left, Mom was still undecided about cycling the rest of the way. It was Bob who persuaded her to let us get back on our bikes. At dinner that night he asked, "Lois, how are you guys getting to South Dakota?"

"I was thinking of driving on Interstate 90, then dropping down to Custer."

I gave a groan, and Bob looked at me as he asked Mom, "Why are you driving? I thought you guys were cycling across the country."

"Well, I don't want the kids on the Interstate, and I just don't see another way across Wyoming from here."

"Lois, the whole state of Wyoming has a population smaller than the city of Portland. You probably won't see a dozen cars on the freeway. You'll be safer on the freeway than any other road you've cycled yet."

"Really?" said Mom. "You think it's safe?"

"Believe me. I work on these roads every day, and I can promise you that you'll be safe. Plus, if at any point you don't feel safe, just load up your bikes and drive."

"If you think it's safe, then we'll give it a try."

God, I could've kissed that man.

Lindsey, Matt, and I left Jane's house at six o'clock the next morning. We hopped on the Interstate and headed east. Bob was right—we probably only saw twelve cars the whole day, and by noon I knew why. Because there isn't a damn thing in eastern Wyoming.

It took us three days to reach South Dakota from Sheridan. Three days of nothing but cows, dust, prairie land, and barbed wire fences. Cycling was better than riding in the car, but by the end of the second day I began to wonder if we'd ever see trees again. At least when we cycled through the high desert in Oregon, I could see mountain ranges on the horizon. In Wyoming, all I could see were more fields of dirt.

Our last night in Wyoming, we were all in the tent when I asked, "How much farther do we have to go until we see something other than dirt?"

Matt piped up, "Tomorrow we should be in the Black Hills, and then we can go see Mount Rushmore."

"Why are you so excited about Mount Rushmore? I just don't get it."

"Come on, Laura," he said. "Haven't you always wanted to see it? Plus, we'll be there for the Fourth of July!"

I said, "It'll probably be a lot better than the crappy fireworks at the Willamette fairgrounds with the scratchy 'Star-Spangled Banner' record that they play."

"It wouldn't take a lot to be better than the fireworks at home," Mom chuckled.

With that, I began to read the next chapter of *Carioca Fletch*.

The hope of finding trees and the enthusiasm of my brothers propelled me the next day. By late afternoon we arrived in Custer, South Dakota, where there were trees. It wasn't the dense forest of the Rockies, but the terrain was much better than the vast majority of Wyoming.

Mom rewarded us for powering through three days of ugly terrain by splurging on a KOA. Showers, laundry, and a swimming pool were the perfect oasis. We arrived on July 2 and planned on heading out on July 5. This gave us almost three days to recover and prepare for the next leg of our journey.

During our time at the camp, it became obvious that other campers were giving us a wide berth. When we'd go to the pool, the other campers would leave. When we walked past other sites and said hello, they just kind of looked at us. I think people were a little leery because of the size of our group and the way we were traveling. In 1985, you just didn't see people cycling across the country, and you sure as hell didn't see a mom and six kids doing it. The reaction of other people only made us more clannish, which didn't help.

There were positives to this situation. We always had the pool to ourselves, and no one ever messed with our stuff. When we'd leave for the day to go sightseeing, we'd lock up our bikes, but I doubt we really needed to.

The morning of the Fourth, Matt woke up before any of us and built a fire. Mom was the next to roll out of bed, and she began to make breakfast. The smell of bacon wafted through the tent and roused me out of bed. Before long, we were all sitting around the picnic table, eating, drinking tea, and talking about the day ahead.

"Listen," said Mom. "Why don't you guys finish eating, go take a shower, and then we'll head up the mountain to the park?"

Matt popped up, grabbed a towel and some clothes out of the tent, and hit the showers with Marc right behind him.

I said to Mom, "I don't think I've seen those two move that fast the whole trip."

"They're just excited. Will you help me clean these dishes? Lindsey, will you take the girls, give them a shower, and help them get ready?"

Lindsey disappeared with the girls and I helped Mom clean up. It only took a few minutes, and when we were done, I ducked into the tent, changed, and went to brush my teeth. I figured if I took the time to shower, the boys would blow a gasket.

Twenty minutes later, we were all wedged back in the car, heading up the mountain towards what I called the four enormous heads. As we got closer to the park, Matt said, "Marc, I'm so excited I feel like my heart's gonna skip a beat."

I looked at him like he was nuts.

Mom looked over at him. "This really means that much to you?"

"It's the one place I really wanted to see on this whole trip. I don't know why. I just think it's amazing."

I was surprised by how high up in the Black Hills we had to climb to reach the park. It was twenty miles of switchbacks from Custer to the park and took forever. At around noon, when Mom finally reached the entrance, I thought Matt was going to jump out before she parked the car.

Once out of the car, Mom said, "Okay, you guys, let's go in and check out the park together. Once we figure out where things are, we can split up."

The seven of us walked into the park and followed a trail towards a viewpoint of the monument. As we came around a curve, we were greeted with a wonderful view of the four presidents. Matt said, "Oh my God. It's *amazing!*"

I really wanted to be a disinterested teenager, but I have to admit Mount Rushmore was pretty cool. I could almost see

Cary Grant scaling down the nose of Thomas Jefferson in *North by Northwest.*

We spent the whole day at the park, capping off the experience that evening with a performance by the Marine Corps Band in the amphitheater. It was a beautiful setting with the band filling the stage and the illuminated monument in the background. The only drawback was the night's speaker, a congressman from North Dakota. He droned on about God, faith, and patriotism to the point that I quit listening. My ears did perk up when he closed his speech with, "And I give thanks that God's an American citizen. Amen." I looked at Lindsey. "Did he really say that?"

"Yeah. I didn't realize God had a nationality."

"Do you think God has a passport? If he does, what do you think his picture looks like?"

The two of us began to chuckle, and an old couple in front of us turned around and the white-haired man said, "Be respectful."

Lindsey muttered, "Sorry."

I whispered to Lindsey, "Some people are so serious," and we began to giggle again. This time Mom gave us a dirty look, so we stopped. At that point, the Marine Corps Band began to play, and we spent the rest of our evening listening to patriotic tunes.

Later that night, in the tent, I said, "I thought God was from Israel. Do you think he had to take a citizenship test to become American?"

We all started laughing, and then Marc said, "Even without the fireworks, it really wasn't anything like Willamette's Fourth of July, was it?"

"Nope," said Matt. "It was awesome."

I fell asleep thinking that the next part of the trip through the Midwest would be a breeze because it was so flat. God, ignorance really is bliss.

Chapter 8

MAY WE NO LONGER BE
IN KANSAS, TOTO

We had six weeks to get to New York City, so our fearless leaders, Mom and Lindsey, looked at the map and created a timeline for reaching our remaining destinations. The next two places were Mom's choices, both in Missouri. She wanted to visit Harry Truman's home in Independence and the home of Mark Twain in Hannibal.

Our navigators decided we'd cycle south through Nebraska into Kansas, then across Kansas to Missouri. When they showed Matt, Marc, and me their plan, it looked appealing. We wouldn't be cycling more than seventy miles a day and each day we'd be camping near a lake. After traversing Oregon and eastern Wyoming, Nebraska and Kansas would be a breeze—or so we thought.

The day we left Custer, we were only going forty miles to Angostura Reservoir, so we took our time leaving the KOA. We went for one last swim in the pool and took showers. It was probably noon before we began riding. Mom and the little girls drove ahead of us to find a campsite.

As soon as we were out of the Black Hills, the terrain turned to grassland and dust, which, on its own, wouldn't have been too bad. It was the headwind that was annoying. I'd rather climb hills than deal with a headwind any day. Hills have a descent, but there's no end to wind. During the ride, I kept telling myself, *It's just a windy day. Tomorrow will be different.*

When we met up with Mom and the girls at the campground, we were all coated in a layer of dust. Somehow, even the little girls were filthy. The campground didn't have showers, so we all went swimming in the reservoir to get clean.

As we washed the day's road grime off of our bodies, Matt said, "That headwind sucked! Do you think we'll have it every day?"

I shrugged. "I was wondering the same thing. I'm hoping it was just a windy day, 'cause facing it all the time will blow."

"Look at it this way," Mom chimed in. "We won't be cycling very far each day, and you can go swimming when you're done. This isn't so bad right now, is it?"

Matt looked at her with distrust in his eyes. "Well no, but how do we know the campgrounds and lakes in Nebraska and Kansas will be this good? What do we do then?"

Mom dismissed him with "We'll deal with it."

The next day the wind didn't let up and, to my chagrin, the ride wasn't flat, but rather a never-ending series of rolling dirt hills. Lindsey, Matt, Marc, and I pushed forward with our heads bent down, unprotected eyes squinting, and backs aching.

At one point I almost ran into Matt, who'd come to a stop. When I looked up, I noticed that both he and Marc were next to a sign that said, "Welcome to Nebraska."

"What's up?" I asked.

Matt looked exhausted. "We're in Nebraska. She's not turning back, is she?"

I think we all knew that this adventure was really Mom's, and we weren't turning back unless *she* decided to. "It doesn't look that way. Why do you ask?"

"I don't know. I guess I thought we'd get to Mount Rushmore and she'd turn around."

Marc, who looked as wiped as Matt, waved his arm, pointing out the landscape. "This is shit. All of it, the heat, wind, dust, and," he made air quotes, "*scenery*."

"Maybe the campground at Box Butte will be better?" I replied. "It's supposed to have a lake, and if we can swim and cool off it'll help."

Matt's skinny shoulders sagged. "Maybe" was his last remark as the boys took off.

I tried to keep pace with them but couldn't. We still had forty-five miles to bike, and they were just too strong for me. Eventually, I dropped back and then took a break to wait for Lindsey.

I sat on the side of the road, drinking some water and looking over the area. Marc was right. It was bleak, and only a handful of cars passed me. Sitting in the middle of nowhere, I began thinking about Matt's attitude. He'd been ready to turn around once he saw Mount Rushmore. What a selfish little bastard. Right then, Lindsey arrived with a big grin on her face.

"Damn!" she said. "We're in Nebraska! Can you believe it?"

"Not really," I groaned. "I didn't think it would be this ugly."

"Yeah," Lindsey laughed. "But just think about how far we've come. Thousands and thousands of miles. It's so amazing." Lindsey was never good with depth perception—or math.

"Well, that's one way to look at it." Then I asked, "Do you actually need to stop, or are you good to keep going?"

Lindsey took a swig of water and squinted at the dusty horizon. "I'm good. I want to get to the campground and go swimming."

I climbed back on my bike and the two of us cycled the last twenty miles together. During that time we didn't really speak. We were too focused on fighting the headwind. However, I did marvel at the difference between Lindsey's and the boys' attitudes. I could see both points of view. The cycling was horrible, but we were making progress. My feeling was that even a windy, hot, and humid Nebraska was better than Willamette.

Unfortunately, when we arrived at the campground, all our hopes for a relaxing afternoon in a cool lake were dashed—there was little shade, and the lake was nothing more than a mosquito-infested pond.

We'd dealt with mountains, freezing cold mornings, and blazing hot afternoons, but we'd been fairly mosquito-free up until this point. The stagnant lake was a breeding ground for the little bloodsuckers. When Lindsey and I found our campsite, everyone was sitting at the picnic table waiting for us. Mom slapped her arm and flicked a mosquito off. "I think we need to find a store and get some bug repellent."

"Can I go with you?" Matt asked. "I need a break from this crap."

Mom looked at all our dejected, sunburnt faces and then suggested, "Let's set up the camp and then we'll *all* go into town and we'll get some ice cream too."

This seemed to perk everyone up and within a few minutes the tent was pitched, car unloaded, and bikes locked up.

We stopped at a nearby Dairy Queen for the promised ice cream treats. We then headed for a grocery store, where we bought supplies for dinner and a can of OFF! insect repellent. When we returned to the campground, we took turns covering ourselves in bug spray and trying to stay cool.

The lack of trees in the campground meant that we huddled in the shade of the tent and tried to keep each other company. Mom and Lindsey took this time to look over the map. Thinking it would cheer us up, Lindsey said, "Look here. We've broken down Nebraska into four nights and then we'll be in Kansas. If we can get through the next four days, I think it'll be better."

Matt asked, "Am I supposed to feel better that for the next four days we have to cycle through this shit?"

Lindsey had had enough of his whining. "I'm trying to help you see that there's light at the end of this tunnel."

"Great," Matt scoffed. He got up, brushed the dirt from his shorts, and walked away.

As I watched his blond head and bent shoulders disappear down a path, I thought, *He just needs a break from all of us.*

Marc, who'd been reading a book while this all happened, caught my eye and shrugged. I think that by this time, even Marc had reached his limit with Matt, because he went back to reading. Deciding to follow his lead, I rummaged through the bag of paperback mysteries, found an Ed McBain *87th Precinct*, and began to read. Mom took the girls for a walk, and Lindsey continued to study the map.

Life around the campsite remained tense. That night we had an early dinner of Kraft Mac & Cheese and watermelon. The usual banter among us was subdued. We just went through the motions of cooking, eating, and cleaning up. We didn't build a campfire that night, choosing to go to bed early. We wanted to get an early start so we could get away from Box Butte. We didn't even read out loud that night.

At some point in the night, Marc got up to use the restroom. As he tried to unzip the front of the tent, he accidentally tore the fly screen. Within minutes, we were inundated with mosquitoes. The repellent may have kept them from biting us, but it didn't stop them from dive-bombing and buzzing in our ears all night.

The next day's ride was sixty miles of the same misery, heat, hills, and wind. Not to mention that we were sleep deprived. We stayed at Bridgeport Recreational Area and campground, which was actually worse than Box Butte Reservoir.

When I arrived at the campsite, Matt was with Mom and he was crying. As a family, we weren't big criers. We all swore like sailors and knew how to throw a punch. It took a lot to make any of us cry, and I figured that Matt must've reached his breaking point. As I approached them, I heard Matt say, "I don't want to do this anymore. I just want to go home. I'm done."

"I'll call Nate and make arrangements for you to fly home when we get to Kansas City. Will that make you happy?" Mom asked.

"I guess so," Matt whined. He then walked towards the lake with Marc right behind him.

"What the hell?" I asked. "You're just going to let him go home? Just let him quit?"

"Laura, he wants to go home," Mom said. "What do you want me to do?"

"Tell him to grow a pair."

"That's not nice," she hissed at me.

I stared at her for a few seconds, and then said, "Fuck this." I threw down my bike and caught up with the boys, who were standing in the lake.

As I approached them, I heard Marc say, "You can't go home. We're almost halfway there. Why do you want to quit now?"

"Because this sucks, and it's stupid. We look ridiculous, Marc. What other reasons to I need?"

"Listen." Marc's voice was low and calm. "I'm not quitting. And if you go home, I'll be the only guy left. You can't do this to me."

I jumped in, my voice louder. "Matt, you can't quit! We'll all get to New York and you'll look like a wuss."

Matt turned on me, full of rage. "Listen, Laura. This is ALL your fault. You're the one who said, 'My teacher goes on bike trips. I think we should take a bike trip too.' If you'd kept your mouth shut, we wouldn't be here right now."

"Go to hell, Matt, you baby!" I turned and left the two boys to work it out. Back at the campsite, I grabbed my book and sat in the shade pretending to read. For the life of me I couldn't figure out why Matt wanted to go home. Did he really think Willamette would be better? Maybe because he and Nate got along better, for Matt it would've been. I just couldn't see the upside for myself.

I don't know what Marc said to Matt, but by the time the boys returned to the campsite, Matt had changed his mind. He told Mom, "I want to finish the trip. I won't go home."

"Good," she said, and left it at that.

Although I was wondering why he'd changed his mind, I decided not to push my luck with him. Considering our history of pissing each other off, I thought it'd be for the best if I just let it go.

The one good thing about the campgrounds in Nebraska was they had indoor plumbing and showers. We didn't have to use outhouses, and we could actually get clean. As for the rest of the amenities? Their campsites left a lot to be desired. There was no shade, and the heat, dust, and bugs were omnipresent. There just wasn't a break from the harsh conditions.

To keep the bugs out of the tent, Mom went to a local market and bought needles and thread to repair the torn screen. That night before we went to bed, she said, "Listen, you all need to go use the restroom now because once we climb in, I'm sewing us in to keep the bugs out."

Marc asked, "How in the hell are we going to get out in the morning?"

"Just pull the thread and it should come undone," Mom replied. "And before climbing in, spray yourselves with the repellent; that should keep the mosquitos off of you too."

Emily, who rarely spoke, suddenly piped up, "Last night you sprayed my fingers and they tasted awful. Don't spray my fingers again."

Laughing, Mom tousled her hair. "Okay. I promise you I won't spray your fingers."

Right before we climbed into the tent, we doused ourselves with OFF! and Mom took Myrtle and Emily aside to spray them. Before spraying Emily, she said, "Okay, Emily, put your hands in your pockets, and that way I won't spray them."

Emily said, "Okay," and put her little hands in her shorts pockets while Mom covered her in a cloud of repellent. When she finished, we all climbed into the tent, and then Mom proceeded to sew us in. As she did that, Matt read the end of *Carioca Fletch*.

When we learned the fate of Irwin Maurice Fletcher, Lindsey turned off the flashlight and we all tried to go to sleep.

Within seconds, Emily shrieked, "Yuck!"

"What in the world is wrong with you?" Mom asked.

Emily screamed in her face, "You sprayed my fingers. You promised that you wouldn't spray my fingers."

"Emily, I did not spray your fingers. Your fingers were in your pockets. Remember?"

Emily took her two fingers, shoved them in Mom's face, and said, "You suck 'em, then!"

At that point we all knew that Matt wasn't the only one at the end of his tether. Little Emily had had enough too.

Mom hadn't cycled since we'd left Custer, choosing instead to drive with the girls to each campground and wait for our arrival. The one morning she did ride, it didn't take her long to figure out why we were all fed up with the state of Nebraska.

That day, we were *only* cycling eighty miles to Lake McConaughy, but it was scorching hot and the wind was relentless. Right away, the boys pulled ahead, and I stayed back to cycle with Mom. I had a feeling that she'd struggle under these conditions. About ten miles into the ride Mom asked, "Has it been like this every day?"

"Actually, now that we're going slightly east, it's better. The wind blows from the south, and we've had a headwind every day."

"I think when Lindsey catches up with us, I'm going to switch places with her. I don't think I can do this."

"If that's what you want to do. Okay," and we continued to push east. But in the back of my mind I was thinking, *What bullshit. At least cycle half of the day's journey.* The only reason we were cycling through Nebraska and Kansas was so *she* could see Independence and Hannibal.

A few minutes later, Mom said, "At least in a couple of days we'll be in North Platte."

I looked over at her, cocking an eyebrow. "North Platte? Really? That's supposed to motivate me—North Platte?"

"I'm just saying we'll soon be out of Nebraska."

"Okay, Mom. Whatever." I shrugged and pulled away. She could get excited about North Platte on her own. The only thing that motivated me was reaching the sign that said, "Leaving Nebraska."

An hour later Lindsey switched places with her, and Mom took off for the campground with the little girls. Lindsey, the boys, and I caught up with them at around four. We were hot, tired, and completely spent.

Two days later, we crossed into Kansas and began cycling east, which slightly improved our riding conditions. The weather was still hot and dry, and the terrain bleak, but at least we were going in the right direction. The biggest drawback to Kansas was their state parks didn't have showers, which meant we had to stay on campgrounds near lakes so we could bathe. The lake water washed off the day's road grime, but in those conditions, all the soap in the world couldn't rid us of our body odor.

Since we were no longer fighting headwinds, Mom decided she'd cycle again and began alternating morning rides with

Lindsey. On the mornings Mom rode, I'd hang back for the first hour and keep her company while the boys went at their own pace. During our time together, Mom talked non-stop about my father, and how he'd been maligned by the city of Willamette. I'd been listening to her narrative for years and knew she desperately wanted me to embrace it. This became clear the morning we cycled from Prairie Dog State Park towards Glen Elder State Park.

It was a gorgeous morning. We'd departed early and watched the sun rise over the horizon. With the wind at our backs, we were practically pushed over the rolling prairies of northwestern Kansas. Mom and I were on our own when out of the blue she said, "Your father, when he was younger, he was a lot of fun. It wasn't until the Oregon Bar tried to have his law license pulled that he changed."

I'd heard this all before and tried to tune her out. But that day, Mom wasn't going to let me off the hook.

"Laura, you can't think of the way your dad was at the end of his life. That wasn't who he was. He changed after the Bar. Anything after that, you need to just forget. You don't need to forgive, just forget it ever happened."

Her advice was so completely fucked up. I really didn't know how to process her craziness. Forgetting without forgiving seemed like a lie to me, because she never actually forgot anything. On one hand, she was affirming that my relationship with Dad wasn't good and that he wasn't very nice. On the other hand, she suggested that he wasn't responsible for his behavior, and I just needed to forget everything. Wow.

I already knew the answer, but asked, "What year did the whole Bar thing happen?"

"Before Myrtle was born. So that would've been '76."

"In '76?" I affirmed. "So, I would've been what, eight?"

"I guess that's right."

"Myrtle's age. The second grade?"

I wanted her to see that she was asking me to forget the last *nine* years of my life, but it seemed to just go right over her head.

"Just remember him like he was, and forget the rest, Laura."

"Yeah, I see what you mean," I said. "I think I'm going to pull ahead now if you don't mind. I'll meet you in Kirwin. Lindsey said she'd switch places with you there." I sprinted forward, trying to get as much distance between us as possible.

Why did Mom have to choose this day for her heart-to-heart with me? It was the first day in a while that cycling had been pleasant. So, why today? Hell, why say anything at all? I never talked about Dad. Whenever Lindsey and Mom talked about him, I stayed quiet.

As the breeze pushed me along, the words "You don't need to forgive, you just have to forget" kept running through my mind. *How can I forget my own father calling me a dyke? How can I forget him looking at me and saying, "Damn, you're ugly"? How can I just ignore sixteen years of cruelty?* I'd spent my whole life seeing myself as my father saw me. I looked in the mirror and saw a scrawny, androgynous, homely person. My innermost self was molded according to his perceptions. I didn't have the ability to forget, and forgiveness wasn't an option.

By the end of the day, I made up my mind to forget Mom's advice. I'd wrestled with maintaining my own reality in the face of her fantasy most of my life. I'd witnessed Mom's bitterness towards me and knew that she never forgot her own part in the abuse. She held onto resentments like priceless treasure and used them to strike when they suited her. Then the real Mom would emerge, and her wrath could be brutal. I thought to myself, *I'll forget when you do.*

We were two-thirds of the way across the state of Kansas and hadn't showered in four days. Fortunately, some campgrounds had running water in their restrooms where we tried to give ourselves sponge baths. Between the dust and sweat, there was just no getting clean. Our hair was stiff with road grime, and our clothes had turned gray. We looked homeless, but of course we weren't. We just weren't home.

One afternoon, we were sitting on the picnic table of our campsite at Tuttle Creek State Park outside of Manhattan, Kansas. Mom had purchased a copy of *The Wichita Eagle* and was reading it.

I asked her, "Why did you get a newspaper?"

"I was looking to see if the Royals were in town this week."

Right away I got excited because the Royals were my favorite team and George Brett was my favorite ball player. "Are they in town?" I asked.

As she put down the paper she replied, "Unfortunately, they're in Cleveland this week. Sorry."

Marc, who was sitting next to me, picked up the paper. "Of course they are. Well, at least you looked."

Mom quickly changed the subject. "I'm thinking that tomorrow we'll spend the night in Clinton State Park and then the next day we'll drive into Kansas City. Let's find a YMCA so we can take showers, go to dinner, and catch a movie."

"Actually do something normal?" Matt chimed in. "Sit in a chair and eat food that isn't fried over a campfire?"

Myrtle and Emily were playing in the tent and must've overheard us because Myrtle popped her head out. "Can Emily and I choose the movie?"

Mom looked towards the tent. "I'll tell you what, we'll find a multiplex. I'll take you and Emily to a movie and the others can see whatever they want to see."

Lindsey, who'd taken a section of the paper from Marc, said, "Hey, according to this paper they made *Fletch* into a movie. We've got to go see *Fletch*." She then looked at the tent and said, "Emily, there's a new *Wizard of Oz* movie called *The Return to Oz*. You should go see that one."

The little girls had been amazing troopers throughout the whole trip. They'd been carted off on this wild adventure and spent their days riding in a hot car and hanging out at campgrounds. While we were in Kansas, Myrtle had crafted this story about Dorothy and Toto to keep them entertained.

When the boys and I would meet up with them in the afternoons, we'd tell Emily that we just might have passed Dorothy's house on the road. Emily would ask, "How can that be, because you said you passed it yesterday?"

"The tornado moved it, Emily," Matt would say. "Don't you remember?"

Even at four years old, Emily was wise for her age and wasn't buying it. She would look at Matt like he was nuts, with her hands on her hips. "I think I saw her house a couple of days ago."

Emily also had a stubborn streak, which was evident when from the tent she shouted, "I'm going to see that movie!"

The Kansas City YMCA was a massive four-story brick building in the heart of the city. From the outside it didn't look like much, but they had showers and that's all that really mattered. I have never had a more cleansing experience in my life. A week's worth of Kansas prairie dust just washed down the drain. The only drawback was that we had to put our dirty clothes back on because we hadn't hit a laundromat yet. That was next on our list, which kind of summed up our whole experience thus far. We tended to do everything backwards.

Finally, with clean bodies and clean clothes, we found the movie theater that was showing both *Fletch* and *Return to Oz*. Walking into the lobby of the multiplex was strange—it had been weeks since we'd done anything so civilized. The smell of our buttery popcorn felt extravagant, and the chance to sit in an actual chair seemed luxurious. I hadn't sat in a chair since the Dairy Queen in Nebraska, which felt like years ago.

The only negative to the whole afternoon was the movie. Our bedtime ritual had been centered on reading *Fletch*. By this time, I knew the Fletch in the books: a young, blond, mischievous, and handsome guy. I'd come to know him. And Chevy Chase was no Irwin Maurice Fletcher. Sorry. At least the popcorn was hot, the Cokes cold, and the chairs soft.

When the credits rolled, the four of us went back to the lobby and found Mom and the girls. They'd enjoyed their movie and were ready to find a place to eat. We found a local diner where we had burgers, fries, and shakes. It was late when we returned to our campsite.

That night in the tent, we discussed all the places the film had screwed up the plot and how casting Chevy Chase was the film's biggest mistake.

"Chevy Chase is funny in a Clark Griswold kind of way, but he's not Fletch," said Matt.

"I agree," Marc replied. "Bad casting. Should we read an Ed McBain next?"

"How about a Matthew Hope book?" I suggested. "I've only read the *87th Precinct* books. Let's try something different."

Lindsey picked up *Goldilocks* and began to share the story of Matthew Hope and his adventures in Florida.

We were only twenty miles from Independence, Missouri, but it was twenty miles of interstate highway and Mom decided to load everything in the car and drive there. Our time in the car together was long enough. The cramped, smelly BO conditions were a gentle reminder of why I liked cycling better.

On the drive into Independence, Marc asked Mom, "Why do you want to see Harry Truman's house?"

Mom looked at us in the rearview mirror. "He was the president of my youth and he reminded me of my own father. I just think of that time as special. Life was easier then, Marc."

"Easier for who?" Lindsey asked. "Not for those he dropped the bomb on."

This pissed Mom off, and she said in her teacher voice, "Lindsey, what was he supposed to do? The war would never have ended."

From there they had a huge debate over Truman's decision to nuke Japan. As the two women in the front went back and forth, I was fascinated by Mom's perspective. Listening to Mom defend her American dream was enlightening. She could only perceive life from the bubble of her very white and privileged position. Her argument was similar to the method she used to defend her husband. All the ugliness was forgotten, leaving only propaganda.

I did find Truman's place interesting in its simplicity. His home was a white, Midwestern, Victorian-style house. There was nothing flashy or ostentatious. It was the kind of house I always imagined Colonel Potter from *M*A*S*H* living in with his wife, Mildred. Seeing Truman's home gave me an appreciation for the man.

Mom loved every minute of our tour and said it made her feel young again. "I needed to go there," she said that night at dinner. "I needed to be reminded of a time when I felt like I could do anything."

"Don't you kind of feel that now?" asked Lindsey. "I mean, we've cycled halfway across the country. Doesn't that empower you somewhat?"

Mom looked at her for a few seconds. "Yes, but it helps to be reminded of what I used to hope for."

That night I lay awake thinking about what Mom said. I wondered what exactly she was hoping for. I felt so hopeless at times. Everyone else seemed to have their own Mecca they wanted to reach. Lindsey wanted to see Mammoth Caves and New York. Matt had wanted to reach Mount Rushmore. Marc was looking forward to Springfield, Illinois, and Lincoln's home. I just wanted to be free of Willamette and the past. More than anything, I didn't want to go home.

Missouri was like somewhere over the rainbow. Their state parks had showers, and the terrain, while still farmland, wasn't nearly as dusty as Nebraska or Kansas. It also helped that it only took us two days to cross the whole state.

In no time at all, we were camping on Mark Twain Lake just outside of Hannibal. It was the day before our mother's birthday, and she wanted to celebrate in her favorite author's hometown.

The campground was wooded and cool. After dinner, the boys ran through the forest playing games while the little girls played outside the tent building fairy houses and creating a world of their own. Mom, Lindsey, and I hung out at the picnic table and watched the boys darting back and forth through the trees.

That night when we were all sewn into our tent, I asked Matt and Marc what they'd been playing, and Matt said, "Robin Hood."

"It was just nice to be around trees again," said Marc. "The forest kind of reminded me of home."

I knew what he meant. Growing up in the Pacific Northwest, we took trees for granted. Cycling for days through prairies and farmland felt bleak. To be back in a forest was refreshing. But the next day, Matt would discover that like Oregon, the woods in Missouri host things that can cause a lot of discomfort.

To celebrate Mom's birthday, we planned to tour the historic area of Hannibal and then go on a paddle wheeler dinner cruise down the Mississippi River. Because we weren't cycling, I planned on sleeping in late that morning. At around nine, Matt rolled over and said, "I think something's wrong. I can't open my eyes."

I lifted my head up. "Let me see."

Matt's face was blotchy, and his eyes were swollen shut. "Oh, my God," I said. "You need to go show Mom."

Matt crawled out of the tent and I could hear Mom scream, "Matt, what in the world happened to your eyes?"

"I don't know! I can barely see out of them. There must have been poison ivy in the woods. I think I need to go to the doctor."

Before I crawled out of the tent, Mom had already headed off to find the campground hosts and a payphone. The six of us kids sat around the picnic table, trying not to look at Matt's obviously uncomfortable condition.

Twenty minutes later, Mom came back. "Okay, Matt. I got you an appointment with a doctor in town, but he can't see you until two o'clock. So, this is the plan. We're going to have breakfast, go into town and hang out, and then I'll take you to the doctor. The boat ride doesn't leave until five, which should give us enough time to see the doctor and get back."

By eleven o'clock in the morning, we were walking around the town of Hannibal, checking out the sights. We went on a tour of Twain's boyhood home and then up to the infamous cave where Injun Joe hid out. It was quaint, and I could see why Mom really wanted to visit the town. At 1:30, Mom took Matt to his appointment while the rest of us stayed behind.

While they were gone, Lindsey informed Marc and me that she'd brought some of her own money to purchase Mom a birthday gift. We discussed what she'd want and decided to get her a leather-bound copy of the complete works of Mark Twain. The plan was to give her the gift during dinner on the boat.

For the next few hours we circled the town, retracing our steps from earlier in the day. I was thinking Mom and Matt would only be gone for a couple of hours. When there was still no sign of them at four o'clock, Marc said, "Do you think they'll make it back in time?"

"I'm sure they'll be here soon," said Lindsey.

By 4:30, I began to have real doubts that they'd make it back. "Should we ask the people who run the boat tours what we should do if they aren't here in time?"

"You stay here," said Lindsey, "and I'll go talk to the ticket people."

She left for the dock while Marc and I stayed with the girls. A few minutes later she returned. "They said they're leaving at five o'clock, with or without us. They won't hold the boat."

"Let's go down to the dock, and if they get here on time, we can all board the boat," said Marc.

The five of us walked down to the dock, where, fifteen minutes later, we watched the paddle wheeler depart without us.

Marc was dejected. "Couldn't just one thing go right?"

Lindsey sighed. "At least we got her a present."

Forty minutes later, Matt and Mom showed up. Mom said the wait at the doctor's office had been ridiculous and the nurse had even called the boat to ask if they'd wait, and they said no.

Matt looked sheepish. "I'm really sorry, guys. It's all my fault."

Mom put a comforting hand on Matt's arm. "Matt, it's not your fault. How about we go find a good place to have dinner and celebrate my birthday that way?"

It wasn't what we'd planned, but we had a nice meal and gave Mom her gift. She looked at all of us and said, "I think we're going to make it."

I didn't know if she meant we were going to get to New York or if she was referring to life in general. I wasn't too sure either way.

Chapter 9

"SNAKES ... WHY'D IT HAVE TO BE SNAKES?"

Crossing the Mississippi meant we were officially leaving the West and entering the eastern part of the country. We were so far away from home that we might as well have been crossing the Nile.

The Midwest prairie lands gave way to never-ending fields of corn, and dry, hot, dusty conditions were replaced with stifling humidity. I don't know which was better, and it didn't really matter. We were beginning the last leg of our journey and that in itself boosted my morale.

The first night in Illinois, I took the little girls to go catch fireflies. From their first sight of the luminous bugs back in Kansas, Myrtle and Emily were fascinated. They'd spend hours trying to capture the flies in jelly jars. It was really peaceful watching the girls with their messy blonde hair and their skinny little bodies doing their best to keep up with the flashing lights.

When we returned to our campsite, Mom and Lindsey were sitting at the picnic table with the map between them, embroiled in a heated discussion.

As I joined them, Mom pointed at the map and said, "Look. Springfield's right here! We're only a day away. Now if we go directly east, we have a straight shot to Washington, D.C."

Lindsey pointed a finger at her. "All I've wanted to see on this trip is Mammoth Caves, and they're in Kentucky. I don't see *why* we can't bike through Kentucky *and then* go to Washington."

"Because we'll be cycling a hundred miles south and then another hundred miles north. We'll be adding two hundred miles to our journey."

Lindsey countered, "Well, you weren't complaining when we cycled north to Yellowstone and then south to get to Missouri. Now that you've seen what you wanted to see, you won't let me go to Kentucky. It's not right."

As they went back and forth, I decided I didn't want to be part of their argument. The evening was about to move from fireflies to fireworks, so I removed myself by going down to the lake. I didn't really care where we went as long as we weren't heading home.

At the lake I found the boys skipping stones. After joining them, I picked up a flat rock and skipped it over the water. "Mom and Lindsey are arguing about going to Kentucky. Mom wants to go straight across to get to D.C."

"No way," Marc said. "I really want to go to Mammoth Caves. How can she change plans like that?"

"Well, you'd better go tell her that you want to go to the caves. I think if you guys tell her how much you want to go, she'll be convinced."

Matt and Marc dropped their stones and hurried back to the campsite, and I trailed behind them.

Marc wasted no time telling Mom his opinion. "Mom, we've gotta go to the caves. It's a national park. We can't come all this way and bypass it now."

"What's so damn special about these caves?" Mom asked.

"There was an article about them in a *National Geographic* at Flossy's house," Matt replied. "The pictures were amazing."

Mom gave us an exasperated look. "Do all of you want to go to Kentucky?"

The boys and Lindsey said, "Yes."

I really didn't have an opinion.

Mom said, "I think it's ridiculous, but if you guys want to go there, then...okay."

Clarifying our route, Matt asked, "When can we go to Lincoln's house?"

"Tomorrow we'll bike to Springfield," Mom answered. "We'll spend the night nearby and the next day we'll go see Lincoln's home and tomb."

Later that night, while we were lying in the tent, I asked, "How many days will we be cycling through Illinois before we get to Kentucky?"

"It will take us the better part of a week," said Lindsey.

I thought about this. "Will we be cycling south that whole time?"

"If we're going to Kentucky, we'll be riding south."

That's when it dawned on me that we'd be fighting a headwind for days. Damn, maybe Mom was right, and we should've just gone straight to D.C. I should've asked for a revote.

Springfield, Illinois was the only destination Marc circled during our initial planning of the trip. Abraham Lincoln was our father's hero, and after Dad's death, Marc had read everything he could about the man. By the time he was thirteen he'd read both Carl Sandburg's and Gore Vidal's books on Lincoln. I swear, he knew more about the 16th president than most teachers. I think it was his way of having a connection with our father, which was something I didn't understand, or want.

At the time, I didn't realize how the death of a father impacted young boys. Matt and Marc were only eleven and twelve when Dad died, and they really needed a father figure. My problem with their desire to connect to our father was that Dad had not been a good parent to them. Maybe Marc thought that by learning about Lincoln, he'd still be able to have a relationship with Dad. I don't know what kind of magical thinking was going on with him. What I do know is that visiting Lincoln's home and tomb was incredibly important to Marc.

Our father's Lincoln obsession baffled me—we even had a bust of him in our dining room—and I really couldn't have cared less about going to his home. Maybe if I'd done the same research as Marc, I would've felt differently. All I knew was that Lincoln had a beard, wore a stovepipe hat, was the president during the Civil War, and freed the slaves. Oh, and we shared a birthday.

Mom drove us to Lincoln's home, which is a national park. In the front of the house, the park ranger informed us the whole neighborhood was the national park. He then explained that Lincoln's house was a small, Greek-revival home. To me, it just looked like a medium-size, drab, brown wooden house. I glanced around the neighborhood, which consisted of a bunch of empty houses, making the area feel oppressive. I really didn't like being there and wanted to leave.

If the outside of the house was bleak, the interior was downright gloomy. It was Victorian in style, so the rooms were small and dark. Even the upholstery on the furniture was black—there was nothing cheerful about the place. As we climbed the stairs to the second floor, Mom began to cry. I don't mean just a few tears. No, she began to sob. As the other people on the tour looked at her with concern, I felt embarrassed and tried to distance myself from her.

Lindsey patted her on the back. "Mom, are you okay?"

Between sobs, she said, "I just feel your dad should be here."

That was my breaking point, and I worked myself towards the front of our tour while Lindsey lagged behind with Mom. Moments later, Marc caught up with me, tapped me on the shoulder, and asked, "Do you think she's all right?"

I really wanted to ignore Mom's theatrics. "I'm sure she is. You know how she gets."

Matt, who had the little girls with him, approached us and said, "I feel kind of choked up being here too. I just feel Dad here."

"Me too," said Marc.

What the hell? Is this contagious?

I looked down at the little girls and chose to keep my thoughts to myself. The whole situation felt so dark, and I didn't want to make it worse. However, I couldn't wait to get away from the area. The bleakness of the house and the, to me, extreme emotions of my family were too much to handle. I was unwilling to open myself up to their perspectives. My mind was made up about our father and a tour of his hero's home was not going to sway me.

Once outside, I waited with the younger kids while Lindsey and Mom finished the tour. It was a hot, muggy day, and I took in my surroundings. The empty neighborhood appeared as if some kind of plague had swept through it. I said to Marc, "Doesn't this place kind of creep you out?"

"Kind of."

Just then Lindsey and Mom emerged from the house, and Mom seemed more composed. I noticed that no one asked if she was okay, and we all pretended her crying fit had never happened. Before things could get awkward, Mom said, "Let's go look at Lincoln's tomb. When we're done with that, you four can cycle on to the campground if you want."

I would cycle through Nebraska all over again just to avoid riding in that car.

Fortunately, Mom didn't have the same reaction at Lincoln's tomb as she had in his home. Maybe it was because the tomb was large and impersonal. It felt more like a memorial than a final resting place. The tour didn't take long, and before I knew it, I was back on my bike, cycling twenty miles south towards Sangchris Lake State Park.

It was only a short ride, but I needed the time to clear my head. I left Springfield feeling conflicted. I couldn't whitewash my dad into some kind of imperfect saint, and I resented those who could. I was continually baffled by how easy it was for my younger brothers to share our mother's image of our father. We'd lived through the worst of his addiction together, and I'd witnessed his total disregard for my little brothers. Christ, for the last two years of Dad's life these boys didn't even have a bedroom. Dad wouldn't make the older boys, Nate and Henry, who didn't live in the home nine months out of the year, share their room. Matt and Marc were nomads; they had the "wandering bedroom" and slept wherever there was a place to lay their heads, which was usually in the basement somewhere.

By the time I reached the state park, I'd decided to try to implement Mom's advice and just forget everything. Although we were on the last leg of our journey, we still had a long way to go, and I didn't want to be pissed off the whole time. But forgetting everything was a lot easier said than done. It just made me more pissed off.

From Springfield to the Kentucky state line, we biked in and out of more small towns than I could count. They all looked the same to me, with a service station at each end of town, a quaint downtown in between, and miles of corn separating them.

Every day in Illinois played out the same way. The boys and I would get up early and cycle with either Mom or Lindsey. We'd bike about forty miles and meet up in a small town with whomever was driving that morning. After a bite to eat, Mom and Lindsey would change places, and we'd finish off the day's miles. It was a monotonous routine, but it worked.

Because the towns were closer together, we came into contact with more people. Also, there were more cars on the road, and I started getting harassed by some drivers. It was always younger guys riding in pickups who'd slow down. The passenger would roll down the window and then ask, "Hey, are you a guy or a girl?"

The first time it happened was between the towns of Centralia and Mount Vernon. I was so taken by surprise that I cried. I'd endured attacks on my gender from a young age. It began with my older siblings calling me Larry or Lawrence, progressing from name calling to outright gaslighting.

When I was seven, my older brothers began to place pornographic magazines under my mattress and then claim I was a dyke. The more I protested that they weren't mine, the worse the harassment became. The worst part was that my parents did nothing to stop them. Quite the contrary. Dad would ask, "Do you still have magazines of naked women under your bed?"

I was fucking seven years old!

By the time I met up with my brothers in a park in Mount Vernon, my eyes were red, and it was obvious that I was upset.

Matt approached me. "Are you okay?"

I didn't want anyone to know what had happened, so I lied, "Yes. I just got something in my eye." Telling them would've been awkward. The abuse I'd received at home was never ac-knowledged. It just happened, and I'd pretend it didn't.

A few minutes later, Mom met us in the car, and we waited for Lindsey to catch up. Mom told us she was going to cycle the remaining miles to the campground and that the boys and I could go on ahead if we wanted to.

I wanted to get off the road and to the campground as soon as possible, so I took off without a word. I could feel my anxiety taking over and knew that the best way to cope was through exercise. It gave me time to think and process.

I'd always been small, wiry, with big blue eyes. However, over the course of the trip I'd developed a deep tan and had lost quite a bit of weight. At some level I knew that from a distance my gender was questionable. Realizing this didn't make it hurt any less, and I spent the next two hours trying to keep the assholes in the present and the past at bay. Truthfully, the rednecks in pickups were easier to ignore than the shameful experiences of my youth.

The '70s and '80s were rough times for any child who didn't fit within the narrow confines of acceptable gender roles. It was even more difficult in Willamette, Oregon and completely intolerable in my home.

Our father did his utmost to keep women in their place. He wasn't at all religious, but he came by his misogyny "honestly" as a cultural norm. As the district attorney, he wouldn't hire fe-male lawyers. I heard him say more than once, "Women lawyers are trying to replace men." The only women in his office were the secretaries, and they weren't allowed to wear pants.

It wasn't until after Dad died that my mother began to wear shorts and pants. Prior to Dad's death she'd only worn dresses and skirts. I don't think she even owned a pair of pants until after 1984.

My two older sisters had to wear dresses every day until they entered middle school. When they turned thirteen, they were allowed to wear pants on Fridays. My mother tried to make me follow the same dress code, but I stubbornly refused.

When I was in elementary school, Mom made all my clothes, which were little dresses with pinafores. God, I despised those dresses. Every day after school I'd take off my dress, find my brother Nate's Levi's and Cub Scout shirt, and put them on. When Mom would see me in his clothes, she'd force them off of me and shove me back into a dress.

I'd try to outsmart her by changing into Nate's clothes in the closet, hiding the dress, and sneaking out the back door to play with the neighborhood kids. When I'd return home, Mom would scream, "What am I going to do with you? You're a girl. Behave like a girl!"

This was when my older brothers and sisters began calling me Larry and Lawrence. It didn't help that Mom kept my hair very short. I could've passed for a very cute boy, and if I wasn't wearing a dress, other people confused me for one.

The truth was, I didn't want to be a boy; I just didn't want to wear dresses. I didn't feel free to run and play in dresses. Plus, western Oregon is wet and cold. Jeans were just plain warmer.

The whole situation was difficult for my parents to handle, especially my mother. In the end, she resorted to shame and humiliation to get me to conform. I think she allowed my older siblings to call me Larry, hoping that their taunts would force me to behave like a proper girl. When that didn't work, she crossed a line by doing something I could never forgive, nor forget.

I was six years old that Saturday afternoon, and the family was getting ready to attend a friend's wedding. I'd been out playing with the neighborhood kids all morning and my mother called me in to change my clothes. She led me into my room, where she'd laid out a frilly dress, black patent leather shoes, and anklets for me to wear. I took the dress and threw it on the floor, saying, "I'm not wearing this horrible thing."

Mom picked up the dress, dragged me into the bathroom, and stripped my clothes off of me. She took a washcloth and began scrubbing the dirt off of my face. When she was done, she said, "Laura, you will put this dress on!"

"You can't make me wear that thing!"

My mother's face turned red. "Do you just want to be a boy? Because I can call the doctor's office and make it happen!"

My eyes got huge, and I became frightened. Mom backed me into a corner and continued, "I have had *enough* of your behavior. If you can't be a normal girl, I'll take you to Portland and they'll fix you."

The look in her eyes told me she wasn't kidding. In between sobs I said, "No. No. I'll wear the dress. I promise. Just let me put the dress on."

Mom dropped the dress on the floor and left the bathroom. I put on the appropriate clothes and walked out of the bathroom to discover that my four older siblings had heard every word. Soon after that, the pornographic magazines began to appear under my mattress.

The memory of my mother's threat lived within every cell of my body. On a fundamental level, I knew that she rejected the person that I was. She couldn't accept a daughter who wouldn't live according to her strict understanding of gender, and I never trusted her after that incident. A few years later when she sent me to live with Mrs. Hall, I knew she just wanted me out of the house.

Over the years I could've just conformed, but there was a little spark within me that always fought back. I refused to be the girl my parents wanted me to be, and I wouldn't pretend for them. I wasn't gay. I had strong sexual feelings for boys. I just wasn't feminine, which made me susceptible to harassment.

By the time I arrived at the campground in Illinois that afternoon, after the rednecks in the truck harassed me, that little spark flared up again. I came to a couple of conclusions. I knew how vulnerable I was on the road, and I couldn't let these guys get to me. So, I decided that the next time another young guy harassed me, I'd just look at them like they were idiots. I couldn't give them the satisfaction of knowing that their words hurt me. They could just fuck off. That was my plan. They could all just fuck off.

As we continued south through Illinois, the tension between Lindsey and Mom heated up. During my morning rides with Mom, she'd bitch about the fact that we were cycling south. She'd say, "If we want to be on the East Coast, why in the hell are we cycling south?"

On my rides with Lindsey she'd say, "I can't believe Mom is being such a bitch about going to Kentucky. We cycled through godforsaken Nebraska and Kansas just so she could see fucking Missouri. It wasn't like Missouri was a treat."

During their rants I'd just listen. In the back of my head, I began wondering when the two women would finally have it out. The only thing preventing an all-out fight was the fact that they didn't see much of each other during the day, and the fact that they could both rant individually to me. It was only in the afternoons and evenings that we were all together. Fortunately, the campgrounds in Illinois had lakes, which meant that we were usually swimming in the afternoons and exhausted by nightfall.

When we reached the Illinois and Kentucky border at Cave in Rock State Park, Illinois, tensions between them had eased. It helped that once we crossed the Ohio River and entered Kentucky, we were traveling east again.

Aside from what I'd been told about Mammoth Caves, I hadn't given Kentucky a whole lot of thought. For the last few weeks, we'd been pushing through wind, dust, humidity, and corn. I was beginning to think that everything east of the Rocky Mountains kind of sucked, but Kentucky changed my mind.

The two days it took us to reach Mammoth Caves National Park were a treat. The wind was at our backs and the road ran along rolling hills and through large swaths of grassland bordered by miles of white fences. The vibrant wildflowers growing in ditches added to the beauty and created a fragrant aroma that hung in the air.

The journey along Highway 62 from Princeton to McHenry, Kentucky felt surreal. The light and colors all mixed together. In many ways the ride reminded me of our very first day of cycling. The blue sky, green fields, and plants brought me back to Oregon and the Willamette Valley. When I pulled into the campground that afternoon, I felt both strong and refreshed.

Everyone in our tribe seemed to be in a great mood that afternoon. It helped that our campground had a huge swimming pool, and that we could cap off our day swimming and lounging. If it hadn't been for Lindsey and Mom's constant maneuvering for control of our group, the day would have been perfect.

We were only fifty miles west of Mammoth Caves, and before turning in for the night, Mom and Lindsey decided that Lindsey would cycle in the morning with the boys and me. Mom and the girls would pick us up in the town of Brownsville just outside the entrance of the park, and from there we'd load up the bikes and all drive in together.

I asked, "How many days are we staying there?"

"We'll spend a couple of nights," Mom said. "And then we'll head east for West Virginia."

"So, how long before we get to Washington, D.C.?" asked Matt.

Mom began to answer, but Lindsey interrupted her. "We have almost three weeks before you fly home from New York, Mom."

Just like that, the tension between the two of them flared back up.

Mom shot Lindsey a nasty look. "We should be in Washington, D.C. in about two weeks. Does that answer your question, Matt?"

Matt, looking like he was caught between two alpha lionesses, shrugged sheepishly and said, "I was just wondering." Then he slinked off into the tent.

A few minutes later, we all climbed in after him. Because of the heat and humidity, we were all lying on top of our bags. In the close confines of the tent, Mom and Lindsey were clearly being overly polite to one another. As Mom sewed us in, Lindsey asked, "Mom, since we just finished an *87th Precinct* book last night, is there one you'd like us to read?"

In between stitches, Mom looked up and in her sweet voice—which was anything but sweet—said, "No, you kids choose. I'm happy just listening."

As I silently lay in my designated spot, eyes closed, I thought, *Oh boy, there's gonna be a huge blowup soon*, and whispered a quiet prayer to myself. "God, let it happen when I'm not around."

At dawn, Lindsey shook the boys and me awake, and we were on the road minutes later. We only had a forty-mile ride that day, but Lindsey wanted to get to Mammoth Caves as early as possible.

I had a feeling she wanted to talk about what had gone down the night before, so I hung back with her while the boys pulled ahead. Once the boys were out of earshot, she said, "I don't know how much more of Mom's bullshit I can take."

Not wanting to add fuel to the fire, I just said, "Uh-huh."

Lindsey continued, "I feel like she has to challenge everything I do and say. I say blue and she says white."

I laughed to myself because that was exactly what Mom said about Lindsey during our morning rides together. Just a few days before, Mom had said, "If I say the sky is blue, Lindsey says, 'No. It's white.'"

In my opinion, the tug of war between the two of them was ridiculous. Mom had all the power. It was Mom who had control of all the decision-making, and the money. At the end of the day, that's all that mattered. We were all at the mercy of Mom's needs, and if Lindsey couldn't see that, she was delusional.

To change the subject, I asked, "Why do you want to see these caves so badly?"

Lindsey looked over at me. "I don't know why. I think the pictures in Flossy's *National Geographic* have a lot to do with it. The caves just looked so vast."

"Do they do tours?" I asked.

"Laura, did you not look at the magazine?"

"No," I replied. "I really don't like *National Geographic*."

Lindsey just shook her head. "If you didn't read the article or look at the pictures, I can't really explain it to you."

I shrugged. "I guess I'll just have to figure out what's so great about it when we get there."

Lindsey looked over at me. "A little bit of research on the places we planned on visiting wouldn't have hurt you."

I fought back with a sarcastic, "Yeah?", followed by, "Well, that sounds like camouflaged schoolwork."

"I just don't get you Laura."

I thought, *Who does?*

Mom caught up with us in the town of Brownsville around eleven o'clock, and soon we were driving up to the entrance of the park. I thought we'd be spending the rest of the afternoon checking out the park's amenities, but Mom's newfound fear of snakes dictated the rest of the day.

The drive from Brownsville to the park entrance was only a five-minute ride, but any time we were all squished together in the little Escort felt like an eternity. Lindsey was driving when we pulled up to the main entrance of the park to pay for a campsite. The ranger gave us a map of the park and a little brochure explaining the different tours of the caves that were available. Lindsey handed the map and brochure to Mom, who began to look through the materials. Tucked inside the brochure was a yellow half-sheet insert with a picture of a snake.

As soon as Mom read the insert, she started freaking out. "Oh, my God. I'm not staying here. They have snakes."

Lindsey looked over at her. "What in the hell are you talking about?"

Matt reached over the front seat, took the insert out of Mom's hand, and then showed it to Marc and me. It was a warning to campers that copperhead snakes were native to the area, and to be on the lookout for them. It explained that snakes like to hang out at the entrance of the caves in the day-time to cool off and will slither out onto the roads at night to warm up.

The three of us gave each other confused looks, and I said, "Mom, there've been snakes during this whole trip. Eastern Oregon is rife with rattlesnakes. At Bruno Dunes there were signs telling us to watch out for rattlesnakes. What about Wy-oming, and every other place we've cycled through? Mom, they all had snakes."

Mom turned in her seat, squinting her eyes. "That was different, I didn't know they were there."

I shot back, "What? That's BS. There were signs all over Bruno Dunes!"

"Tough shit, Mom," Lindsey said. "We're staying here, so you'd better come to grips with it now because here is our campsite."

"I'm not getting out of this car!" exclaimed Mom.

Lindsey pulled the car into our spot and looked over at her. "Do what you damn well want," she said, and slammed the car door.

There was no way I was going to spend another minute in the car, so I hopped out too. Matt, Marc, and the girls scrambled out behind me, leaving Mom alone in the passenger seat.

Finally, Lindsey did what she'd been dying to do the whole trip: She took control. As we gathered near her, she said, "Okay, guys, let's set up camp and then figure out what we want to do."

Within minutes, all our gear was out of the car and the tent pitched, but Mom was still sitting inside the car. I walked over to her and asked, "Are you really going to stay in the car the whole time?" I didn't buy her phobia of snakes. I felt like she was being childish, and her behavior was starting to piss me off.

Through the open window she said, "I'll get out when you guys can guarantee me there are no snakes in our campsite."

I turned around and said to everyone, "Mom will get out of the car only if we can promise her there are no snakes around."

Matt, Marc, the little girls, and I walked around the site looking for snakes. Lindsey, who thought the whole situation was bullshit, sat at the picnic table drinking a Coke.

When we were done looking, I went back to the car and said, "Mom, there are no snakes. Will you get the hell out of the car now?"

"Are you sure?"

"Yes." I swear to God I wanted to smack her. Here she was, our fearless leader taking us across the country, and now she was afraid of an unseen snake. *Give me a break!*

Mom opened the car door, ran to the picnic table, and practically jumped on top of it. I shut the car door and joined her.

Mom stayed on top of the table for the remainder of the afternoon. The rest of us tried to ignore her and even went for a long walk around the park.

We found the main lodge and asked what times the cave tours began. We also found the park's amphitheater and learned there'd be a presentation on snakes that evening. I thought that maybe if Mom just got a little information about the snakes, it might calm her fears.

Mom was still perched on top of the table when we got back to the campsite. I climbed up with her and said, "Mom, the park rangers are putting on a show tonight and we're going. Are you going to come with us?"

Her face turned white. "Will there be snakes?"

"I don't know," I lied, "but you can't stay up here the whole time. Mom, there are not snakes slithering around all over the place. We just walked all around the whole park and didn't see a single one."

"I'll think about it," she said, running her hands through her bushy, curly hair.

"Well, eventually you're going to have to go to the bathroom. What are you going to do then? You might as well get down now."

"I said I'll *think* about it, Laura," she barked.

"Okay," I said, leaving her perched on the table.

About an hour later, Mom did have to go pee, and she made me walk with her to the restrooms. She wouldn't even go into the stall until I checked it for snakes. When we returned to the campsite, Lindsey had laid out all the food for that night's meal on the table, thus taking away Mom's spot.

"We need the table," said Lindsey. "Just sit on the bench."
Mom gave her a nasty look and sat down.

The next few hours were spent getting dinner ready. Matt and Marc took the little girls to gather firewood while Lindsey and I cut up tomatoes, onions, and lettuce for soft tacos. When we got the fire going, we browned some ground beef and warmed up some refried beans. I rolled a taco for Emily while Lindsey made one for Myrtle. With the girls fed, the rest of us dug in, including Mom. After dinner, we cleaned up the dishes and put everything away. During this time, Mom never moved from her spot on the bench.

The park ranger's program was scheduled for 7:30, and when the time came, I asked Mom, "Are you coming?"

As she sat on her spot, she thought it over for a second and then said, "I'll go."

Within minutes we were at the amphitheater and found a row of empty seats towards the back. We all sat and waited for the show to begin. Mom leaned over to me and asked, "What is this program about?"

Matt looked shocked. "Didn't you tell her?"

"Tell me what?"

"The ranger's going to talk about how to identify snakes and know if they're dangerous or not," I said.

Mom looked aghast. "You've got to be kidding me!"

I hissed, "No! Get over it. You can't sit on the damn picnic table for the rest of our time here. What are you going to do when it's time to leave?"

Just when she was getting up to leave, the ranger took the stage and Mom sat back down. Looking at her, I began to realize just how childish her behavior had been. This had nothing to do with snakes. She never wanted to go to Mammoth Cave, and she didn't want to cycle through Kentucky. I knew this was all because Mom wasn't getting her way, so she was ruining our whole experience.

My feelings were confirmed the next day when she claimed that she was also claustrophobic and refused to go on any tours. She chose to stay back with Emily while the rest of us went on a four-hour tour of the caves. By this time, I was more than happy to spend four hours separated from her and her phobias that seemed to only materialize over the last couple of days. She sure as hell wasn't claustrophobic when we were all jammed into the car together, and she wasn't scared of snakes as we rode through eastern Oregon and the deserts of Idaho. It was all bullshit.

Our tour through the caves took us along a wide path that wound through stalactites and stalagmites. It felt like we were walking through middle earth, and I wouldn't have been surprised to happen upon a dwarf or dragon along the way. The ranger escorted us in and out of large caverns. Some caverns'

ceilings were so high that the stalactites looked like chandeliers. Other caverns had underground lakes with an eerie glow. I could see why Lindsey and the boys wanted to visit the park. I don't know if it was worth cycling 200 miles out of our way, but I don't regret the experience. I learned more about geology that day than I had in eleven years of schooling.

At the end of the tour, Mom and Emily met us at the main lodge. They'd spent the day walking around the park, enjoying the sights. There was a part of me that wanted to ask, *So you're over the whole snake thing now?* But I chose not to say anything. I felt it was better to just ignore her behavior and move on.

That night, Mom and Lindsey plotted a course across Kentucky through West Virginia. When they were done, Mom had the boys and me huddle around the map and said, "Okay, guys, we're almost to the end. We have three more days in Kentucky and then we're in West Virginia."

I knew we had at least one more mountain range to cross. "When will we be climbing again?"

Lindsey looked down at the map. "I don't think we face a mountain range until eastern Kentucky, and then West Virginia has the Appalachian Mountains."

"Yeah, but they won't be as high as the Cascades," said Matt, "and it's almost August, so it'll be warmer, too."

"So, for the next couple of days it's relatively flat?" I asked.

"It looks that way," Lindsey said. "I think we're on a good course and we should be in Washington, D.C. before we know it."

I went to sleep thinking the next few days of cycling would be a breeze, unaware of obstacles far bigger than the mountains lying in wait.

Chapter 10

WEST VIRGINIA – FIGHTING MAMAS (I STILL DON'T WANT TO GO HOME)

We continued to follow our daily routine as we biked through Kentucky. The only indication that we were nearing West Virginia was a change in the vegetation. The tidy, white-fenced, bluegrass fields gave way to overgrown, winding roads as we climbed into the Daniel Boone National Forest.

Throughout our trip, I'd taken for granted the overall security I felt on the road. In the back of my head, I knew we were vulnerable, and in Illinois, I'd experienced verbal harassment. That being said, from Willamette through Kentucky I can honestly say I was never fearful of other drivers. That all changed in West Virginia.

We crossed the West Virginia state line near Huntington, where ironically, we had to cross the Ohio River again. I felt like we'd entered some kind of cosmic loop. We'd crossed it when we entered Kentucky, and now we crossed it again to leave the state.

The day we entered Kentucky felt like riding through a beautiful landscape painting, but when we crossed over into West Virginia, the sheer wildness of the area stirred up strong feelings of vulnerability.

Where Kentucky's roads had been wide and well cared for, West Virginia's roads were narrow and poorly maintained. The roadside vegetation was so overgrown that it reminded me of the movie *Invasion of the Body Snatchers*. Out of fear that a tentacle might reach up and grab my ankle, I cycled faster than my typical pace.

If the conditions of the roads weren't bad enough, the drivers really put our safety into jeopardy. Old, beat-up trucks with shotguns on gun racks buzzed past me with little to no consideration for my safety. As the drivers approached me from behind, they would honk and gun their engines, making me jump. Later that afternoon when I arrived at Beech Fork State Park, I realized I wasn't alone in my assessment of the Mountain State.

I found Mom and the boys sitting at the picnic table of our campsite drinking Cokes while the little girls were hanging out nearby doing their own thing. As I dismounted my bike, I said, "Man, that was one hairy ride!"

Matt waited for me to sit down and then said, "You're telling me. The first sign of banjos and I'm out of here."

Mom didn't catch the *Deliverance* reference and asked, "Why would you hear banjos?"

Matt looked at her. "Mom, it's from a movie, and trust me, banjos in the middle of a holler is not something you want to hear."

"I still don't get it," said Mom, looking even more confused.

Ignoring Mom's inquiry, I asked to look at the map, and Marc went to the car to get it. While he was gone Mom asked, "Why do you want the map?"

"Because I just want to see how long we'll be in this state. I didn't feel safe riding today."

Mom didn't take my concerns seriously until Lindsey biked in, threw down her bike, pointed back towards the entrance, and said, "Oh, my God! These drivers are assholes!"

As she joined us at the table, Lindsey reached for the map. "Let's find the fastest route out of this state—give me the map."

The five of us put our heads together and decided to cycle straight east and enter Virginia near Warm Springs. In total we'd only bike in West Virginia for three more days. We went to bed that night thinking that we could power through the state and everything would be fine. It was a good idea—but it didn't work out that way.

Our next stop in the land of coal mining was a campground outside of Charleston. Mom woke the boys and me up early and before we knew it, we were back on the road. That day we broke from our routine and cycled closer together. We did this instinctively. After almost two months of cycling on state highways and back roads, we'd become somewhat road savvy. We were alert and aware of our surroundings. From a distance I could tell what kind of vehicle was approaching, and how much space they needed. That day, we were extra cautious. For instance, the boys didn't pull so far ahead of us that we couldn't see them.

That day's ride, while dodgy, went without incident, and I was beginning to feel a bit more secure about our cycling conditions. The trucks still passed a little too close and the roads were full of potholes, but no one harassed us. That night we had a mini meeting to discuss plans for the next couple of days.

We looked at the map and decided that the next day we'd push ourselves, cycling ninety miles to Watonga State Park in the Monongahela National Forest. "That should be doable," said Matt. "We don't really start to climb into the Appalachians until we get closer to Virginia, so I think we should go for it."

"Okay," Mom agreed. "But I want to ride the morning leg because the afternoon humidity kills me. Lindsey, you meet me at noon somewhere along the way and we'll switch places."

Lindsey didn't object to the idea. "That should work."

We all crawled into the tent early that night, knowing the next day would be long and arduous. It would also be explosive.

Mom woke the boys and me up at around six, and we were soon on the road. Since we hadn't encountered any real problems the day before, the boys pulled ahead of us and were quickly out of sight. I chose to hang back and ride closer to Mom.

As the sun rose over the lush, green mountains, the wildness of the area felt almost subdued. There were relatively few vehicles on the road, so Mom and I cycled side by side, talking about Washington, D.C. and the sites we wanted to visit.

Every Christmas, Flossy would give my parents a subscription to *Smithsonian* magazine. Each month a new issue would arrive, and for the next few weeks all of us kids took turns devouring the articles. Unlike *National Geographic*, I found *Smithsonian* fascinating. The vastness of the Smithsonian seemed overwhelming. I was really looking forward to visiting the National Museum of American History and taking in all that it had to offer, from the enormous flag that inspired our national anthem to Fonzie's leather jacket. I wanted to see it all.

About an hour into the ride, as we passed by a small house that sat back from the road, a barking little white dog jumped out of the bushes in front of us, blocking our path. The dog wasn't a threat. We just wanted it out of the way and began telling it to shoo. Within seconds, a pickup truck came barreling down the road towards us in the opposite direction. My instincts told me to get even farther off the road. As Mom and I moved farther back, the dog remained rooted to its spot. As the truck came closer, the driver crossed the double yellow line and swerved towards the dog, killing it instantly. As Mom and I looked at each other in shock, an older man in overalls and work boots appeared behind us and said, "Don't worry about it. Just keep going."

Mom asked, "Are you sure? Do you want us to help you?"

"No," the man said. "I'll take care of it. You two just get going."

He didn't have to tell me twice, and I began cycling up the road. Mom and I didn't say anything for a few minutes and then Mom whispered, "That driver did that on purpose."

"I know. Just be thankful he didn't hit us."

"I think we just need to get the hell out of here. When we meet up with Lindsey, we'll load up all the bikes and drive to the campground."

Lindsey and the girls passed us about an hour later. She didn't stop to check in, which annoyed me because she knew how dodgy the conditions were. I figured she'd simply drive twenty or so miles and wait for us. When Mom and I arrived in the town of Summerville, we found the car parked at a grocery store with only the boys and little girls waiting. Lindsey had chosen to leave the younger kids to go cycle on her own. Mom hit the roof.

As she peered into the window, Matt explained, "We tried to tell her to wait, but she said she was sick of waiting and just jumped on her bike."

Marc added, "She can't be all that tough to find. She left about twenty minutes ago."

"What the *hell* is she thinking?" Mom asked. "No one should be cycling on their own right now!"

I jumped into the mix. "She probably just wanted some time on her own."

"I don't give a damn what she wanted," Mom said. "She should've at least waited until I got here. Put your bikes on the rack, climb in, and we'll pick her up along the way."

That's when I realized that Marc looked a bit shaken. As he climbed into the back of the car with the little girls, I asked Matt, "What's wrong with Marc?"

As Matt was securing a bike to the rack, he said, "Some guy in a pickup pulled up next to him, called him a *spic*, and ran him off the road."

That made my dog incident seem minor. "No fucking way!"

Matt leaned in closer. "Yeah. The guy slowed, rolled down his window, then grabbed Marc's head and pushed him into the ditch."

When the bikes were secure, I climbed into the front seat and told Mom what had happened. Marc said, "I don't want to talk about it, I just want to get to the campground."

Mom looked back at him. "Are you hurt?"

"No," Marc mumbled, "I'm just pissed off. Can we just go?"

As we were driving down the road, Mom looked back at the boys through the rearview mirror. "That's another reason she shouldn't be riding by herself. Jesus Christ, she drives me crazy."

I figured we'd catch up with Lindsey within a few minutes, but that wasn't the case. As Mom drove the forty miles, she slapped the steering wheel every few minutes saying, "Where the hell is she? Where the *hell* is she?"

We arrived at the campground without passing Lindsey. Mom paid for a site and dropped us all off. Her plan was to find the sheriff's office to see if anyone had passed Lindsey on the road. Before she left, Mom said, "If she finds you guys, tell her to stay put."

As Mom drove away, I thought she was overreacting. Lindsey had a tendency to get off course. There had been a few times during the trip that she'd made a wrong turn, and it hadn't been an issue. We wouldn't even have known if she hadn't mentioned it.

Matt suggested that we put up the tent while we wait. For the next few minutes we set up the camp, which is when I told the boys about the dog. Marc said, "No wonder Mom's pissed off."

As we were putting the sleeping bags in the tent, Matt asked, "Where do you think she is?"

"Knowing Lindsey," I said, "she probably took a wrong turn somewhere and got lost."

Marc looked at me. "How in the hell could she make a wrong turn? We were on a state highway! All she had to do was follow the signs."

I looked over at him. "Really, Marc? Lindsey sucks at directions. She's on her own, and all she has to do is *not* follow the signs."

At that moment, Lindsey came blithely cycling up to our site and said, "You won't believe this, but I got lost."

I gave Marc a look. "Told you so."

"Mom's pissed, Lindsey," Matt informed her. "She went looking for you."

Lindsey threw down her bike, kicked it, and said with a toss of her long hair, "She is such a bitch. Why couldn't she just let me be?"

I'd had enough. I yelled, "I don't know, Lindsey, maybe because Mom and I watched a driver purposely kill a dog and

Marc got run off the road. Maybe you should've waited for us before you just took off."

Lindsey got in my face. "You're such a sanctimonious bitch, Laura!" she yelled, and stormed off with her dark mane flying behind her.

I yelled back, "Fuck you!"

Marc looked at me and said quietly, "Could you not shout? Everyone is looking at us."

Sure enough, the campers across from us were staring. I didn't really care. "Whatever!" I said as I headed off in the opposite direction from Lindsey. I found a quiet spot at the far end of the campground to alternate between fuming and feeling sorry for myself. It wasn't until I calmed down about twenty minutes later that I finally became aware of the beauty surrounding me.

The red mist of my rage receded to reveal that the campground was in the gorgeous foothills of the Alleghenies, which are part of the Appalachian Mountain Range. I was sitting in an empty campsite looking out over a rippling stream shrouded in the shade of ash and birch trees. Through the leaves, the sun dappled the water, giving it the appearance of fairies dancing on the surface. At that moment, I realized just how far we'd traveled and began to realize the real source of my anger—a combination of fear and anxiety.

We'd traveled through ten states, and West Virginia was the first time I'd felt defenseless. Watching the dog get hit, then hearing how Marc was run off the road, followed by losing Lindsey, made me acknowledge a few things. First, what we were doing was batshit crazy. More importantly, over the last few weeks, I hadn't really had to deal with life. Granted, there were challenging times, but the trip had been like Neverland. I didn't have to think about growing up.

The events of the day slapped me back into reality. The awareness that our trip was coming to an end hit me like the truck that killed the dog. I'd be returning to Willamette and beginning my final year of high school. I had no idea of what I'd do after graduation, but I knew I was trapped in a mess of my own making. Looking at the void of my near future was uncomfortable, so I chose what came naturally, and ignored my feelings. Instead of owning my shit, I stuffed everything back down and returned to our campsite.

Walking back towards our tent, I could hear Mom and Lindsey shouting at each other. As I got nearer, I heard Mom say, "What in the hell were you thinking? Anything could have happened to you."

"Oh, like you care?" Lindsey shouted. "Give me a fucking break."

Matt and Marc spied me from a distance and Matt gestured for me to stop. The boys rounded up the little girls and walked over to me. "I think we should disappear for a while," said Marc. "Those two are about ready to come to blows."

I looked over at the two women standing toe to toe. "Yeah, let's go for a walk."

As we walked away from the shouting match, I asked, "When did Mom show up?"

"About ten minutes ago," said Matt. "Before she parked the car, she saw Lindsey sitting at the table and slammed on the brakes, jumped out, and the shouting began."

"God," I said, "you're right. Let's just keep our distance for a while."

"I just want to get out of this damn state," said Marc.

Looking him over, I asked, "Are you okay?"

"Yeah. It just freaked me out. I heard the truck behind me, and the next thing I knew, a hand was on my head and this crazy guy said, 'Get off the road, you little *spic*.' I was scared shitless."

Matt gave him a sly look. "Amigo, have you looked at yourself in the mirror? You *are* really dark, and your hair *is* really bushy."

"What difference does that make?" said Marc. "Jesus, because I look Hispanic it was okay? Jesus Christ, Matt, that's sick."

As the boys were going back and forth, I took a good look at all of us, and we did look a mess. The girls' hair was overgrown, the boys were in need of haircuts, and all of our clothes had the gray tinge that comes with being overworn. Plus, we'd lost so much weight that our clothes hung loosely on our bodies. We looked like vagabonds on bikes.

At the far end of the park, we found an empty campsite and hung out for a while. We were surrounded by trees, and the sound of the water was soothing. While the boys and I sat on top of a picnic table, the little girls gathered sticks to make little fairy houses.

"At least tomorrow we'll be in Virginia," I said. "We're in the Appalachian Mountains now, and it is kind of beautiful."

"Well," said Marc, "I'm not riding again until we're out of this state."

"I don't blame you," Matt replied. "Hell, I wouldn't blame you if you didn't want to get back on your bike at all."

"I am seriously thinking about it," Marc said.

"Do you really want to ride in the car the rest of the way?" I asked. "I mean, it stinks."

Marc looked out over the forest. "I'll decide once we're in Virginia, but I'm not getting back on my bike in this state."

"That sounds like a good plan," I said. "Should we go back and see if they're done fighting?"

"Sure," said Matt, and he turned towards the girls. "Hey, let's go back, okay?"

Myrtle stood up. "Do you think they're done shouting at each other?"

She looked so earnest it almost made me laugh. I realized then how much the little girls had grown up on this trip. They were only four and eight years old and had spent most of their time in the car. At the beginning of the trip, I'd decided to let Mom and Lindsey take care of them. I'd been their caregiver for so long and felt I was done. Granted, I'd spent some time with the girls, but it was at that moment that I realized how much they'd matured.

I said to Myrtle, "Let's hope so," and then we all began walking back to our site.

As our tent came into view, we didn't hear any shouting, which I took as a good sign.

"Maybe they made up?" asked Marc.

"Maybe they just got tired of yelling," I said.

When we walked into camp, it appeared that it was a combination of the two. They were sitting together at the picnic table, drinking sodas and talking to each other. When we joined them, neither mentioned the blowup, and we all acted like nothing had happened. To avoid the subject of their enormous fight, we began to discuss the next day's ride.

I looked at Matt and Marc and just shrugged, kind of saying, *What the fuck?*

They each looked back at me with a wry smile that said, *Just go with it.* So, I did.

Looking back over the events of that day, it strikes me as odd that we all instinctively knew that we had to fend for ourselves. There wasn't a male father figure who would *save the day*. All the talk about how Dad would have loved the trip was just talk. The reality was that Dad wasn't viewed as a protector or someone to turn to when things got tough. I didn't hear my mother say, "If your dad were here, everything would be fine." Maybe deep down even Mom knew that Dad couldn't be counted on in times of trouble.

Marc stuck to his guns and refused to spend another day cycling in West Virginia. Early the next morning, Lindsey, Matt, and I headed east on Highway 39, hoping to cross from the hicks and hollers of West Virginia into genteel Virginia by midday. The three of us chose to cycle together that day to avoid any problems. We couldn't prevent assholes from killing dogs or running us off the road, but maybe, by sticking together, there'd be safety in numbers.

The three of us took off at dawn, and as we climbed higher into the Allegheny Mountains, I felt compelled to stop and take in the scenery. The mountains were shrouded in mist with the tips of the trees poking through. The sun had just risen above the clouds, creating the illusion that we were suspended in midair. As I took in my surroundings, tears welled up in my eyes. The view captured my feelings perfectly. I was in limbo—stuck between hope and anger—and it felt like anger was winning.

Lindsey shattered the silence of the moment when she pulled up behind me and said, "Isn't it gorgeous?"

I turned back towards her and gave her a half smile. "Yes, it is. Makes you want to sing John Denver songs all day."

Lindsey looked out over the trees. "Thanks. Now I'll be singing 'Take Me Home, Country Roads' all day."

I laughed. "Come on, mountain mama, let's get going," I said, and pedaled on down the road.

Later that morning, Mom and the younger kids met up with us in the town of Minnehaha Springs, right on the border of Virginia. She asked if we'd run into any problems, and we told her so far it had been smooth riding. To celebrate surviving

West Virginia, she took us to lunch at the local Dairy Queen. While we were eating burgers and fries, Matt asked Marc, "We only have another twenty miles to go today. Do you want to bike the last leg with us?"

Marc stared at his fries. "Nope. Let me know how the rest of the day goes and I'll think about joining you tomorrow."

Matt took a drink of his soda. "Will do."

Mom decided to drive ahead to the campground at Lake Moomaw near Hot Springs, Virginia and set up camp. Lindsey, Matt, and I jumped back on our bikes and followed. By the time we reached our campsite the tent was up, and Mom left a note on the table telling us that they'd be down at the lake.

The three of us dropped our bikes and followed the signs to the water. We found Mom and the little girls sitting in the shade on a small beach. The girls were playing in the sand, and Marc waved at us, already swimming. We dropped our stuff near Mom and joined him.

With a huge smile on his face, Marc said, "This is amazing."

"So, you're feeling better?" Matt asked.

"God, yes," Marc responded. "I spent the time in the car looking at the map, and tomorrow we'll be in Charlottesville! Can you believe it? Mom said maybe we'll stay at a KOA."

I asked, "Are you gonna bike the rest of the way?" I hoped so, but didn't want to push.

"I think so," Marc said. "But if I run into problems again, that's it. I'm done."

As he was talking, I looked back over at where Mom and the girls were. "They look a lot happier today," I noted.

"Yeah," Lindsey said. "I think our fight kind of cleared the air some."

"Maybe," I replied.

"What does that mean?" Lindsey asked.

I didn't want to get into another argument. "Nothing. I was just talking."

What I was thinking was that if Lindsey thought yesterday's spat had cleared the air, she was nuts. Mom never just let bygones be bygones. But if Mom wanted to call a truce for a while, who was I to bitch?

We spent the next few hours at the lake, swimming and sunbathing. As the sun began to set, Mom said, "How about we go up to our site, build a fire, and then fix dinner?"

As a sign of consent, we all began to put on our shoes and collect our things. On the way back to our campsite, we picked up sticks for the fire, and by the time we got there, we had a large stack of firewood. Matt and Marc built the fire, and Mom sent me to the restrooms to fill up a pot to boil noodles while Lindsey emptied a jar of Ragu into a pot. In no time, we were all sitting around the picnic table slurping spaghetti. Matt looked up at all of us. "I am so fucking glad we're out of West Virginia. No more banjos."

Mom let out a huge laugh. "Matt, I couldn't agree with you more."

Chapter 11

I CAN DREAM TOO

The distance from Hot Springs to Charlottesville was over a hundred miles, so we decided to break it up by biking to Staunton and camping just south of there at Sherando Lake Campground in George Washington National Park. That night, Mom made the executive decision that we'd load everything up and drive the remaining forty miles to Charlottesville. I asked why, not wanting to spend that much time in the car. Her answer: "Because the route into the city seems to be all interstate and I'd rather we just drive in."

"Are we staying at a KOA?" Matt asked.

"I think so," Mom said. "They'll have a laundry and a pool. That way we can get cleaned up and enjoy our time there."

When we climbed into the tent, I asked, "What are we gonna do in Charlottesville?"

Matt looked over at me. "Laura! Sometimes you drive me crazy. It's where Thomas Jefferson's from. Don't you know that?"

"I do now!" I snapped. Dripping with sarcasm, I said, "I figured that there's something interesting in Charlottesville because you're *so* excited about going there." Turning to Mom, I asked again, "So what *are* we going to do there?"

"Ugh," Matt grunted, hiding his tanned face in his hands.

Mom said, "Well, we're going to tour Jefferson's home and then maybe visit the University of Virginia and then visit the old town."

I looked over at Matt and raised my eyebrows. "Okay. That's all I wanted to know."

Lindsey butted in. "Are you two done? Can I read now?"

Matt and I said in unison, "Sure," and she began to read Agatha Christie's *A Crooked House*.

Around noon the next day, we pulled into the KOA just outside of Charlottesville. Mom grabbed a load of brochures for different local tourist attractions for us to look through. We spent the rest of the day doing laundry, swimming in the pool, and browsing through the brochures to decide what we wanted to go see first. As we lounged poolside, we made the unanimous decision to make Jefferson's home, Monticello, our first destination.

The next morning, we ate a quick breakfast of cold cereal and fruit, then tidied up and headed out for a day of sightseeing. On the way to Jefferson's home, I once again found myself wedged in the backseat between the boys with Myrtle on my lap. We weren't our normal smelly selves, but Myrtle's butt still dug into my thighs.

Matt turned to me and asked, "After looking at the brochures, do you get why we want to visit Jefferson's home?"

I adjusted Myrtle a little bit so I could see Matt better. "Yeah. Actually, it looks pretty cool."

Marc piped up, "I feel like we've kind of made it now. I mean, we're in Virginia, and before you know it, we'll be in D.C."

I turned to Marc. "You're feeling better about things."

"It helps that we're visiting cool places now. We're riding *to* places and not just *through* places. I know that sounds weird, but it's how I feel."

I thought about what he was saying, and it made sense, but I saw it differently. All summer I'd been biking away from Willamette—and home. I was excited about reaching these destinations, but it also meant that we'd be returning home soon. I leaned back and tried to glimpse the passing scenery. As we drove towards Monticello, I thought to myself, *The trip is not over yet, so enjoy it while you can, Laura.*

A few minutes later, Mom pulled up to a parking lot outside the visitor center, and we all climbed out of the car. We toured the center while Mom got in line to purchase tickets to tour the home. The next thing I knew, we were all seated on a shuttle heading up towards the house. As I looked out the window of the shuttle, my first impression of Jefferson's property was just how wealthy he must've been. The land surrounding his home was vast and the outbuildings numerous. You could fit most of our downtown into his property. I'd never seen anything like it before.

When the shuttle stopped outside of the mansion, we were ushered off and told to wait for our tour guide. Out of nowhere, a college-age girl who looked like she'd just stepped out of a Laura Ashley catalogue appeared and told us she'd be our tour guide. Before leading us through the house, she informed us that she was a University of Virginia student and a Daughter of the Revolution.

Right away, I decided not to like her. Why? Because she was everything I wasn't, and I resented her for it. She was articulate, put together, and obviously well bred. I, on the other hand, was a mess. My curly hair was bushy and in need of a haircut. My clothes were dingy, and when I looked down at my once-pink canvas topsiders with holes in the toes, I felt both ignorant and poor.

Before entering, our guide explained that she'd walk us through the house, and once we were done, we'd be free to explore the rest of the property on our own. As she led us from one room to another, she definitely came across as condescending, but my own insecurities were probably the real problem. I felt clueless about my surroundings and chose to hang towards the back of the group and just enjoy learning about the house.

I knew very little about Jefferson, but from observing the wine dumbwaiter in the fireplace of the dining room and the lazy Susan reading table that held five books, I was beginning to like him. He appeared to have been both eccentric and intelligent. By the time we were escorted out of his house, I appreciated why people were enamored with him. But those thoughts were quickly tempered when I found the burial place of his slaves.

Even learning that he freed *some* of his slaves made me cringe. It made me look at his property in a different light. I thought, *Damn, he had enslaved people do ALL this work.* As I walked back towards the shuttle, I began to wonder if our whole country was built by really intelligent assholes. It was beginning to look that way, and it pissed me off.

We spent the remainder of our time in Charlottesville visiting the University of Virginia and walking around the old town. Mom allowed the boys to get much-needed haircuts and let us pick out some new clothes. I got a pair of Bermuda-length white Adidas shorts. I loved them because they were clean (an odd contrast with my John Mellencamp concert shirt and filthy shoes). I think Mom wanted us to look presentable for when we arrived in Washington, D.C. We'd be staying with relatives of one of Mom's coworkers in both D.C. and New York, and Mom said, "I don't really want word to get back to her how rough we all look."

With new and freshly laundered clothes, we left Charlottesville for Fredericksburg. It was only a sixty-mile bike ride, and by mid-afternoon we'd arrived at the campground, which was also the site of a Civil War battleground. As Matt and I were setting up the tent, he said to me, "Man, we're at a real Civil War site."

"I really don't get the whole Civil War thing," I said.

Matt stopped hammering in a tent peg. "Laura, is there anything you really want to visit? You haven't really cared about anything."

I looked at him. "You know what I want to see? I want to visit D.C. I want to see the still from *The Swamp* in *M*A*S*H*, and Indiana Jones's whip, and all that stuff. I don't know why, but I want to visit D.C. more than New York."

"There. At least you want to see *something*."

I watched him pound in the last stake and thought, *What I really want is to keep going on this trip, and never return home.*

With the tent up and all our stuff out of the car, Mom suggested we take a walk around the park. She needed to find a payphone to call the couple in Alexandria that we'd be staying with to ask when it would be okay for us to arrive the next day.

I really didn't want to go on a group walk. "I think I'll just hang back, if you don't mind."

"Suit yourself," Mom said, and everyone took off, leaving me on my own.

While they were gone, I decided to check the air in our bicycle tires. I did this from time to time mostly as a distraction. While I was pumping more air into Mom's front tire, I heard a voice ask, "Hey, are you guys really from Oregon?"

I looked over and was surprised to see a young, attractive guy near our car. He was lean, with curly blond hair and a friendly smile. He was straddling a bike that was decked out in gear. There were two black bags hanging from a bike rack, with a sleeping bag and tent strapped to the top.

"Yeah, we are," I said. "Where are you from?"

"I'm from California. Did you guys bike here?" he asked.

I pointed at the car. "Kind of. We have the car too because my little sisters are with us."

"Man, that is so cool. I took off from San Diego back in June. When did you guys take off?"

"We left in June too."

He was so easy to talk to, and for a few moments I felt like a normal girl. I was a little disappointed when Mom and the others returned and joined in on our conversation. For a few happy minutes it was just me and a nice guy hanging out.

He told us his name was Jason and that we were the first people he'd met that were cycling across the country too. We invited him to join us for dinner, and we spent the rest of the night swapping stories about our trips.

At one point he asked us, "Did you guys find it weird that you didn't have to pee all that much in the Midwest?"

Mom laughed so hard that it caught us by surprise. She said, "I *did* notice that. We were drinking gallons of sun tea and Kool-Aid each day, and it just seemed to sweat right out of us."

"The weirdest thing was that it was so hot that I'd put my Top Ramen noodles in a cup with water, set it in the sun, and they'd be ready in minutes," said Jason.

"God, I hated Nebraska," Matt said.

I looked at him. "Really? We didn't notice."

Before Matt could say anything, Jason said, "Oh, man, that state was awful. Just the mosquitos were enough to do my head in."

It was so refreshing hanging out with Jason. He was the first outsider we'd truly engaged with throughout the trip. He was also the first person who grasped what we were doing and didn't look at us like we were freaks. I was kind of sad when we said our goodbyes because it was nice to talk to someone who wasn't family.

That night when we were tucked away in our tent, Mom said that she'd called the people we were staying with in Alexandria, Ray and Lisa, and they were expecting us around four in the afternoon. Therefore, we'd bike to Mount Vernon, have lunch there, then cycle on to Alexandria.

Before I could ask, Matt looked at me and said, "Mount Vernon is George Washington's home, Laura."

"Thanks for the tutorial, ass wipe," I said.

Mom butted in. "Knock it off. Try to be on your best behavior when we get to their house. Okay?"

"I'll give it my best shot," I said. A moment later, I added, "You guys realize that we haven't slept in a house since Sheridan, Wyoming?"

Marc popped up from his sleeping bag. "I don't know what I'm more excited about, Washington, D.C. or sitting in a chair."

We all busted up laughing, and then Matt said, "Who knew we'd ever miss sitting in a real chair so much?"

Mom replied, "We don't really know these people, so try to remember how to be civilized."

"We'll give it a try," I said. "But I can't make any promises."

The ride to Mount Vernon was a fast, flat forty-mile stretch along the Potomac River. With the wind at our backs, I barely had to pedal and was able to enjoy the ride. The river was to our right, and through the trees I spied boaters enjoying the warm summer weather. Trailheads led down to the river. The paths were an open invitation to go sit on the banks, but we all wanted to get to Washington's home as quickly as possible, so we pushed on.

With perfect riding conditions, we reached Mount Vernon about forty minutes quicker than expected. Since we didn't have any cash on us, we had to wait in the parking lot for Mom and the little girls to arrive. We found a shaded spot under a tree to hang out and watched cars from varying states pull in to visit the estate.

I looked over at Lindsey. "What a bunch of wusses. They drove here."

We fell on our backs laughing, and then Matt said, "God, I think we've done it, you guys."

"It wasn't pretty, but we're almost there," said Marc.

I sat up and leaned back against the tree, feeling conflicted. I was proud of our accomplishments so far, but a little voice in my head told me that the return to Willamette would suck.

When Mom and the girls arrived, we put our bikes on the rack and walked up to the formal entrance of Washington's house. We were led around the estate by a clone of our tour guide from Monticello. From their Laura Ashley dresses to their pretentious attitudes, these two could've been twins. I hung towards the back of the group with Lindsey and asked, "Do they go to tour guide school where they learn to be obnoxious?"

"Oh, get over it. Just enjoy the house," Lindsey replied and walked ahead of me.

She was right, but the tour guide still annoyed me.

The house itself was right out of *Gone with the Wind*. It was a white, wooden plantation home with a wraparound porch and large pillars. The rooms were light and airy, but the house lacked the eccentricities of Monticello. However, what it lacked in character it made up for in location. The mansion sat on the Potomac River, and after touring the home, I detached myself from our group and relaxed on the grassy bank.

The rippling of the water almost lulled me to sleep. There was something about the river that seemed familiar. It was almost like I'd been there before. I felt like I belonged there, but I couldn't quite figure out why. Just when I began to nod off, Marc tapped me on the shoulder. "Hey, we're going to have lunch in the cafeteria. Do you want to join us?"

I got up and took one last look out over the water. "Yeah, I'm hungry."

The two of us walked back to the house and found the others waiting for us. "Where did you go?" Mom asked.

"I just sat down by the river. It's really great down there. If we need to kill a little time before we leave, it's a great place to hang out."

"We only have a few miles to Alexandria, so maybe we'll do that," said Mom.

We ate hamburgers and fries in the little café; then we went back to the river and lazed about on the riverbank for an hour. We decided Mom would ride the rest of the way with the boys and me while Lindsey would take the girls in the car.

Before we left for Alexandria, Mom gave Lindsey our hosts' address and phone number and told her, "If you get lost, just call this number from a payphone and Ray will come find you." Which was a good thing, because she had no idea where she was going. Come to think of it, neither did we.

Fortunately, there's a bicycle trail that goes from Mount Vernon through Alexandria and on to Washington, D.C. We followed the trail, which led us along the river and past large, stately homes. In no time we were in Alexandria, where we were grateful to discover that Ray and Lisa's house was only a couple of blocks from the bike path. By some miracle, we didn't get lost and neither did Lindsey. As we cycled up to their house, we found Lindsey and the girls sitting on the front porch with the couple who were crazy enough to let us stay with them.

I liked Ray and Lisa right away. They were younger and didn't have any children of their own. I did wonder how they'd handle six kids invading their space for a few days, but any reservations I had about them were wiped away by the bright smiles on their faces. They were beyond gracious, and there was none of that awkward sizing-each-other-up period that tends to happen with new people. Ray had an open expression and cheerful demeanor that exuded kindness. Lisa was a petite woman who seemed genuinely happy to host us. After our initial greetings, they showed us where to store our bikes, and then gave us a tour of their house.

They lived in a three-story row house in one of the oldest sections of town. The inside was comfortably decorated. The living room had an overstuffed sofa and chair, which I secretly wanted to sit on for the remainder of the evening. There were also bookcases jammed full of books, a great stereo system, and shelves upon shelves of record albums. The upstairs had three bedrooms—a primary bedroom, guest room, and study. Mom and the little girls were to sleep in the guest room, while Lindsey and I were to share the study. The finished basement was set up for the boys. They'd even begun to make dinner for us. It felt like we'd walked into a really nice bed and breakfast.

After the tour of their home, Ray found some sodas for the boys and little girls, then turned to Lindsey and me and asked, "Would you guys like a beer or a glass of wine?"

I'd been dry all summer, which was the longest time I'd gone without alcohol since I was fourteen. I looked at Mom to see if it was okay, and she just nodded yes. I said, "I'll take a beer."

Lindsey had a glass of wine and I drank a Budweiser from the bottle. I didn't really like beer, but man, did it taste good. The beer made me feel included as an adult.

I was given a glass of wine with dinner, and over spaghetti they asked us questions about our trip. They really wanted to hear all of our stories and listen to our experiences. Aside from Jason from California the night before, we hadn't had a chance to tell anyone about our adventures. They seemed in awe of our journey, and Lisa said, "I can't believe you guys made it this far."

"We're not done yet," I said, "but we did get this far."

"Would you guys like me to drive you around D.C. tonight and you can see it all lit up?" Ray asked.

Without hesitating, we all said, "Yeah!"

We helped Lisa clear the dishes, and then Ray led us to his four-door Honda Accord. "I don't know if we'll all fit."

"Trust me," said Matt. "We'll fit."

Marc added, "Dude. You have, like, four doors. We'll be riding in style."

Ray smiled. "Okay. Get in."

Lindsey, Matt, Marc, Myrtle, and I all squeezed in the back while Mom and Emily took the passenger seat. Ray got in, looked at Mom, and said, "I guess you guys have done this a lot?"

Mom replied, "You could say we have it down."

As we crossed Key Bridge into Georgetown, Ray explained that D.C. was built between Georgetown and Alexandria. I thought Georgetown was just a university that had an awesome basketball team. Actually, Georgetown is an old area of D.C., and two things about it really caught my attention. First, the buildings were amazing. The shops still had the style and feel of early America. The second thing was the pubs. They looked like places our Founding Fathers would have stopped in for a beer. Judging by all the young people waiting in line at the various clubs, Georgetown obviously had an incredible nightlife.

The people looked college-age, dressed in shorts and polo shirts. I envied their potential. Even from the car, I could sense their amazing energy and wanted to tap into it. A desire to be in their position awakened within me, but the goal seemed completely out of reach.

As we were leaving Georgetown, Ray explained that we'd be passing the Watergate Hotel building soon, and then he'd park up near the Lincoln Memorial. As the lights of the National Mall came into view, I tried to get my bearings. I'd seen pictures of the Washington Monument and Lincoln Memorial but didn't really have a grasp of how the Mall was laid out. When we passed behind the Lincoln Memorial, I was shocked by its size—it's enormous.

Ray parked across the street from the Memorial, and we all climbed out of the car and ran up the stairs of the monument. When we reached the top, we jumped up and down with our hands in the air like Rocky.

Before stepping in to view the statue, I looked out over the reflecting pool towards the towering Washington Monument. People were walking around taking in the sights, and I thought to myself, *This. Is. Amazing.* The sense of accomplishment outweighed the fact that it was my dad's hero's memorial. Getting from Willamette, Oregon to Washington, D.C. had nothing to do with Dad, and I was owning the moment.

What moved me wasn't the statue of Lincoln or the Gettysburg Address. What really grabbed me was the commemoration of Martin Luther King's March on Washington. In the shadow of Lincoln, engraved in the marble, was Dr. King's speech. I stood there reading the words, looked back at Lincoln, and thought—*I can dream too.*

A few minutes later, I went back to the steps and sat down, which is when I noticed the Vietnam Wall. Among all this white marble was this open, black granite scar with the names of 58,000 service people who'd either lost their lives or were missing in action. The memorial looked like a book carved into the ground that refused to be closed or hidden from view. The honesty of the contrast between power and death spoke to me.

I had this sense that D.C. would play a significant role in my life, but I didn't know how. I wanted to be a student waiting in line in Georgetown and had no idea how I could achieve this goal. I was barely getting through high school, and any chance of a higher education seemed remote. Even with everything working against me, I tucked this dream away in the back of my mind and hoped for a miracle.

Chapter 12

NEW YORK, NEW YORK

The next morning, we jumped back on the bike path and rode into D.C. via Arlington Cemetery, with Emily and Myrtle balanced on the seats of Matt and Marc's bikes, hanging on for dear life. It wasn't the safest mode of transportation for the girls, but safety hadn't been a priority all summer, so why start now?

Mom wanted to see the burial sites of John F. Kennedy and Robert Kennedy and visit the Tomb of the Unknown Soldier. I thought we'd just pop in, take a look around, head over the Memorial Bridge, and spend most of the day visiting the Smithsonian museums. Instead, we were treated to another one of Mom's meltdowns.

Our first stop at Arlington was the Eternal Flame, where Mom began to weep. In between sobs she said, "It really was Camelot for your father and me. When Kennedy became president, we were so young and hopeful." I'd had enough of Mom's drama and snuck off to look at General Lee's home.

Lee's house was giant, with white columns, and overlooked the Potomac River with an amazing view of the National Mall. The other side of the house looked out over rows and rows of white tombstones. In some ways the setting was quite creepy, but it also gave me some perspective. We were in the middle of Arlington surrounded by the memories of thousands of people who'd made the ultimate sacrifice. I told myself that I needed to show some respect, that not everything was about Mom's or my feelings. But even in the midst of that thought, the feelings of resentment were buried just under the surface.

A short time later, Matt came and found me. "Hey, we're going to watch the changing of the guard at the Tomb of the Unknown Soldier and then we're heading for the Smithsonian."

"Good," I said, and followed him to where the others were gathered. As we made our way to the tomb, Mom asked, "Where did you go?"

"Just up to Lee's house. I wanted to stretch my legs."

"Doesn't it just make you want to cry?"

The truthful answer would have been no, but I said, "Yep."

The changing of the guard was fascinating, but I was antsy to see the Museum of American History.

I was full of anticipation as we pedaled over the Memorial Bridge, weaving among joggers, tourists, and other cyclists. It was an amazing combination of tourists and locals. On the D.C. side of the bridge, we saw brown pedestrian signs pointing us to different sites and followed the directions to the American History Museum.

There was a rack outside the main entrance to the museum where we locked up our bikes and then climbed the steps to the front entrance. As we walked into the main hall, we were greeted with the giant flag that had been the inspiration for Francis Scott Key's "The Star-Spangled Banner." The sheer size of the flag was jaw dropping. It felt like we were being pulled over to the flag, and we stood there staring until a large curtain dropped over it. We later found out the flag was only on display for a few minutes every hour to protect it from the elements.

When the flag disappeared from view, Mom said, "Okay, guys. I'll take Emily and Myrtle with me and you guys can go whatever direction you want. Just meet me back here in two hours and then we'll have lunch."

Matt and Marc took off in one direction while Lindsey and I went in another. As we entered the main area of the museum, I said, "Damn. I don't even know where to begin."

"Let's just take one floor at a time and see where we end up."

"As long as we see the pop culture stuff, that sounds good to me."

As we meandered our way through each room, the sheer volume of objects on display felt overwhelming. I said, "I feel like I could spend days in here and still not see everything."

"I know what you mean," Lindsey agreed. "It makes me wish we had more time in D.C."

"Do you know how long we're staying?"

"I think three days. Mom said she wants to be in New York by the end of the week."

I thought about the timeline. "We can't bike to New York in two days."

Lindsey replied, "I think we're done biking. I heard Mom say something to Ray and Lisa about driving to New York."

I couldn't believe she was okay with this. In utter disappointment I responded, "Man. I guess we only biked to D.C. then?"

"Isn't that good enough? We made it clear across the country."

"Yeah, it is, but it kind of seems like we quit right at the end."

"Laura, we didn't quit. Look where we are. We're in Washington, D.C. We didn't quit."

"Okay, if you say so. Can we go find the pop culture stuff now?"

Lindsey sighed, "I think it's on the next floor," and we made our way to the stairs.

Even at the time, I knew that my desire to see the movie and television paraphernalia display was a bit silly, especially in comparison with all the other historical artifacts on display. I mean, what is Fonzie's leather jacket compared to George Washington's uniform? Or Archie and Edith's chairs compared to Abraham Lincoln's hat? I just felt like all the personal possessions of different presidents spoke to our nation's history, while the props from television shows spoke to my past. Those silly '70s sitcoms were the things that had kept me company during all the lonely nights I spent at Mrs. Hall's house. George Washington didn't give me nearly as much comfort as, say, Jack Soo's coffee cup from *Barney Miller*, which actually choked me up when I saw it.

Plus, I found it affirming to see all the movie, television, and sport objects on display. I felt like the Smithsonian was saying that pop culture was important in our society and needed to be remembered and celebrated. Given the fact that Dorothy's ruby slippers were one of the most viewed objects in the whole museum, I guess the Smithsonian knew what it was doing.

At noon, Lindsey and I made our way back to the entrance of the museum and met up with the rest of our group. Emily and Myrtle were bouncing with excitement, and I asked Mom, "What's gotten into them?"

"They saw Judy Garland's shoes, and they know there's an old-fashioned ice cream place here."

Myrtle butted in, "Mom said we can have lunch at the ice cream place."

I smiled at her. "Really?"

"Why not?" Mom answered. "We might as well get the *full* experience."

I was surprised by Mom's willingness to splurge because she'd been pretty frugal up to this point. I was even more surprised when I saw the prices on the menu and plucked up the courage to ask why we were really eating there.

"We're celebrating," said Mom. "Plus, I need to let you guys know that we're not biking to New York." And there it was. The other ruby slipper dropped.

Matt perked up for the first time in weeks. "So we're done biking?"

Before Mom could answer, Marc said, "Thank God. I am so sick of my bike."

I looked at Mom, my eyes wide with disappointment. "Why?"

"I just don't think we have enough time to get to New York and really visit the city if we bike the rest of the way. I've already called the lady we're staying with and she's expecting us at the end of the week."

"Well, it sounds like you have it all planned out," I replied. I really didn't want to spend a day riding in the car with *everyone*. Even today, just the memory of the stench makes me gag. However, I knew the trip was ending on the fifteenth of August, and it was already the sixth, the same day we dropped the bomb on Hiroshima, and now I had to deal with the fallout of Mom's decision. Then again, it didn't really matter how we spent our last days, since all roads led back home.

Mom followed up her reasoning with, "I think in the end it is the right idea."

"How long will it take to drive to New York," I grumbled.

"Not long. If we drive straight there, four or five hours. But I want to make stops along the way, so it'll be longer."

Great, I thought. *All day shoved in the car together with all our stuff.* At least we wouldn't be sweaty and smelly the whole time. But by this point, the car itself reeked. The upholstery had absorbed our stink and sweat for the last two months. Trust me, there wasn't an air freshener strong enough to mask that odor. At that point, despite the special meal, I lost my appetite.

We spent the rest of the day visiting the Natural History and Air and Space museums.

It was dark by the time we descended the Washington Monument (Mom stayed back, having suddenly developed a fear of heights), and we had to navigate our way back to Ray and Lisa's house. We didn't have lights on our bikes, but thankfully, the path was illuminated the whole way. When we pulled up to their house, Ray was sitting on the front porch waiting for us.

Mom asked him, "Were you a little worried about us?"

"I was," he replied. "I think it would be for the best if you guys just took the Metro into town tomorrow. I should have told you there's a station two blocks from here."

"I think you're right," Mom said as she dismounted from her bike. "That way we won't have to lug the bikes around with us all the time."

Mom had us lock up our bikes on the back patio and then joined Ray and Lisa in the living room. Lisa asked if we'd like pizza for dinner and Mom said, "If you order it, I'll pay for it."

Lisa asked what we wanted for toppings and then went into the kitchen to place the order. While she was gone, all of us kids vied for a seat on their sofa. We were still getting used to sitting on something soft and comfortable. Ray just stood back and watched as we worked out who got to sit where, and then said, "I've never seen anything like this."

I laughed, "I know. I wish I could say we behave better at home, but the truth is, we fight for seats at home too."

Matt added, "Yeah. At home you have to say, 'Place is saved by me' if you get up from your seat. If you don't say it, you lose your spot."

Laughing, Ray asked, "How long does that save your seat?"

In unison we answered, "Ten minutes!" God, it seemed like an age ago since we even had a seat to save.

When the pizza arrived, we all gathered around the table and shared stories about our day. Ray asked us what our plans were for the next couple of days and Mom said, "I think we'll visit the Capitol, maybe Ford's Theater, and then spend the next day at the zoo." The little girls' eyes widened, and Myrtle asked, "Are we going to see panda bears?"

Ray explained that we could get to all those places on the Metro, and after dinner he took us on a short walk to show us where the Metro station was and how to get to the places we wanted to go. He really didn't want us biking in the dark again. It was odd to have an adult male truly concerned for our safety. I guess that what it's like...?

We spent our remaining time in D.C. visiting as many sites as possible. From the National Archives to the National Zoo, we tried to see everything. On our final Metro ride back to Ray and Lisa's house, Matt said, "Man, we could spend another two weeks here and still not take it all in."

"It just makes me want to come back," I said.

Matt looked over at me. "So, was it everything you wanted?"

"It was. I really like this place. Sure beats home."

Mom ignored my dig and changed the subject. "Is it a good place to quit biking?"

"I guess so," I sighed. "I still wish we were biking the last part, but I understand why we're calling it quits here."

Back at Ray and Lisa's house, they'd prepared a small farewell dinner of chicken fettuccine. The heavenly smell of creamy garlic wafted up from a steaming bowl in the center of the table. We gathered around and took our seats, struggling to be polite even though we all wanted to dig in. Ray asked us if we knew much about the lady we'd be with in New York.

As Mom served the little girls (we had a rule that the youngest ate first), she explained, "She's my friend Joan's mother, and Lisa's aunt."

Ray and Lisa gave each other sly looks and then Lisa asked, "So, Joan didn't tell you much about her mother?"

"No," said Mom. "Joan set it all up for us and I spoke to Muriel on the phone before we left, and then again today. Is there something we don't know?"

Ray paused a moment before he spoke. "Let's just say she's an interesting woman. Also, keep an open mind when you meet her."

I was only half listening to this conversation and more focused on my meal. It was so nice to be sitting at a real dining room table, eating off of real plates and having a real home-cooked meal. The first bite of that fettuccine was indescribable. Needless to say, there were no leftovers. It was only when I met Muriel that I began to wonder what Ray and Lisa had been trying to tell us.

Mom decided to take a multi-stop route to New York, wanting to waste as much time as possible before reaching Muriel's. The first place she took us to was an Amish market outside of Baltimore, where I asked her, "When does this lady expect us to arrive?"

"Tomorrow sometime."

This was the first time that I heard we weren't expected until the next day. I asked her, "Are we going to find a campground and spend the night somewhere?"

"I don't know what we're doing yet. I'll figure something out."

"Mom, wouldn't it be better if we figured out what we're doing now so we don't end up stuck later on?"

Mom looked at me and said, "Oh, Laura, we'll be okay. Just enjoy the day."

I was left with a nagging feeling the day wasn't going to end with enjoyment, and I couldn't understand why she wouldn't just look at the fucking map and find a place to spend the night.

That feeling was validated hours later, when at two o'clock in the morning, she pulled up to the entrance of Jones Beach on Long Island. The gates were closed, and Mom looked back at us and said, "Get some sleep. When the gates open up, we'll spend the day there and then go to Muriel's."

I said, "Are you fucking kidding me! Mom, we're in New York. We don't know where in New York, and you just want to sleep in the car!"

Mom glared at me in the rearview mirror. "Damn, Laura. Go to sleep."

I looked over at my brothers and sisters, assuming they would agree with me. But Matt and Marc were already getting comfortable, Myrtle and Emily were asleep, and Lindsey was sitting in her front seat throne.

Lindsey looked back at me. "Jesus, Laura, shut up and go to sleep."

"I'll shut up, but I'm not going to sleep."

For the next seven hours I sat wedged between Matt and Marc with Myrtle lying across our laps. I couldn't have fallen asleep even if I'd wanted to. I spent the time thinking about what I'd be facing once I got home. I was in a pickle and I knew it. Up until that night I'd been able to avoid these tough realities by focusing on the trip. Whenever a kernel of truth made its way into my thoughts, I could just change course. Squeezed into the backseat of a smelly car, I couldn't even adjust my position, let alone my train of thought.

Back at Willamette High School, I had about thirty unexcused absences to account for—days spent finding a buyer for alcohol and partying at our house while Mom was at work. I didn't even know if I'd be allowed to register for my senior year. Plus, my junior high school plan of *barely* graduating was working well, but it would be coming to an end soon. I seriously doubted that our trip across America would be seen as "extra credit" or make up for three years of not giving a shit.

By the time the sun rose over the Atlantic, I'd come to the exhausted conclusion that I was screwed. All I could do was try to enjoy the rest of the trip and deal with the consequences when I got home.

The park opened at seven in the morning, and Mom pulled in and bought a day pass so we could spend the day on the beach. We found a picnic spot, unloaded some of our stuff, and then went down to the water to hang out. I sought out a shaded area under a tree and passed out for a couple of hours.

I woke up to discover that Mom had gone to a grocery store and got orange juice and donuts. I grabbed a donut and said, "Funny. This is how we began this trip. We had donuts the morning we left home."

Mom asked, "Do you feel better now?"

"Kind of, but I still think you were crazy to have us sleep in the car last night."

"No one attacked us, Laura, and we all lived," said Lindsey.

With a mouth full of donut I said, "Maybe that was because I was awake all night. You don't know."

"You are so full of shit," said Lindsey, and she went to wade in the ocean with the others.

I looked out at the five of them playing in the water, wondering if the Atlantic was as cold as the Pacific was in Oregon. I shouted at them, "Is it warm or cold?"

Matt shouted back, "It isn't as cold as the Oregon Coast!"
I decided to kick off my shoes and join them.

Before we left Jones Beach, Mom called Muriel and told her where we were. Muriel said it would take us about forty-five minutes to reach her house in Queens and gave Mom detailed directions. We left the beach at around three o'clock with only Muriel's directions and a vague idea of where we were headed.

Mom drove us into Queens just fine but proceeded to get lost once we were in the borough. We saw more of Queens than we anticipated. Actually, we saw more of Jamaica Avenue than we wanted. I have no doubt we passed Archie and Edith's home more than once. After an hour of driving around in circles, Mom finally pulled over and asked for help from a pedestrian. With a new set of directions, she proceeded to get lost—again. Lindsey convinced her to pull into a gas station and asked the attendant for directions. This time she got it right and we soon found ourselves in front of a little house on a tree-lined street.

Mom parked the car and was just about to get out when she noticed a man and woman standing at the front door. It appeared as if the gentleman was saying goodbye, so Mom waited a minute before approaching the woman. During that time, Mom looked back at us and said, "Listen, we don't know this woman. This is her house, and you all need to be respectful. Be on your best behavior."

The gentleman began to walk to his car just when Mom was done giving us her directive. As she got out of the car, she poked her head in and said, "I mean it," and then went to introduce herself to Muriel.

When the coast was clear, Lindsey said, "What the hell does she think we're going to do?"

"Obviously," I said, "she thinks we're going to destroy that woman's home."

"Whatever," said Matt. "I just want to get out of the car now."

From the window I could see Mom and the woman talking. The woman was heavyset and appeared to be in her seventies, with short gray hair and a flowery house dress. She kind of looked like Edith Bunker, only bigger. Eventually, Mom waved us out of the car. She didn't have to tell us twice—we piled out and joined them at the front door. The woman introduced herself as Muriel and invited us into her home.

Before going inside, Mom asked if our bikes were safe and Muriel said, "Um. I would move them to my backyard if I were you."

Mom commanded, "Matt and Laura, would you guys get the bikes off the rack?"

Muriel pointed at the side of her house and said, "Just take them in the back through the gate there. When you're done just knock on the back door and I'll let you in."

Matt and I went to do what we were told while the others all went inside. Back at the car Matt said, "Maybe this will be the last time we have to deal with these damn bikes."

"God, that would be nice," I said. "Do you think you'll ever ride a bike again?"

"Not any time soon."

With the bikes put away, we knocked on Muriel's back door and Marc let us inside.

The back door led us into the kitchen, where we found everyone sitting around Muriel's Formica kitchen table in her vinyl chairs, drinking sodas and chatting. When we joined them, Muriel said, "Okay. Let me show you guys where you'll be sleeping."

Muriel's house was larger than it appeared from the outside because it had a finished basement where she told us there were two bedrooms. She didn't take us down there but indicated she would later.

On the main floor, there was a guest room, and the living room had a sofa bed. Muriel told us we could decide for ourselves who would sleep where.

Mom stepped in fast. "Matt and Marc, you two get the sofa bed. Lindsey, take the guest bedroom up here, and I'll take Myrtle and Emily in one of the rooms downstairs, and Laura, you take the other."

With the room assignments settled, Muriel said, "Well, how about I take you for a drive around Queens?"

The last thing I wanted to do was get back in a car, but Mom replied, "That would be wonderful."

Fuck, I thought, *we've been driving around Queens for hours, can't we just stop?* Instead of relaxing here, I found myself squeezed in the back of Muriel's car, driving around the area, thinking, *Why are we doing this?* There really isn't all that much to see in Queens.

When we returned to Muriel's house, Mom offered to take her to the grocery store and purchase supplies for our stay. She also offered to pick up take-out for dinner. Muriel took Mom up on her offer and the two women left us alone in the house while they went shopping.

With the older women gone, Matt and Marc decided to go down into the basement and check out the other rooms. As they were descending the stairs, Lindsey said, "Don't get into anything that you shouldn't."

Matt yelled back up the stairs, "Okay, *Mom*, like we'd do something like that!"

To be a smartass, I shouted back, "Yes!"

With the boys in the basement, Lindsey and I took the girls into the living room, turned on the television, and tried to find something for them to watch. Just when we'd found a channel with cartoons, Matt came running into the room wearing a blonde wig under his Detroit Tigers baseball cap, saying, "Go, Tigers! Go!"

"What in the hell are you wearing?" I asked.

Marc was right behind him. "Come downstairs and check this out."

As Lindsey and I followed the boys down to the basement, Matt said, "This is the weirdest place. There are two rooms, but one room is full of wigs, shoes, and clothes."

At the bottom of the stairs there was a door that opened into a bedroom. The room was very masculine, decorated in dark blues and browns. In one corner was what looked like an Air Force uniform. Nothing appeared strange about the room, and I was kind of disappointed.

Matt said, "We're not talking about this room. Look over here, there's a secret door," and he pushed open a narrow door leading into another room. From where I was standing, all I could see was that it was painted pink.

"You've gotta check this place out," said Marc.

Lindsey and I walked through the door into a room that looked like what I pictured an actress's dressing room from the '40s would look like. At the far end of the room were three large racks of women's clothes, and next to the racks were shelves of women's high-heeled shoes. On the other side of the room was a dressing table and mirror that had more makeup on it than the cosmetics counter at Macy's. Next to the dressing table was a stand full of wigs and a full-length mirror. In the middle of the room was a king-size bed—with a pink bedspread!

I walked over to the shoe rack and noticed the shoes were really big. I picked one up and saw it was a size ten. "Man, Muriel has really large feet."

"For a woman wearing a housedress, I can't see her wearing these clothes, but who knows," said Lindsey.

Matt said, "I know we shouldn't have been snooping around, but this is just too crazy."

I felt like we really shouldn't be in there. "Let's get out of here, okay? She might not want us in here."

"Yeah," said Marc. "Let's shut the door and pretend we didn't come in."

Matt took the wig off and hung it back up on the rack. We turned out the lights, shut the doors, and went back upstairs to wait for Mom and Muriel to return. When they came home, we were all sitting in the living room watching cartoons with the little girls. To the ignorant eye we must have looked like a nice, polite bunch of kids, not a nosy group of amateur detectives.

Mom had purchased Chinese food, which we scarfed down in no time. While we were cleaning up our dinner mess, Muriel asked if we knew any card games. I said, "Kings Corners or Crazy Eights?"

She asked, "Do you guys want to play Crazy Eights?"

"Why not?" said Mom.

The little girls asked if they could go back and watch television, and the rest of us played cards. During the game, we became aware of what Ray and Lisa had been alluding to.

For the first two games we were all chatting. In the middle of the third game, Muriel was dealing when she said, "Um. I have something I need to tell you."

"Okay," said Mom. "I hope we haven't already done anything to upset you."

"No. No. You're all fine. It's just I need to let you know that I have a boarder, and the rooms in the basement are *his* rooms."

Lindsey, Matt, Marc, and I all exchanged looks. I don't know if they too had heard Muriel say, "*His* rooms." *Both* rooms were his rooms?

Muriel continued, "He knows you're staying here for a few days and he's fine with you using his rooms. He's a commercial pilot and lives out of state. He just stays here when he's flying out of New York." She picked up her cards and cleared her throat. "Well, I don't know how to say this, but he's a… transvestite and, well, one of the rooms is where he changes and sleeps when he wants to be…you know, a woman."

Silence. We all just stared at our cards. Laughing was out of the question.

Lindsey nudged me and nodded her head towards Matt and Marc. Their faces were slack and their mouths open. It took all I could muster to not crack up. I could almost see the wheels in Matt's head spinning. He had to be thinking, *I was wearing his wig*.

Muriel continued matter-of-factly, "I just needed you to be aware of what you'll see downstairs. He's a nice man, and he brings his friends here to change their clothes too. The gentleman you saw earlier, his name is Jim, but his female persona is *Danielle*."

Mom looked like she was caught between being shocked and trying to come off as sophisticated. Finally, she settled on flattery. "Um. Well. I think it's wonderful that you provide a place for these people."

Muriel asked, "Would you like to see some pictures of my friends?"

Mom slapped down a card—the queen of hearts. "Sure."

Muriel got up and left the room looking for the pictures. While she was gone Mom whispered, "Be polite. Don't say anything rude."

I whispered back, "What the hell do you expect us to do?"

Muriel waddled back into the room carrying a large photo album. She sat down at the table, opened it up, and proceeded to show us pages and pages of men dressed in drag. As she flipped through the album, I watched my mother's demeanor. This was the woman who flipped out because I refused to wear a dress. How was she going to cope with this situation?

In truth, Mom seemed to handle it pretty well, and I was much more uncomfortable with the whole situation. Here were these men, who seemed to know who they were, embracing their fluidity. I, on the other hand, felt ashamed for wearing Levi's.

As Muriel showed us more pictures, I began to wonder if these men were comfortable with who they were, or did they live double lives? Her boarder had two rooms, one masculine, one feminine. Maybe the whole issue was messy and complicated, and just thinking about it made me incredibly anxious. In the end, I decided to laugh at the whole situation for a couple of reasons. One, it was funny. We make it to Queens and we're staying at a changing house for transvestites. Archie's worst nightmare. And people thought we were strange as we pulled into campsites. Fucking irony!

But the overriding reason for my laughter was because I didn't know how to deal with my own issues. I'd experienced harassment my whole life because I refused to be appropriately feminine according to the standards of my family and hometown. Fuck, during my freshman year, three senior varsity football players cornered me in the student center, held me down, and threatened me just because I was wearing a polo shirt and Levi's. Just being myself was always met with scorn and rejection, bordering on violence.

That night, Mom chose to sleep in the feminine room with the girls while I slept in the masculine room (of course she put me in there). As I lay awake looking at his things, I noticed a number of pictures on the dresser. I got up to inspect and realized that the man must've been married with children. There was a picture of a bride and groom in front of a church. There were also pictures of young children next to the wedding picture. I thought, *You poor guy*, and went back to bed. It was all so complicated.

The next morning, Muriel treated us to bagels and lox with schmear—her word for cream cheese—for breakfast and told us the easiest route to get into Manhattan. She said, "Really, just follow the signs and you should be okay."

"How do I get out of this neighborhood so I can *follow* the signs?" asked Mom.

"Just go the same way you came in."

I thought, *Here's to another lost hour.*

Fortunately, we didn't have nearly as much trouble getting out of Muriel's neighborhood as we had trying to find it. In no time, we were crossing the Queensboro Bridge and entering Manhattan.

Driving into Gotham City was exciting and intimidating. Cruising up and down the streets of Manhattan in our Escort, I felt so small. In comparison with the buildings and the yellow taxis, and the crazy number of pedestrians, we seemed so insignificant. We were just a little bug crawling on the skin of the Big Apple.

Mom parked the car in a garage in Times Square, and we made our way out onto the street. New York has a particular smell in the heat of August—a mix of exhaust, sweat, urine, and steaming street vendor food. Even the streets themselves—or it seemed like the sewers—were steaming, and hot air blew up out of the vents as the subways rattled by underground.

When I walked out onto 45th Street, the energy of the city was overwhelming. Everyone must have felt the same way because we just stood on the sidewalk looking up at the buildings. When the third person told us to "Get the hell out of the way," Mom pulled us closer to the building and asked, "Where do you guys want to go to first?"

Lindsey said, "The Empire State Building."

Marc said, "Let's just walk around Times Square."

I said, "Damn, I have no idea."

"Okay," said Mom. "We're in Times Square. Let's find the Empire State Building and then you guys can go up to the top—without me."

For the next half hour, we walked around aimlessly looking for the famous building that should have stuck out like a sore thumb, but we just couldn't find it. Finally, Mom asked a guy selling t-shirts where the building was. He looked at her funny and said, "Lady, you're standing right in front of it."

Sure enough, we were right in front of the entrance, the giveaway being the huge lettering above the doors that read EMPIRE STATE. In our defense, all the buildings were enormous, and we couldn't tell one building from another.

"Listen, I really don't want to go up there," said Mom. "I'll stay down here with Emily, and the rest of you go up to the observation deck. When you come down, we'll decide what to do next."

The five of us walked into the building, purchased our tickets, and found the elevators to the observation deck. Riding up the elevator to the 102nd floor was a little uncomfortable. The biggest building in Willamette with an elevator was only three stories. While we were standing in the elevator, Marc said, "I don't know about you guys, but this is kind of freaky."

"Yeah," said Lindsey, "but just think about the view we'll see when we get to the top."

The other people in the elevator with us kind of gave us strange looks, so I said, "He's never been in an elevator before."

An older lady looked over at him and said, "You'll be okay."

Marc whispered under his breath, "You bitch," and I just smiled back at him.

The view from the top gave me an appreciation for the density of Manhattan. Everywhere I looked seemed packed with buildings, cars, and people. The only place that looked green and inviting was Central Park. I turned to Matt. "You know, I think I could hang out in the park all day."

"I know. It's the only place that there's anything growing."

Lindsey butted in, "Yeah, but there are so many other places we could go see. Neighborhoods to visit and other parts of the city." *Like Queens*, I thought.

"I think I'd feel better if I knew where we were going," I said. "Let's head to the park and try to get our bearings."

Despite being huge, the city was making me feel claustrophobic. The weather was muggy, the buildings towered over us, and there were just so many people. The wide-open spaces of the park looked like a safe refuge.

When we exited the building, we found Mom talking to a couple of hustlers who were running a shell game. One of the guys was holding Emily, saying, "Baby needs a new pair of shoes."

Mom said, "These guys are really funny. Watch how they work the crowd."

We stood around and watched them take a couple of people's money. Matt said, "I think I could win."

"Matt, you idiot," said Marc. "It's a con. They want you to think you'll win. Think about it."

Before Matt could lose any money, Mom took Emily back and then we walked up Fifth Avenue to the park, where we spent the rest of the day hanging out at the boat pond and scouting out the different sculptures in the park, and that's how we happened upon Strawberry Fields.

Towards the end of the day, Mom had Emily and Myrtle's portraits painted, then had Matt and Marc's portraits drawn by the artists hanging out around the Metropolitan Museum of Art. As far as I know, the portraits still hang on the wall in Mom's basement. On the way back to the car, we stopped off for a slice of pizza and soda at Ray's in Times Square. It wasn't the most exciting day in Manhattan—but it was fun.

On the last day that Mom and the younger kids were in New York, we went to a Mets baseball game. The Mets had a young and exciting team—little did we know they'd win the World Series the following year. That day, Darryl Strawberry played in the outfield and Dwight Gooden pitched. Both players were just starting out, and it was before their professional meltdowns. We ate hotdogs and popcorn and drank sodas. Mom even bought us Cracker Jack. In other words, we had the full ballgame experience.

As we sat in our seats, I looked at our ragtag group, and a sadness washed over me. They were so excited about returning to Willamette, and I never wanted to go back. Just the thought of being back home cast a dark shadow over my mood. This trip gave me a glimpse that the world was bigger than Willamette, and the last thing I wanted to do was go back to where we started. I just wanted to keep going—but unfortunately that wasn't an option.

Muriel wanted to give Mom a chance to have a night out without kids and had made reservations for the two of them at an upscale restaurant that night. There was just one little problem—Mom didn't have any nice clothes to wear. So, Muriel suggested she go downstairs and pick out an outfit from her boarder's wardrobe. I could actually see Mom's internal struggle play out on her face. She really wanted to go out, but she didn't want to wear the transvestite's clothes. In the end, the desire to have a nice meal with another adult won the day, and Mom went down to the basement to pick out an outfit.

When Mom ascended the stairs, she was dressed in a conservative suit and had even borrowed some of the boarder's makeup. Actually, she looked pretty good. "Muriel, the only problem is my feet are small, and all the shoes down there are a size ten," said Mom.

Muriel offered, "You can use a pair of my shoes. I'm a size six. Will that work?"

"Perfect."

Right before they left, Mom told Lindsey and me to do some laundry so the younger kids would have clean clothes to wear on the flight. The plan was for us to take the rest of their things back with us in the car.

Matt watched through the front window as Mom and Muriel drove off. He turned around and said, "I fucking can't believe she's wearing his clothes!"

"Oh, Matt, get over it," said Lindsey. "She wanted to go out to dinner."

"It's just weird."

As they were going back and forth, I thought Mom wearing a crossdresser's clothes was fucking perfect. I wondered if our dad could see her right now. Just the thought of Dad watching this all play out warmed my heart.

Lindsey and I dropped Mom and the kids off at LaGuardia Airport and sent them on their way back to Portland. Meg's husband, Jake, would fly in the following afternoon, and then we planned on heading towards Oregon the next day. This gave the two of us a day and a half to do whatever we wanted, so we headed back to Manhattan. Without four younger kids in tow, we had a lot more freedom to enjoy the city.

On the way into Manhattan, we decided we wanted to go back to the Metropolitan Museum of Art. We parked in the same garage in Times Square and walked towards the Met. As we walked along Fifth Avenue, Lindsey said, "You know what? I could live here."

"I don't think I could," I said. "It's too crowded and there isn't enough green. It's all concrete."

"That's what I like about it. It's so different than Willamette."

"I liked D.C. better. More open spaces and trees."

The two of us went back and forth on the merits of each city, and before we knew it we'd walked nearly forty blocks to the museum. As we climbed the front steps, I asked, "Why didn't we go in here the other day?"

"I don't know," said Lindsey. "At least we're here now," and we climbed the stairs, went inside, paid our five dollars, got our little metal MMA tab, and began touring the exhibits. I knew the reason we hadn't gone in earlier. Mom didn't trust us to behave. *What were we going to do? Destroy a painting or something?*

Being from a small logging town, I'd not been exposed to fine art. Willamette's idea of fine art was mounted game heads and chainsaw sculptures. This was the first time I'd ever been in an art museum, let alone seen the works of masters. When we entered the Impressionism hall, I felt compelled to sit down on a bench and just experience the paintings. Sunflowers, dancers, poppies, and lilies were reflecting light and beauty all around me. I just wanted to stay in that room forever.

Lindsey said, "Isn't it all so gorgeous?"

"It is," I said, soaking it all in. "I would love to just crawl into one of these paintings and disappear. It makes our mill town look pretty dank."

"Yeah, but we don't have to stay there, Laura. We can leave."

Maybe Lindsey believed this, but I doubted it was true. I just let the words "We can leave" hang in the air.

We picked Jake up at JFK Airport at five o'clock the following night. We stood at the gate and waited for his plane to land. When he entered the waiting area, I was surprised by how happy I was to see him. He'd been our biggest champion before we set off on the bike trip, so it was only fitting that it'd be Jake driving back with us. When he saw us, he dropped his bag and gave me a huge hug. "You guys did it!"

"I know!" I said. "Did those guys get home okay?"

"Yes, Meg, Henry, Nate, and I picked them up at the airport. They were so happy to be home."

"Now we need to figure out how *we're* getting home," said Lindsey.

Jake asked, "Can we go into Manhattan for a while first? I've never been to New York City."

Considering he'd just flown across the country and was willing to drive back to Oregon with us, we didn't think that was a huge ask. When we got into the car, he said, "Oh, my God! This car stinks."

"Really? We hadn't noticed," I said. For a second he thought I was serious. So I said, "Tell me about it. The good news is that after a while you get used to it."

"I think we'll drive the whole way home with the windows rolled down," he said, laughing.

"Trust me," Lindsey said. "You don't want to drive in this thing any other way."

The three of us drove into Manhattan, parked the car, and walked around the city for the next few hours. On the way back to Queens, we picked up a pizza and a six pack of beer. That night, we came up with a plan to send the bicycles back to Willamette. We also figured out what route we'd take home.

The next morning, Muriel told us where there was a bicycle shop. We took the bikes to the shop, where they were boxed and shipped back to Willamette (where they would stay boxed up in our garage for more than a year). With that job done, we got in the car and began our trek home. It'd taken us eight weeks to reach New York City and would take only three days to drive back. When we pulled up in front of our house in Willamette, I felt like I'd gone a long way to get absolutely...nowhere.

Chapter 13

CRASH LANDING

When we arrived home, Mom and the younger kids had already been back for the better part of a week, so the real celebrations had already happened. When we pulled up to the house, people were happy that we'd made it home safe, but that was the extent of our homecoming.

We'd been driving for three days straight without stopping, and I was just happy to get out of the car. Plus, I stank and wanted to get clean—to scrub the trip away. I went up to my room, sat down on my bed, and took in my surroundings. I was torn. Should I crawl under the covers and fall asleep, or take a long, hot bath? The need to get clean won out. I went to my dresser and pulled out some clean clothes. They felt brand new. I'd been wearing the same handful of shorts and t-shirts all summer, and everything I'd taken with me was threadbare and trashed. My pink Sperrys had reached their end, and I kicked them under my bed.

For the next hour, I leaned back in a sudsy, steamy bath and tried to scrub the stink and grime off my skin. When I drained the water, there was a dirt ring around the tub. I put on fresh clean clothes and threw my dirty clothes down the laundry chute, wondering if I'd ever wear them again. Probably not.

In the living room, I caught a glimpse of myself in the full-length mirror and became fully aware of the extent of my weight loss. My old clothes were barely hanging onto my body, and I was emaciated. It wasn't a good look.

As I stood there, Nate walked into the living room and said, "So, you're back?"

I said, "So, you're still here?", turned, went into the kitchen, picked up the phone, and called my friends Macy and Tami to see if they wanted to hang out.

I didn't keep in contact with them on the trip because it wasn't practical. I bought postcards with the best of intentions, but they didn't make it into the post. This was decades before cell phones, and calling them collect on a payphone wasn't an option. Only Mom kept in contact with home. She called Nate a couple of times just to let him know what state we were in, but that was it for communication.

As I dialed Macy's number, I looked around the kitchen. Dad's old cigarette burns served as a reminder that even after roughly 8,000 miles of travel, nothing had really changed.

Macy, Tami, and I had been friends since grade school. We were an odd trio. Macy and Tami came from working-class families. Their fathers worked at the lumber mill and their families were fully immersed in our hometown's mill culture. My middle class, white-collar family knew little about that aspect of our town. What we did have in common was a lack of ambition and a desire to have fun.

Macy said she would get Tami and then they'd pick me up.

About an hour later, Macy pulled up with Tami in her dad's old Bronco. Both looked sun-kissed and well. The three of us drove around town, talking and listening to music. Later on, we found someone to purchase us a bottle of vodka, snuck back into my house, and spent the rest of the evening hanging out in my room, drinking Smirnoff and Coke.

At one point Macy mentioned that one of our mutual friends, Angel, had dropped out of school.

"What? She only had a year left."

"Well," Macy said. "You know she's been using crank for a while."

Tami added, "Yeah, weed is one thing, but crank is just plain bad."

I looked at Tami and said, "Maybe Mrs. Johnson was right, and one third of us *won't* graduate."

Macy asked, "I wonder who'll make it through the year? I'm on thin ice. I don't know if I'll have enough credits to graduate on time."

I looked at her. "Don't you know?"

"I have a ton of unexcused absences and I don't know if I passed enough classes. I'll find out when I register for school next week."

"I'm dreading registration," I said. "I always start in a hole."

Tami commented, "Laura, if you would just try, your situation would be a lot better."

"That's the thing, Tami. I don't want to try."

School registration day. God, I knew this day was coming and I'd avoided thinking about it all summer. With my poor grades and attendance, it would be a day of reckoning. The school's policy was that they wouldn't send report cards home if the student owed money or had unexcused absences. Since I had around thirty unexcused absences, my report card hadn't been mailed to my house. The last thing I wanted to do was confront the reality of my predicament.

This wasn't the first time I'd faced these obstacles. The previous two years I had had to write an essay explaining my truancy for Mrs. Johnson, who'd followed our class from junior high school to high school. I also had to meet with her one on one. The only silver lining I could see around this dark cloud was that it'd be my last visit with Mrs. Johnson. If I could just get through the next nine months, I'd never have to face her again.

Macy came over to pick me up, and she and I walked the half mile to the high school together in the lingering August heat.

On the walk from my house, Macy asked, "How many days did you miss last year?"

"My guess is around fifty, but only thirty were unexcused. What about you?"

"I'd guess around twenty," she said. "What was your essay about last year?"

"That writing an essay was stupid."

"My guess is we won't be given an essay assignment again."

As we walked through the glass front doors of our dilapidated 1950s high school, I said, "We'll know soon enough."

I stepped up to the school office's main counter to speak to the school secretary. She had a daughter in the class below us who played varsity basketball with Macy and me. In the past she'd made a few snide remarks about my school record and indicated that I shouldn't be allowed to play ball. Aside from Mrs. Johnson, she was the last person I wanted to see.

Before I could say anything, Macy took the lead. "Hi. We're here to register."

The secretary, decked out in her best Jaclyn Smith K-Mart pants suit, gave me an insipid smile and said, "Oh, Laura, you're back. We've been waiting for you. Go over to the counselor's office and Mrs. Johnson will speak with you. Macy, you can join her."

The desire to tell her to fuck off was overwhelming, but Macy grabbed me by the arm, pulled me out of the office, and whispered, "Laura, just shut up. We knew this was going to happen."

"Yeah," I said. "But she doesn't have to be a bitch about it."

Mrs. Johnson, dressed in her customary tweed suit and sensible shoes, stepped out of her office and said to the both of us, "Okay, girls, this year you won't be writing an essay. Instead, you'll work your absences off by cleaning the school. Macy, you have to work twenty-five hours, and Laura, you have fifty hours. Come here tomorrow and speak to Mr. Jones, the custodian. He'll put you to work and keep track of your hours. When you're done, you can register for school."

On our walk back to my house, I said, "I'd rather clean the school than write a paper."

Along the way we stopped off at another one of my buyers, got a couple of bottles of cheap rum, and again spent the evening getting drunk in my room. The two of us showed up for our first day of work hungover. My senior year was not beginning on a good note.

In a blink of an eye, I was right back where I'd left off: hanging out with the same group of friends, drinking too much, and dreading school. The night before the first day, I sat on the window ledge in my room, looking out over the roofs of our neighbors' houses and wondering if I'd ever get out of this place. I'd only been home for two weeks, but it felt like I'd never left. To top it all off, the trip had changed our mother, and I didn't know how to deal with her.

The year before, Mom had been all over the place emotionally, and I'd felt like the lone adult in the house. The bicycle trip allowed her to regain control over the younger kids, which meant that I was off the hook for childcare. I'd been their care-giver from the age of eleven and was more than happy for her to be their mother. But her newfound authority didn't include me. That ship had sailed a long time ago.

I found her metamorphosis from conservative Stepford wife to the eccentric ditzy mom to be the most challenging. She'd changed almost everything about herself, from how she wore her hair to how she dressed. Over the summer, her pixie hair-cut had grown out and was bushy, and for some reason she decided to keep it that way. Long, flowing skirts, oversized sweaters, and beads replaced her stylish, conservative dress-es. I knew all of these changes were just window dressing, and underneath *nothing* had really changed. I knew this because our relationship had not changed. I was still the thorn in her side that forced her to deal with the reality that a bicycle trip doesn't change the past. I was still the daughter who knew too many secrets and wouldn't conform.

I went over to my closet and dug out a bottle of vodka that I'd stashed there the night before, poured some into a half-full Coke bottle, and sat back down on the window ledge. Sipping my drink, I thought of my options for getting out of Willamette. I couldn't see any. I looked up at the night sky and said, "You're so screwed."

During the first week of school, it was obvious that about half of our classmates had dropped out. Kids that I'd sat next to since first grade were nowhere to be seen. It was like those who were missing had never existed at all.

As the semester progressed, the obvious divisions within our class grew more apparent. There were those who were headed off to college, and their shared experience of taking SATs and waiting for acceptance letters to varying universities seemed to strengthen their bonds. Then there was the rest of us, who were just kind of floundering. Our bonds were tenuous because we didn't know from week to week who'd still be around. The guidance counselors were calling people into their offices and telling seniors to drop out because they didn't have enough credits to graduate.

One Friday night before a football game, Macy, Tami, and I were drinking in my bedroom when I asked, "Do you guys know what the people who've dropped out are doing?"

Tami said, "I know some were given applications for the mill when they left."

"Really? That's harsh."

"Well, at least they have jobs," Macy replied.

"I get that," I said, "but it seems like the mill is feeding off of the failure of the high school."

"They probably would've gone to work there anyway," said Tami. "This way, they get a head start."

Looking back, I'm amazed at how ignorant I was about the socio-economic structure of our little mill town. The lumber mill and logging industry needed laborers. The mill didn't need high school diplomas; it needed strong young guys who worked hard and for cheap. I thought I knew everything about Willamette, but from my privileged perch I didn't understand how our town really functioned. I came to realize that there were kids destined for higher education, and those marked to work the green chain. I didn't fit into either category. I fell between the cracks.

Throughout the fall, I'd developed a foolproof system for procuring alcohol for my friends and me. I could count on a number of my older siblings' friends to do a booze run about once a month. Plus, every few weeks I'd head over to Oregon State and hang with Lindsey. On those trips, I'd bring Macy and Tami with me and we'd spend our time hitting different parties, playing drinking games, and getting bombed.

Mom was oblivious to my activities. She was so busy creating a new persona and social life that she wasn't privy to what I was up to. It was all fun and games—until one night I binged too much and my whole house of cards came crashing down.

When winter arrived, I was counting on basketball to keep me on the straight and narrow. It had always worked in the past, but by my senior year, even basketball couldn't bring me around. I just couldn't see the point of the whole endeavor. We weren't that great of a team and I spent more time on the bench than on the court. My disposition rubbed off on some of the other players, and we began to gather for parties on the weekends. I wouldn't say that I instigated the parties, but I provided the booze.

By February, our parties moved from occasional weekends to me bringing vodka hidden in a Big Gulp on the team bus, where we'd pass the cup around before and after the games. How our coach never caught on to what we were doing was mind-blowing. Our flagrant disrespect of him actually emboldened me to push my luck. On a return bus ride from an away game, a group of us decided to get hammered the following night before the boys' game. Each teammate gave me five dollars and placed their booze order.

The next afternoon, I found a buyer, gathered the drinks, and snuck them back into my house before Mom returned from work. Mom had made plans to take the younger kids out to dinner and a movie that night. After they left, Macy came over and we began drinking early. Later on, my teammates came over to pick up their orders.

My last clear memory was Macy saying, "Laura, I'd slow down if I were you. You're really drunk."

I was hammered, but said, "Oh, Macy. No one will notice. No one ever does."

"Well, I can tell, and if you plan on going into the school that fucked up, we're all screwed."

Elisa, who was the captain of our team said, "Don't worry about it. We'll stick together and it'll be okay."

The next thing I knew, I found myself lying on my couch, wrapped up in a blanket, with a large bowl on the floor beside me. I looked up at the ceiling trying to figure out what had happened, but it was all just a giant blank. It wasn't until Mom walked in the room that some of the pieces began to fall into place.

I saw Mom and stretched. When I ran my hands through my hair, I found chunks of vomit tangled in it. At that point I could smell myself and wanted to gag. I asked, "What happened?"

Mom wasn't upset; she had an amused look on her face. "Don't you remember?"

"I remember a little bit, but not much. I don't remember leaving the house. Did I leave the house?"

Mom laughed. "Oh, you left the house all right. You ended up behind the high school, passed out in the parking lot. You weren't breathing and one of the teachers had to do CPR on you."

Totally confused, I asked, "What?"

"Yeah, they wanted to take you to the hospital, but I said you could sleep it off at home. Also, don't worry about getting in too much trouble. The police aren't going to cite you because they think you've suffered enough. The school, on the other hand, I don't know."

"Did anyone else get in trouble?"

Mom said, with not an ounce of sympathy, "Oh, all of you girls are in a load of trouble."

I leaned back on the couch. "Shit," I said, and then got up to go take a shower.

The hot water stung my arms and legs, and I realized I had scratches all over my body. I wondered where the hell I'd been the night before. To this day I have no idea how I got so scratched up.

When I emerged from the shower, Lindsey, who'd come home that day from college, lit into me. She demanded that I tell her where I had gotten the alcohol. I told her, "From one of your high school friends."

Once Lindsey deciphered who purchased me the booze, she stormed out of the house to find her friend and chew her out. As I watched her leave the house, I thought, *Lindsey, you fucking hypocrite. You've been my primary buyer for years.*

Later that afternoon, I called Macy to see if she got in trouble. Her dad answered the phone. "Laura, I think you and Macy need a break from one another," he said, and hung up.

Monday morning, I had to swallow my pride and do the walk of shame. No one had called or spoken to me since Friday night, but I was sure everyone knew what had happened. I figured if this didn't get me kicked out of school, nothing would.

I walked into the school just a few minutes before the final bell because I didn't want to linger around the halls. Feeling that my punishment would be swift, I went right to my first period class. Sure enough, less than a minute after the bell, a call from Mrs. Cross came over a speaker in the classroom, instructing me to go to Vice Principal Brill's office.

Someone said, "Yeah, I wonder why?" and others snickered.

I stood up and said, "Well, it was nice knowing you guys. See ya later." I was almost out the door when someone called out, "Hang in there, Laura."

I poked my head back in the classroom. "Thanks. I'll try." I don't know who said those words, but at that point, it meant the world to me.

As I made my way to the office, I saw our coach standing in the middle of the hallway. He was a smaller man, with a stocky build and ruddy complexion. Even from a distance I could see his red face. He was furious. He stepped towards me. "I only have two questions, and I want the truth."

I knew from this point on I had to be honest about my own actions, and not throw anyone else under the bus. I said, "Okay."

"Did you find the buyer?"

"Yes, I did." He turned a darker shade of red.

"Were you drinking on the team bus?"

I answered, "Yes," and with that, he stormed off down the hall.

His second question threw me, and I realized that someone had talked. I had some ideas who, but I had bigger issues to contend with at that point. I took a deep breath and walked into the school office, where I was confronted with the wrath of the school secretary.

Unbeknownst to me, her daughter had been a recipient of the booze I'd purchased. She and some others had gotten drunk *and* caught. As soon as I walked through the door, the secretary said, "Sit down. The vice principal will be with you soon." She got up and knocked on the vice principal's door and told her I was there.

The secretary, in the same outfit she'd been wearing for years, took her seat, looked at me, and said, "Well, I hope you're proud of yourself. All of you girls, including my daughter, have been suspended from the basketball team."

"I guess that's fair," I said just to shut her up. I already felt guilty, and didn't really want to have *this* conversation with her.

She continued, "Until my daughter met you, she never drank alcohol. I have said for the last two years you shouldn't be allowed to play."

I wasn't going to give her an inch. "Yep. You're probably right." Just then, the vice principal called me into her office. Once I entered, she had me sit down in the chair opposite her desk.

Mrs. Brill had a kind disposition and didn't come across as a disciplinarian. Maybe this was because she always appeared slightly disheveled. Her gray-blonde hair was mid-length and a bit frizzy. Her clothes, while stylish, needed an iron. Her whole look was disarming.

Mrs. Brill looked at me for a couple of seconds and then asked, "How are you?"

Her question caught me off guard. She was the first person to ask me how I was doing. Everyone else had made a point to tell me how I'd screwed up, and how stupid I was for getting that drunk. I'd spent the weekend feeling humiliated and ashamed. Those feelings were a consequence of how I was doing.

The bitter truth was that I wasn't doing well, but I didn't think she wanted to hear the truth. So, I went the safe route and said, "Oh, I feel better. I'm okay."

She looked at me for a few seconds and then said, "Well, I've given this a lot of thought and I'm going to suspend you from school for one week. Your coach will decide what to do about basketball. Do you have any questions?"

"Not really. I mean, I did it. Actually, I thought you would expel me."

She gave a half smile. "Laura, we don't expel people for getting drunk."

I thought about all of my peers who were no longer in school and wondered what the hell they'd done to be kicked out. I knew at this point I'd graduate regardless of my grades, behavior, or attendance.

She continued, "Okay. Why don't you go get your books out of your locker? I've arranged it so you can turn in your school-work while you're gone. When you get your things, come back here and then I'll drive you home."

Later that evening, my coach called me at home and told me I was off the team. That was the extent of my punishment. I was suspended from going to school for a week and couldn't play ball. *Big deal*. I hardly went to school anyway and I'd been warming the bench all season.

There are some hard and fast rules in my large family. The most important rule being that you never snitch on a brother or sister because there'll be serious repercussions. I applied this code to the situation I found myself in. I'd owned my own shit with our coach, but I found the mere idea of telling on anyone else abhorrent. So, when the coach told my teammates that

I was the snitch, that hurt more than getting suspended. I'm sure he did it to protect the real whistleblower, but he didn't have to throw me under the bus.

On my first full day back at school, the team captain took me aside. She was close to six feet tall and hoping to get a basketball scholarship. A scholarship that was put in jeopardy because she'd been suspended from the team for a week.

I'd always gotten along with her, but on this day, she was fuming. She backed me into a corner and asked, "Why couldn't you have just kept your mouth shut about the rest of us?"

"What? I did! I only said what I did. I never mentioned names. Coach already knew everything when he spoke to me, so maybe *you* want to find out who told him."

She looked down at me and said, "You bitch. You told and you know it. You're a fucking liar," and then stormed off.

During lunch hour, Matt, who was a freshman, told me he was embarrassed to be my brother. "People keep coming up to me and asking how often you get passed out drunk at home," he said.

"Matt," I said. "I really don't give a shit."

"That's your problem," he shot back. "You don't give a shit about anyone but yourself."

"Okay, Matt, you're right. But right now all you care about is you! So, fuck off."

"Just don't even look at me," he hissed, and then walked away.

By the end of lunch hour, I'd never felt so alone. My family, friends, and teammates were all either ashamed of or pissed off at me. No one gave a fuck, so why should I? I walked out of the school, found a different buyer who bought me a fifth of vodka, and went home.

By spring break, I was going through a few bottles of vodka a week, and no one noticed. On the days I went to school, I'd pick up a 32-ounce soda, pour half out, and add vodka. I'd put the cup in my locker and sip on it between classes.

The one person who seemed to reach out was my sociology teacher, Mr. Stiers. He was the one who had performed CPR on me the night I overdosed. Every Friday he'd ask what I had planned for the weekend. I'd smile and say, "Probably what I did last weekend," and leave the class.

My weekends were spent either visiting Lindsey, who still supplied me with alcohol, or hanging out with Macy. Macy's parents had allowed us to hang out together, believing that we'd learned our lesson. But the only lesson I learned was that there really were no consequences for my behavior.

My friend Maris was the only other person who seemed to notice that I was sliding into darkness. Maris and I had been best friends through junior high school right up until my father died. After Dad's death, I pulled away from her because she made me uncomfortable.

Maris was popular, a cheerleader with a classic southern California girl look, and was one half of the cutest couple in the school. I was none of those things and always felt like the pretty girl's ugly friend. On top of all that, her parents had been Pentecostal missionaries in Brazil, and I just couldn't cope with all that Jesus. To Maris's credit, she never gave up on me and was the only one willing to be honest with me.

One Sunday evening in April, Maris called and asked if she could take me to lunch the next day. I was surprised to hear from her, but also kind of glad. I'd missed Maris and looked forward to hanging out with her even if it was only for lunch. She told me to meet her in the Student Center and then she'd drive us over to the Dairy Queen.

We each ordered chicken strip baskets and sodas and then found a booth. While we waited for our food, the conversation was light and friendly. After our food arrived, Maris looked at me and said, "Laura, you're a mess. You barely make it to school. When you do you look horrible. Your clothes are dirty, and you always have that Big Gulp with you, and don't tell me it's just soda in there." Before I touched my first chicken strip, I was served up a meal of brutal honesty.

I decided to be honest back with her. "I don't know what's going on. I just feel like I'm in a dark hole and I can't get out."

"I know you don't want to hear this, but there is a way out."

"If you say 'Jesus' I am going to throw this soda in your face."

She said, "Yes, I was going to say Jesus, but that's not all. You've been like this since before your dad died. I just want you to know that I remember your dad. He was not nice. I hated going over to your house because of him. He said humiliating and mean things all the time and he wasn't nice to you."

Tears began to well up in my eyes. "Thank you. I live in this la-la land where he's seen as a saint. I have all this anger pent up and I don't know what to do with it."

"Laura, I know your mom, and she isn't going to change. *You* need to change. What you're doing isn't working."

"But I don't know what else to do," I said, looking out over the parking lot with tears streaming down my face.

"Well, it's going to destroy you, and I hate watching it. I just wanted you to know that I see you."

No one had ever been this honest with me, and I felt exposed. I couldn't even look her in the eye.

"That's all I wanted to say, really. You're gonna do what you want, but just know I'm your friend."

I looked up at her and said, "Thanks. It does mean a lot to me, Maris."

I wish I could say that I saw the light, climbed out of my hole, and changed my ways. But I can't because I was too afraid of the light. Instead, I sunk deeper into depression. It took another few weeks before I finally reached out for help.

I sought out Mr. Stiers, hoping that he'd point me in the right direction. I waited until after school and knocked on his door. He saw me, smiled, and said, "Come on in, Laura."

Mr. Stiers was a younger guy. He'd been Nate's basketball coach. Not too tall, with dark hair and blue eyes, he looked the part of a teacher. My mom had even been his fifth grade teacher. There was something about him that I instinctively trusted. Maybe it was because he'd saved my life the night I almost died.

I told him that I had a problem and needed help. He listened to me for a while, and then said, "Laura, this is kinda more than I can help you with. I think you should speak with Mrs. Johnson, the school counselor."

His suggestion made me laugh out loud. "Mrs. Johnson has been telling me for years I'm on a path that would only lead to ruin. I'm not going to talk to her."

Mr. Stiers grinned. "Okay. I'll meet with you for a while and see what we can do."

I met with him once a week for a few weeks. Mr. Stiers wanted me to quit drinking altogether; however, that wasn't going to happen. During our meetings we never discussed why I was drinking. He just tried to fix me, but I really didn't want to be fixed. I just wanted someone to listen to me.

One weekend while I was visiting Lindsey, I made the mistake of telling her that I was talking to Mr. Stiers. The next day she called Mom and told her everything I'd shared with her. *Talk about a rat.* It was at this point Mom drew a line in the sand and let me know exactly how she felt about me, my problems, and my father.

Mom picked me up from Lindsey's apartment. On the drive home she began reading me the riot act. She said, "I can't believe you've been talking to your teachers about what's gone on in my house. Those things are private, and they stay in the house."

"I didn't know what to do," I said. "I needed someone to talk to."

Mom looked over at me. "Tomorrow you and I are going to go speak to Mr. Stiers and put an end to all this crap."

I began to say something, and she said, "Stop. Just stop," and then didn't speak to me again for the rest of the drive home.

Back at the house, I went up to my room and stayed there. I felt vulnerable and wanted a drink, but I was out of alcohol. I was also tired, so I climbed into bed and went to sleep. When I woke up the next morning, the house was empty. There was a note on the dining room table that read: *Meeting tonight with Mr. Stiers at six o'clock. Be there.*

I got dressed and went to school. For the rest of the day, I felt like an angry anvil in the shape of my mother was hanging over my head. She was pissed, and I didn't know what to expect.

At school, Mr. Stiers approached me and said Mom had called him the night before. He said, "Your mother cried and cried. I think this meeting will be good for the both of you."

My gut told me he was wrong, but I said, "I don't know. Maybe."

What he didn't understand was that there were two sides to my mother. First, there was her public persona, Mrs. Jacobson, the widowed mother with nine children, the hard-working, crazy mom that rode across the country. Then there was Lois, the woman that I knew only too well. I would be dealing with both personalities that night—Mrs. Jacobson in the meeting, and then the real Lois at home.

Mr. Stiers, Mom, and I met in his classroom that evening. The three of us sat around a table to discuss my problems with alcohol. Mom began crying right away and opened the meeting saying, "I just don't know what to do."

Mr. Stiers offered her a sympathetic look. "Lois, I know these last couple of years have been difficult. I am here to help you."

When he said "help you," I knew this meeting was going to be about Mom. Sure enough, the next ninety minutes were focused exclusively on Mom being a victim of my behavior. At no point did he discuss my problems. The whole meeting was about Mom, and Mom's struggles. It wasn't until Mom and I returned home that the real Lois reared her ugly head.

When we walked into the house, she looked at me and said, "Sit down. You and I are going to talk."

I took a seat at the dining room table and she sat down at the head. She ran her hand through her bushy hair and gave me a look that could pierce iron. "This is over," she said. "You've been walking around this house like a beaten puppy for months. No more."

I felt drained, and empty, so I began to cry. I looked her in the eye. "I feel like a beaten puppy."

"Oh, give me a break, Laura!" she shouted. "What do you want from me?"

My emptiness was filled with rage. Something snapped in me and I shouted back, "You're incapable of giving me what I want from you!"

She said, "You know what? You quit trying when you were in the third grade. You quit trying at school. From that point on you just quit."

"Maybe that's about the time you sent me to live with Mrs. Hall." I wanted her to acknowledge what she'd done to me.

"Oh, please," she said. "I just had you sleep over there. You weren't living there. Don't be dramatic."

"You kicked me out of the fucking house! At eight! Why? Was it because Dad couldn't stand the sight of me?"

She shot back, "Listen to me! You do not mention your father! Let me tell you something right now. If your father were to walk in the door and ask me to leave all of you, I'd do it. Gladly!"

"You think I don't fucking know that?" I screamed.

"And let me tell you something else, Laura," she said. "I know when your dad was dying in the hospital that you were here in Willamette acting like nothing was happening. You are a selfish little bitch."

I got up and looked at her. "Man, you are an amazing piece of work," I said, and stormed up to my room.

I lay down on my bed, too angry to cry, and a little relieved that everything was out in the open. Nothing was resolved, but we both knew where we stood. Forget about love. I didn't like her, and she didn't like me. The real question was how to live under the same roof with all that honesty. I knew there was no way I could do it sober.

Chapter 14

REHAB HAS MULTIPLE MEANINGS

Throughout the months of April and May, Mom's blossoming flowers, meticulously planted throughout her yard, marked the passage of time. In March, the bright yellows of daffodils trumpeted the arrival of spring. Around Easter, the reds and purples of tulips took their place. Spring culminated in May and the blooming explosion of her thirty rose bushes. As she fed and tended her flowers, our relationship was dying on the vine.

We maintained an uneasy truce that spring. As long as I planned to graduate in June, she stayed out of my affairs. The situation was far from perfect, and I felt trapped. I resented every minute I lived in her house, and even fantasized about leaving home. Fear and alcoholism kept me rooted in the unhealthy confines of my family system. The silent victims of our battle were my younger brothers and sisters. I no longer felt any obligation or responsibility for their welfare. My apathy towards them created a chasm that took years to mend.

At 7 p.m. on the first Thursday of June 1986—a comfortable, early summer evening—I found myself wearing a cap and gown sitting on a folding chair in the middle of Willamette High School's football field, feeling like a hypocrite. Tami sat on one side of me and Maris on the other. Macy was conspicuously absent—she'd not earned enough credits to graduate and had fallen victim to the dreaded call to the counselor's office. I knew that if I'd come from a working class family, I wouldn't have been sitting there either.

An example of WHS's double standards happened earlier in the day when I'd been called to the office. I had forty-two unexcused absences that needed to be rectified before I could receive my diploma. Before entering the office, I wrote a note that read: *Please excuse Laura Jacobson's absences on (list forty-two dates). She was ill. Thank you, Lois Jacobson.*

I walked into the school office and said to the secretary, "I'm here to see the school's attendance director."

She chose not to speak to me; instead, she got up, knocked on the attendance director's door, said, "Laura Jacobson is here to see you," and sat back down.

The attendance director met me at the counter. "So what do you want to do about these absences?"

I handed him the note and said, "That should cover it."

He took the note and read it. "I am going to accept this note only because I never want to see you again."

"Well, I never want to come back here again, so I guess this'll make us both happy." I left the office.

Now, all the school administrators were sitting on a makeshift stage, listening to the chair of the school board and the mayor give speeches about the wonderful education we'd received from Willamette High School. Even in the midst of my cynicism, I knew that the school did provide a quality education—to those who took advantage of the opportunity.

Looking around at my peers, I knew that a number of them were headed to college. I also knew that I had a snowball's chance in hell of following suit. I'd made a conscious choice to only do the bare minimum required to graduate. What seemed like a smart-alecky decision in junior high school didn't feel too bright that evening. I had a signed diploma, but no real future to get excited about. I had no idea that in four years, doors would open and opportunities would arise. From my seat on the fifty-yard line, all I could see was Willamette and the land of no opportunity.

At the conclusion of the ceremony, my family found me on the field and the first thing my mother said to me was, "Let me see that your diploma is actually signed."

"It was the first thing I checked," I said. "It's signed."

Maris was standing near me and said, "Mine's not. I just received a note that says I have two unexcused absences to make up before they'll give me my diploma."

Mom said to her, "That doesn't seem fair."

It wasn't fair. If life were fair, I would've been in the same boat as Macy. To this day I have anxiety about the veracity of my high school diploma making my bachelor's and master's degrees null and void. In my nightmares, Mrs. Johnson tells me I need to pass algebra before I can graduate. I have to go back to high school, where my math teacher informs me he doesn't accept assignments turned in thirty years too late.

After graduation, Mom told me I had to find a job. The only one I was really qualified for was the cannery. Right away I drove over to Salem to apply for a seasonal job, thinking that I would start work in a week. When they called, they told me they wouldn't hire me because according to their records, I'd lied about my age two summers ago.

When I told Mom that the cannery wouldn't hire me and why, she said, "Well, whose fault is that?!"

"Actually, it's your fault!" I yelled. "You forced me to work there when I was sixteen!" I stormed out of the house.

For the next six weeks, I bounced from one friend's home to another, doing all I could to avoid my mother. I only returned home to change clothes and steal a few bucks from Mom's purse. Mom must have figured that a twenty here and there was a small price to pay to keep me out of the house.

If I wasn't hanging out at Macy's, I was going to parties and crashing at various homes. Sometimes I was gone for more than a week. This pattern continued until the end of July, when Mom left a message at Macy's asking me to come home that night. When I walked in the front door, my whole family was waiting for me. Lindsey and Mom had decided that it was time for an intervention. What a load of bullshit.

Mom, Flossy, Junior, Meg and Jake, Lindsey, Nate, Matt, Marc, Myrtle, and even five-year-old Emily participated in the meeting. Mom had me sit down and proceeded to tell me how my drinking was having adverse effects on the family. "Your behavior has cast a horrible shadow over this family. I am embarrassed to go into the grocery store. People are talking, Laura, and it isn't good."

"Really," I said. "This is all about how *you* look!"

"No, Laura," Meg said. "This is about *you* needing help. No one knows where you are most of the time. You show up every now and then and disappear again."

Lindsey piled on, "I found a bunch of empty rum and vodka bottles in the closet. You have a real problem."

I almost laughed in her face. They were old bottles, which *she'd* purchased and helped drink. Her hypocrisy was beyond belief.

The only people I believed were Meg and Jake. They talked about how my drinking was affecting *me*. Everyone else talked about how I was soiling the family name. Nate and Henry talking about how I was an embarrassment to them angered me the most. They didn't like me, and I didn't like them, and I couldn't have cared less if my behavior had embarrassed them. If it did, then good!

If only their own behavior had ever embarrassed them just a little, I'd have felt differently. The shame I carried because of their humiliation of me was a big part of my drinking problem. If I could have just summoned the courage to call them out, maybe it would've been an authentic intervention. Instead, it was a sham.

My drinking was only the obvious problem. The real issues were not discussed. Dad wasn't mentioned. The neglect and abuse I'd endured wasn't mentioned. All that was discussed was how my drinking affected *them*. I had a problem and I needed to fix it.

By the end of the meeting, I knew where I stood when Mom said, "Tomorrow you're going to a rehab in Salem. You'll spend a month there and when you get back, I want all of this nonsense to stop."

I said, "Fine. Whatever makes you happy."

Westover Recovery Center was on the outskirts of Salem. It was a typical residential treatment facility for drug and alcohol abuse following the 12-Step System, based on the idea that a spiritual conversion can create sobriety. I was to achieve this enlightenment through a progression of steps beginning with the realization that I was powerless over my alcoholism and needed help.

I had no problem with these first two steps. Alcohol had taken over my life, and I was pretty powerless. It was the other steps that tripped me up, and I had absolutely no intention of doing them honestly.

Step three required a spiritual awakening, where I was to ask God for help. My past experiences with God had revealed that God didn't give a damn. There was no way I was going to ask God for help. Steps four through twelve dealt with owning my sins, seeking forgiveness, and then making amends to all the people I had harmed in my life. *What about all the people who had harmed me?* If I honestly progressed through all the steps, then I would have a spiritual awakening and God would change my life. The key word here is *honestly*.

At eighteen years of age, I wasn't going to honestly address the reasons why I abused alcohol because I was scared. The abuse I'd experienced at the hands of my parents and older siblings had left deep, humiliating scars. My overriding fear was that the counselors would tell me that my family was right and that I was a freak. So, I chose to lie about everything. I said I drank because I wanted to have fun and I didn't want to grow up. I apologized to my mother for all the harm I caused her and the family and promised to change my ways.

Over the course of twenty-eight days, the only friend that came to visit me was Maris. One Saturday afternoon, she showed up at the facility and we spent an hour talking about my situation. She said, "Laura, this is really an opportunity for you. The people you've been hanging out with aren't healthy. Just stay away from them." Maris was talking about my social circle, but the real source of unhealthy behavior was my own family.

"Maris, I have no intention of returning to my old ways."

"That's good because it really wasn't working."

"I know. If it were, I wouldn't be here right now."

"Just call me when you get out. We'll hang out."

"That sounds good. Thanks for visiting me. You're the only one who has. I thought Macy would."

She replied, "Macy has her own problems. I think this place would be really intimidating to her."

"Yeah, you're probably right."

I didn't make any real friends at Westover. Oh, I hung out with some people, but I didn't create any strong bonds. The most important thing I gained from Westover was the AA Blue Book, and the knowledge of where to turn when I *wanted* help. Years later, when I sought out recovery, I used *that* book when I turned to AA.

A couple of days before the end of my stay, Mom and Lindsey attended the little graduation ceremony the facility held for finishing their program. At this time, they were both given the opportunity to address me. Mom said, "I hope that you will do right by your family from here on out."

Lindsey began to cry and said, "I just think you can achieve so much if you turn your life around."

The counselor asked if I wanted to say something, and I said, "I know this hasn't been easy. I promise you things will be different."

Yes, things would be different. I would lie through my teeth, put on a big smile, and do what I damn well pleased. I wouldn't drink at home. I'd change my friends, and I'd spend every day of my life trying to figure out how to get the hell out of Mom's house and Willamette.

By the time the new school year had begun, there were eight of us living at home because Lindsey and Nate had graduated from college and moved back in. Nate could barely look at me, and when he did speak to me, it was to inform me that I was a loser.

Lindsey spent most of her time in our room, writing about her experiences on our bicycle trip. I just wanted to get out of the house. So, I unpacked my bicycle from the box in the garage and assembled it. I missed the freedom I'd felt while cycling and wanted to get that feeling back. I spent most of my days riding around the Willamette Valley, trying to get up enough nerve to ride out of town and never return. For all my bravado, I was really a coward. I couldn't leave without some money and a plan. I just needed money and a plan. Once I had them, I'd get the hell out of town for good.

During my time at home, I began to hang out with a more reputable group of friends. I still drank with them, but they were clean-cut, all-American kids who met with my mother's approval. I knew that with Mom, image was everything.

I also tried to find a job but was unsuccessful. Locally, my reputation was working against me, and without a car, I could only look locally. Mom had me enroll in the nearby community college, but it was in Salem and she wouldn't let me use her car, so I barely attended classes and eventually dropped out. I was as lost and screwed up as I'd been before going to rehab but was able to hide it much better. Rehab taught me how to lie and manipulate really well, and over the course of the year, I'd perfected those skills. By the spring of 1987, I was beginning to give up all hope—and then Maris showed up.

Maris called me up and asked if she could come over and talk to me. I was surprised to hear from her. In January, she'd enrolled in a Bible college in Santa Cruz, California and moved south. She told me she was home for the week and that she had a proposition for me. I told her to come on over.

When she arrived, we went up to my room. She sat down on Lindsey's bed and said, "How about the two of us go to Brazil for three months?"

It was like the door of opportunity had flown open and all I had to do was walk through it. "When were you thinking about going?" I asked.

"I was thinking January. That would give us eight months to save up enough money for tickets and other expenses."

"Where would we stay?"

"I have connections all over Brazil. We can stay with family and other friends. I'll set that up before we leave. What do you say?"

I didn't hesitate for even a second. "I'm in. I don't know how I'll raise the money, but I'll figure out a way."

She beamed. "I knew you'd go for it."

That night I told Mom our plans and she said, "I'll let you go." I looked her in the eye and said, "I'm not asking you for permission. I'm telling you I'm going." She was shocked but said nothing. From the look on her face, it appeared I had gained a measure of control.

Finally, I had a plan. Now I just needed the money. I'd struggled to find a job for months. But now, with a plan in place, I applied to a different cannery and was hired. I spent the next eight months working the graveyard shift, canning pears, saving my paychecks, and preparing for a South American adventure.

Chapter 15

BRAZILIAN JESUS

Through the summer and fall of '87, the goal of a Brazilian trip kept me on the straight and narrow. I was pulling the graveyard shift seven days a week at the cannery. I had neither the time nor the energy to party and really didn't want to at that point. My goal of leaving home became my new addiction.

While I was focused on going to Brazil, Mom and Lindsey began planning a European bicycle trip for the following summer after I returned from South America. Their idea was that the old gang would spend three months cycling through western Europe. I had my doubts that the trip would happen and even greater doubts about spending three months living in a tent with Mom.

Our relationship was fractured, but our conflicting schedules meant that we rarely interacted. The only time I really saw Mom was during the few hours in the evening before I left for work. At those moments I did my best to stay out of her way, which was easy because she was usually busy with the younger kids or planning the trip with Lindsey. There was no Rand-Mc-Nally map of Europe, so once again, the voyage was all about destinations. Sometimes Lindsey and Mom would include me in their planning—which was just a bunch of chatting—but they obviously didn't really want my input. Plus, in the back of my mind, I couldn't see a European bicycle trip with all seven of us working. We wouldn't have a car, which meant that Myrtle and Emily would have to cycle. The little girls were only seven and eleven years old at the time. Then again, I hadn't thought we would make it all the way to New York the last time they'd planned a trip. So, what did I know?

If we did go on the bicycle trip, then there was a possibility that between Brazil and Europe, I'd be away from home for the better part of a year. These two trips gave me a glimmer of hope that maybe there was a way out of Willamette—I just needed the courage to seize those opportunities when they arose. Going to Brazil was the first step.

Maris and I decided that flying from Miami, Florida to Rio de Janeiro would be the most cost-effective way to get there. In November, we bought our tickets for a January 4 departure, returning on April 4. The problem of getting from Oregon to Florida was resolved when her brother, Titus, offered to drive us to Georgia. Titus was in the Marines and stationed in Washington, D.C. He planned on purchasing a car while he was home for the holidays and needed someone to help him drive across the country.

Mom solved my problem of getting back to Oregon from Florida when she offered to buy me a plane ticket as a combination Christmas and birthday present. The only condition was that I had to visit Nate, who'd joined the Army the previous summer and was stationed in Georgia. I asked her why I couldn't just fly home from Miami.

Her response was, "If you're clear on the other side of the country, you have an obligation to see your brother."

Since Nate had been gone for a year, we'd been getting along brilliantly.

"Sure, if I was landing in Georgia, but I'm landing in Florida."

"I'll get you a bus ticket to Georgia."

I agreed to her conditions, but thought, *Fuck me. Why does there always have to be a string attached?*

Maris and Titus picked me up at six o'clock in the morning two days after Christmas 1987. As we drove out of town in Titus's brand new Toyota Corolla, I had the biggest smile on my face. Aside from my month in rehab, this was the first time I'd been separated from my family. With each passing mile, it was like all the strings that attached me to home were being cut. I realize now that geographical relocation doesn't really solve problems. But putting some distance between me and the people and places that had left so many scars felt liberating.

During the car ride to Georgia, Titus and Maris spent a lot of time telling me about their friends and church community in Brazil. I'd resigned myself to the fact that I'd be spending a lot of time with Christians and going to church at least once a week. What I'd gathered from these conversations was that faith and church were going to be a central aspect of our travels. I just hoped I'd see more of Brazil than the inside of Pentecostal churches.

Maris knew that I was not religious and really didn't put a lot of stock in Jesus. I'd been looking for a savior for years, only to be left wanting. I didn't see him on the crucifix in the hospital chapel where Dad died. The morning of his death, I looked for signs in the ice patterns on my windows and only saw neglect. During the hard times when I sat on my window ledge searching for answers? Nothing. And I sure as hell didn't experience Jesus at the church services Maris dragged me to in junior high school.

Maris's parents were ordained Four Square pastors. As such, the gifts of the Holy Spirit, including speaking in tongues, were central to their worship. Not to mention that the music was loud and repetitive. I mean, how many times can you sing the same verse over and over? As for the sermons, they were full of fire and brimstone and went on forever. The Jesus they proclaimed during these services didn't ring true. Their Jesus just didn't sit right with me, but I couldn't put my finger on why. It would take years before I figured out what was wrong with their Jesus, but at the time, I didn't know enough to put the pieces together.

Maris had made arrangements for us to stay at the home of a family friend who lived just outside of Atlanta. The family was away on vacation, but they left us a key to their place so we could spend the night.

As we approached Atlanta, Titus said, "These people are loaded. Just wait until you see their house."

Maris added, "Yeah, their house is really amazing. They even have a swimming pool and tennis court."

In my mind's eye, I envisioned a large house on an estate, so when Titus pulled into a trailer park, I was just a little surprised and asked, "I thought you said they lived in a mansion?"

"They do, but they own this trailer park," said Maris. "Their house is at the far end of the property."

As we drove past one run down single-wide trailer after another, I was beginning to realize that Maris's rich friends were simply slum lords. When Titus pulled up outside a large Tudor-style home, I thought, *Good lord.*

While Titus and I unloaded the car, Maris went to find the key. As we stood on the porch, she put the key in the door and said, "Wait until you see the inside."

Not wanting to reveal my initial thoughts about their friends, I said, "As long as they have a bed to sleep in, I'll be happy."

Maris swung open the door, found the light switch to the living room, and said, "See, I told you it's gorgeous."

Gorgeous isn't really the word I'd use. It looked like a Christian gift shop had exploded in their living room. A large picture of Jesus hung on the wall, and not just any picture of Jesus—this Jesus had long blond hair and blue eyes with a large

American flag in the background. This was an all-American Jesus.

One side of the living room had cabinets filled with crosses and angels, with a huge Bible on a wooden music stand on the other side. I didn't want to offend Maris and Titus, so I said, "Wow. This place really is something else."

"Yeah," said Maris. "I just feel the Spirit here."

I looked over at her and realized just how different we were. Maris saw everything through her faith. Where I saw hypocrisy, she saw honest devotion. What I viewed as godawful, Maris saw as Jesus. I was cynical and she was sincere. We'd be spending the next three months together, but I had yet to come to terms with this reality.

Titus spent the night with us, then headed for D.C. early the following morning. Maris and I slept in, and then made plans with Greyhound to catch a bus to Miami, where we'd spend two days getting our passports stamped with a Brazilian visa and make arrangements for the first few weeks of our trip. The first place we were going to was an orphanage outside of São Paulo, but we were landing in Rio and didn't really have any plans for our time there. The night before we were to fly out, I asked Maris, "Where should we stay in Rio?"

"I think we'll just land, then go and find a hotel. Let's worry about it when we get there."

"I'm kind of worried about it right now."

"Trust me, Laura. We'll find someplace to sleep and then we'll get a bus to São Paulo. Don't worry. We'll figure it out."

Figure it out? That didn't work out so well when we all slept in the car at Jones Beach.

So I was worried and tossed and turned that night thinking about how we'd manage in Rio on our own.

We landed in Rio on the morning of January 5. I'd worked so hard to get to this point but didn't really have a grasp of the country that I'd be exploring for the next ninety days. I knew Brazil was tropical and that we'd be there during their summer. Beyond these two basic truths, I didn't know much about the nation I'd learn to love.

As we stepped out of the airport, I was hit with intense heat and humidity. The combination of sunlight and colors made me feel like an animal emerging from hibernation. The fragrance of the tropics seemed to bring this three-dimensional experience to life. I always thought the tropics would smell like Coppertone suntan lotion. In reality, their unique scent is a combination of overripe fruit mixed with perspiration. It wasn't a horrible smell, but I could see why Coppertone stuck with coconut.

As I tried to get my bearings, Maris hailed a taxi. Soon we were sitting in the back of a yellow cab careening into the congested center of the city with no apparent regard for our safety. While Maris was talking to the driver in Portuguese, he flew through two red lights. When she was done talking to him, she turned to me and said, "He knows an inexpensive hotel in Copa Cabana. He's going to take us there."

The driver beeped his horn twice and flew through another red light. I said, "I guess I shouldn't have worried after all. Now if we can just get there in one piece."

"You'd better get used to it. This is how Brazilians drive. When a light changes to yellow they beep the horn twice to let the other drivers know they're not stopping."

"Gee. That makes me feel a whole lot better." I sunk down in the seat because I couldn't bear to look.

"It's how they all drive. We're not in Oregon anymore, Laura."

No shit, I thought.

True to his word, the driver took us to a hotel near the beach. We weren't flush with cash, but we felt that, after driving across the country and riding a Greyhound bus from Atlanta to Miami, then flying to Rio, we deserved to have a good night's sleep.

Once we were settled in our hotel room, we changed into swimming suits, grabbed our towels, and hit the beach. The two of us found an empty spot in the sand and spent the rest of the afternoon laying out. The water was too rough to go swimming, so we spent most of our time people-watching. Being from Oregon, where the ocean is freezing-ass cold, I wasn't used to seeing people so scantily clad. "Why do they even bother with swimsuits?" I asked Maris.

"It's because they aren't Christians."

"What does that have to do with anything?"

"Laura, these people are all Catholics. They aren't Christians. If they were, then they'd have more respect for their bodies."

Wow. That was a new one. Taking another look around, I said, "I think they have a lot of respect for their bodies because they're showing a lot of 'em. But those thongs look pretty uncomfortable."

Maris laughed, "They look like they're walking around with a permanent wedgie."

I started laughing too. "That's because they are."

I thought about what Maris had said about who was and wasn't a real Christian, and it didn't sit right. I didn't want to get into an argument with her, but at the same time, I wanted to experience Brazil through my own lens.

The next afternoon, we took what was supposed to be a six-hour bus ride from Rio to São Paulo. At the bus station, Maris called the couple we would be staying with, Fracco and Fatima, to let them know when we were arriving.

As the bus wove in and out of traffic leading to the highway, I saw poverty on a shocking scale. Hundreds of makeshift shacks constructed of corrugated iron, plywood, and cardboard were wedged in between palm trees. From the safe distance of my bus seat, the wash of colors looked almost beautiful—until the realization that people actually lived in those shacks hit me.

I'd heard about the slums of Rio but hadn't really given it much thought. Poverty had not figured into my Brazilian expectations. I thought Brazil would be full of tropical beaches, exotic foods, and colorful people. I had no idea that the vast majority of Brazilians were so destitute.

In Willamette, poverty on this level was hidden away in the foothills of the coast range. The people who lived there were basically off the grid. Their homes were little more than shacks, and they survived on what they could grow, hunt, and fish. There was almost a pride in their minimalist lifestyle—a fierce sense of independence. What I saw from my bus window in Rio wasn't that kind of poverty. The poverty I was seeing left me feeling powerless, and for the first time, privileged. I turned to Maris and said, "I didn't think it would be like this. They're so poor."

Without batting an eye, she said, "If they'd just find Jesus, they wouldn't be living like that."

Maris's answer to everything—Jesus. Something in my gut wanted to call bullshit, but my ignorance of the Christian faith and scripture held me back. I turned and looked back out the window, thinking that Jesus must be pretty damn petty if he caused that much suffering. If that was the case, I really didn't want to have anything to do with him.

The bus ride from Rio to São Paulo was my first lesson in Brazilian time. Our six-hour bus ride took eight hours. We were scheduled to arrive in São Paulo's bus station at six o'clock in the evening but didn't pull in until after eight. When Maris called Fracco to let him know we'd arrived, he said it'd be at least an hour before he could pick us up.

Maris said, "I'm starving. Let's go get something to eat while we wait."

"Thank God. I could eat a horse."

Maris pointed at the station's mezzanine. "I think there's a diner up there."

We hauled our oversized, canvas duffle bags up the stairs and sat down at the counter of the diner. The menu was written on a blackboard in Portuguese. "I'll let you order," I said, "because I have no idea what any of that says."

Looking at the menu, Maris stated, "Mostly you want to stick with rice, beans, and chicken. Also, try guarana, I think you'll love it."

Maris ordered the meals. The guarana arrived first, and it looked like ginger ale. "Go ahead," said Maris. "This is the best drink in the world."

I took a swig. "Dang, that's good. What is it?"

Maris grinned. "It's made from a berry that's grown here. I can't really explain it, but it's delicious."

I took another swig. "I can't believe they don't sell this at home."

When the food arrived, we scarfed it down. It was the first real meal we'd eaten since dinner on the airplane. When we were finished, we went back down to the entrance of the bus station to wait for Fracco.

I asked Maris how many years it had been since she had last seen Fracco. She said, "I think it was about seven years ago."

"So, you were twelve? Do you think he'll recognize you?"

"No, but I'll recognize him," and she pointed at a small dark man with curly hair wearing cutoff shorts and a t-shirt.

Maris ran up to him and said, "Ciao, Fracco."

Fracco said, "E Maris?" and then gave her a hug.

Maris said something else to Fracco and then he walked over to me and said, "Ciao, Laura."

I gave Maris a sideways look. "Ciao, um, I guess."

Fracco reached down, picked up both of our bags, and led us to his van. Maris jumped in the front seat, and I sat in the back. The two spent the whole ride to the orphanage chatting in Portuguese while I tried to fall asleep.

It was almost eleven before we reached the orphanage and were greeted by Fracco's wife, Fatima, a large black woman who pounced on Maris when she got out of the van. When Maris introduced me, Fatima pulled me into a huge embrace and kissed my cheek. While being smothered, I looked over at Maris and said, "I'm not really used to this."

Fatima said something to Maris in Portuguese and Maris laughed. I asked, "What?"

"She said, 'I don't think this one is used to hugs and kisses. Brazil's going to be hard on her.'"

"You think?" I said.

Fatima allowed Maris and me to sleep in the following morning. It was after nine before I stumbled out of bed and followed Maris's voice into the kitchen, where she sat at a large round table with our host, drinking coffee and enjoying fresh bread and jam. Maris looked over at me and asked, "Do you want a café com leite?"

"Café what?"

"Coffee with warm milk. You'll love it," and she poured me a drink and passed me a bowl of sugar.

Having been raised on Lipton's tea, my only previous coffee experience had been at the cannery. The plant's break room had one of those machines that, for twenty-five cents, brewed shitty coffee in a cup with playing cards on the front and a wild card on the bottom. My coworkers and I used the cups to play poker during our 2 a.m. break. Therefore, I had no idea coffee could taste so good, and from that point on I was hooked. Brazil prepared me for the coffee explosion that would occur in the northwest a few years later.

High on caffeine, Maris and I walked outside and toured the orphanage, a sprawling facility with cream stucco walls and a red tile roof sitting on top of a hill. There were dorms for older boys and girls and a nursery for the younger children. Between the kitchen and the dorms was a cafeteria. Detached from the main buildings were apartments for the staff and extra classrooms where the children received extra tutoring. About twenty kids chased a ball around a giant soccer pitch on a field below.

"Let's go join in," said Maris.

"I don't know how to play."

"Oh, come on. If the ball comes to you, kick it. These kids just want some attention."

We ran down the field and Maris said something to an older boy who was shirtless, barefoot, and wearing Bermuda shorts. The boy spoke to the others and before I knew it, I was running around the field without a care in the world.

For the next week, this ragtag group of kids became my solace. While Maris spent her days catching up with her friends, I tried to learn how to play soccer and understand Portuguese. The kids called me "Tia," which means auntie, and laughed at my sad soccer skills and inability to pronounce words.

I had an affinity for these kids. We didn't speak the same language, but we understood each other. I knew what it was like to be cast aside. Granted, not to the degree that these children had been abandoned, but I knew how much it hurt to not be wanted by your family.

Fracco and Fatima's unconditional love towards the children moved me. They treated each child with dignity and respect. I was in awe of their ability to keep all the children in line and do it with a smile. Each day Fracco would make the time to play soccer with the older kids, while Fatima was constantly surrounded by the younger children clamoring for her attention.

Towards the end of our visit, I said to Maris, "Fracco and Fatima seem so calm and peaceful with these kids."

"They were both raised in my parents' orphanage. They know what it's like to be abandoned."

"I've just never seen such patience and love before. It's different."

"That's what happens when you have a calling. Your work becomes a joy."

I had no idea what she was talking about. *What the hell is a calling?* I really didn't want another Jesus conversation and chose to let her comment dangle.

Years later, I'd learn what it means to be called. It's a blessing to be led to a vocation of service that brings joy and makes living more meaningful. Fracco and Fatima's love for those they served has been a reminder that in God's hands, even a crappy childhood can have a beautiful outcome.

Once we left São Paulo, we spent the better part of a month jumping from one family friend's home to another. We landed at a beach house for a couple of weeks followed by a few weeks in the city of Curitiba. During this time, our church attendance was minimal, and I was beginning to hope it would stay that way. However, that all changed on February 11, the day before my twentieth birthday, and right before Carnival. Maris informed me that her father was in Brazil and would be driving us to their mission, Hesed.

I asked her how far of a drive it was from Curitiba, thinking it would be a short journey. I was shocked when she said, "Not far. Maybe ten hours."

"Ten hours is not far!? Are you kidding me?"

"Listen, Laura, it's Hesed's annual revival, and we're going to help them get ready. You knew we'd be doing church stuff before we left."

"I get that, but man, I thought we'd experience a little bit of Carnival. It's Brazil's biggest festival."

"Carnival is Satan's festival. The only thing that can combat it is Jesus. Real Christians use this time to bring people to Jesus."

As Maris was speaking, I realized that arguing would get me nowhere and became resigned to the fact that I'd be at a Bible revival during the biggest party in the world. So, under my breath, I said, "Fuck me."

Chapter 16

WHAT WOULD JESUS DO?
(Probably Not That!)

The following morning, Maris's father, Wayne, picked us up in a VW Bus. Maris and I had been friends for ten years, and this was only the third time I'd ever met Wayne. He was a short, heavyset man with an elfish quality about him. The other two times I'd met him, he seemed nice enough—the problem was he was rarely around. He spent most of his time doing mission work in Brazil, and when he was in the States, he worked as a long-haul trucker for his brother. His absences left Maris and her family in financial straits. To make ends meet, her mother worked days at a local fast-food joint and cleaned offices in the evenings.

What really drew Maris and me together, I think, were the similarities in our home lives. Both of our mothers worked multiple jobs to make up for their husbands' lack of support. Both of our fathers were negligent and absent. The big difference was that Maris's family adored Wayne. They supported his ministry and understood his absences as part of God's work. I did not share those feelings for my father.

As we drove along, Maris and Wayne talked about their family, about Hesed, and about different people that they knew. I felt like a third wheel, so to feel included, I asked, "Why did you name your mission Hesed? It's kind of a weird name."

Wayne looked back at me and said, "It's Hebrew for kindness."

"That's pretty cool. How long are we staying?"

"About a week," Maris answered. "And then, as a treat, Dad set up a stay at a beach resort for us."

With the promise of a week at the beach, I figured a few days at their mission wouldn't be too difficult.

Hesed was fifteen miles from the nearest town, with the last five miles on a dirt road. As we pulled into the compound, Wayne proudly showed me the church, the outdoor amphitheater church, the Christian college, and the dorms. He then drove around to show me the quaint houses of his sister and nephew before pulling up in front of a modern two-story, A-frame home that he'd built. Surprisingly, all the houses were Western in appearance. Wayne's older brother Robert now lived there with his family. Before getting out of the van, Wayne turned to me and said, "We'll be staying here for the camp. You and Maris can share her old room."

We carried our bags into the house through a side door and were greeted by Wayne's brother Richard, his wife, Vera, and their twenty-two-year-old daughter Sarah. From the look on Maris's face, it seemed Sarah's presence was an unpleasant surprise.

Richard was enormous, with a gut hanging so far down over his jeans it was a wonder he could stand up straight. Vera was his opposite, thin with a permanent scowl on her face. Sarah was a younger version of her mother.

Vera had made a cake and prepared coffee for our arrival. We all sat down at the kitchen table and talked about the drive over from Curitiba. From there, Maris and I were told what was expected of us to prepare for the revival. We were to help clean the dorms, set up the rooms, and clean up the kitchen.

Maris turned to her cousin and asked, "So, Sarah, are you going to help us too?"

Before Sarah could answer, Vera interjected, "No, Sarah needs to take care of her horses and help me here in the house. I have things that need to be done."

I was beginning to understand why Maris wasn't too happy to see her cousin. Later that night, Maris told me Sarah was a princess and was not expected to do anything beyond care for and ride her horses. Furthermore, Vera had a few orphan girls come up to her house to clean.

"There's still an orphanage here?" I asked.

"Yeah, it's the one where Fracco and Fatima met. It's about a mile down the road. Dad didn't take us there, but I'll take you tomorrow."

"Why is the orphanage so far away?"

"Dad and Richard thought it would be a good idea to separate the mission from the orphanage."

Maris's answer sounded a bit like segregation, and I was beginning to question the kindness of Hesed.

We spent most of our first full day at Hesed cleaning the dorm rooms and bathrooms of the Bible college. Towards the end of the day, Maris walked me over to the orphanage to see the facility and maybe play soccer with the kids.

The palm-lined dirt road connecting the orphanage to the mission passed through cow pastures and alfalfa fields. As we ambled along the road, Maris explained that the crops and livestock belonged to the mission.

I had not seen any farm laborers around. "Who does all the work?" I asked.

"Well, the orphans do. They need to earn their keep."

Maris had told me earlier that the government paid the mission for the care of each child. "Why would they need to work for what the government is paying for?" I asked. "Isn't the money already theirs?"

"Laura, you don't understand. These kids need to learn that nothing is for free. They have to work."

At that moment, I saw something red move in the field and realized it was two boys in red tunics who appeared to be about twelve years old. They were leading the cows towards a barn. I pointed them out and asked, "What are they doing?"

"I think they're taking the cows in to be milked. It has to be done twice a day."

"Does the orphanage use the milk?"

"The mission sells it to the orphanage."

It took a second for Maris's words to sink in. The mission received money from the government to take care of the kids. The kids had to earn their keep by working in the mission's fields and milking its cows; then the mission sold the milk back to the orphanage. I asked her, "Doesn't that seem wrong to you? It's like the mission is profiting off of the orphanage in more ways than one. What do the kids get out of this?"

"More than if they weren't here. They get a place to sleep, and food to eat. Most importantly, the gospel is preached to them."

Maris had a point, but it still reeked of fraud in my book. When we reached the orphanage, I looked around and thought, *You bastards.*

The orphanage consisted of five filthy, single-story buildings with a muddy square in the middle. Two of the buildings were for the older boys and girls, one was for the infants, one was a kitchen and cafeteria, and the other housed some of the staff. Later on, I'd discover that only two of the buildings had toilets and running water.

Everywhere I turned, there were kids in red tunics busy doing some chore or task. I asked, "What's up with the red clothes?"

"Oh, it's just a uniform," said Maris. "They have to wear it while they're here. It helps us keep track of where the kids are on the property and what they're doing."

At that moment, I heard a motorcycle coming up the road and turned to see Maris's uncle Richard, who pulled up next to us. He turned off the bike and said, "I'm here to get some of the boys to help Sarah round up her horses. She wants to go for a ride later and the horses are out in the field."

Maris replied, "We're just here to say hello to the kids and maybe kick a ball around with them for a while."

"Just make sure they're done with their chores first," he said. Then he started the bike back up and drove off.

As he rode off down the road, I thought, *Sure thing, asshole.*

We played soccer with some of the kids that day, but I got the sense that kicking a ball around wasn't really encouraged. These kids were there to work. Therefore, I didn't get the opportunity to get to know the kids the same way I had in São Paulo.

The Hesed orphans lacked the joy and happiness of the kids in São Paulo because the orphanage lacked the kindness of Fracco and Fatima. I found it hard to believe they'd been orphans here. It seemed impossible that such a horrible place could produce two such lovely people.

On the first day of the revival, I sat on a bench at the back of Hesed's outdoor church, watching Wayne literally thump his

Bible. He'd been shouting for close to an hour, with perspiration stains under his armpits and sweat rolling down his face. I had no idea what he was saying but deciphered a pattern to his speech and movements. He'd shout a sentence, hold up his black Bible, then swing it down to hit the lectern with a loud smack. The church, packed with people in their early twenties, would shout "Oh, Deus" and "Amen" at the end of each statement.

As Wayne professed his understanding of the teachings of Jesus, I caught a glimpse of two of the orphanage girls walking away from the camp, their distinct red tunics giving away their status within the compound. I figured they must be the girls who cleaned Vera's house. I looked back at Wayne and thought, *Nope, buddy, I am not buying what you're selling.*

On the second day of the revival, Wayne led the revelers down to a pond, walked out into the water, and said something in Portuguese. I turned to Maris and asked, "What's your dad doing?"

"Oh, he's baptizing people. Most of these people were baptized as infants, so they haven't *really* been baptized."

We watched as person after person walked into the water and was dunked three times by Wayne. Maris then turned to me and asked, "Have you been baptized?"

"Yep, when I was about seven."

"Was it full immersion?"

"No, Presbyterian."

"So, you weren't pushed under the water three times?"

"Nope, just sprinkled."

"Then you weren't really baptized. You need to be re-baptized."

"Maris, I think I'm good."

Wayne was in the process of dunking a young man when she turned to me and said, "I just worry about your salvation."

"Okay. But I think I'll run the risk with just being sprinkled. Thanks."

By the last day of the revival, I came to understand why the faith practiced at Hesed was so flawed. Hesed's underlying belief was in the superiority of its American leaders' gender, faith, race, and nationality. Their arrogance permeated the whole ministry. Hesed wasn't a community of believers; it was a male-dominated hierarchy. The American males were at the top, followed by American women, then Brazilians, and finally the orphans at the very bottom. I was left wondering why Hesed had even been formed.

At each service, I found myself moving further and further towards the back of the sanctuary. By the final night, I sat outside of the sanctuary, watching from a tree stump. Maris, who'd helped her father act out the story of Lazarus rising from the dead, was up on the stage. As I sat on the outside looking in, it was the first time I really missed my family, especially Matt and Marc. I missed our quirky sense of humor, the levity of their banter, and our inherent irreverence.

As I created an imaginary dialogue between the three of us, the whole assembly jumped up, raised their hands in the air, and began babbling at the top of their lungs. The urgent desire to flee wiped out all thoughts of Matt and Marc, but before I could bolt, I felt a tap on my shoulder. I looked up to see Vera standing near me. With a prideful look on her face, she leaned down and said, "They're speaking in tongues. It's the only way to receive the Holy Spirit."

"What?"

"They were all baptized yesterday, so they only received Jesus yesterday. Today they are receiving the Holy Spirit by speaking in tongues."

I thought, *This is completely bonkers. I am sitting in the middle of the fucking jungle, at a Pentecostal revival, while they're all shouting and yelling trying to catch the Holy Spirit.* All I wanted to do was run away. Silently I said a prayer: *Please God, get me the hell out of here. Amen.*

When I finished my petition, Wayne said something and the whole congregation stopped speaking and sat down. I thought, *Thank God.*

After the service, all the Americans gathered back at Richard and Vera's house for ice cream. As we sat around a table, Maris's family congratulated one another on a successful revival, measured by how many people were baptized—and how much money they pulled in.

I was ignoring their conversation when Wayne addressed me. "Laura, did you see how many people accepted Jesus?"

Not wanting to offend him, I said, "Yeah. It was pretty amazing."

He then asked, "Why weren't you speaking in tongues? I told everyone to do it and you didn't get up."

"It's just not my thing. Let's say the Spirit didn't move me."

"Laura," he said, leaning in towards me, "if the pastor says to do something, you're to do it."

"Like I said, I didn't feel moved."

"According to the Bible, if you don't follow the pastor's instructions, you're practicing witchcraft."

I noticed that everyone had fallen silent and was looking at me.

"Oh, well," I said and raised my eyebrows. On the outside I looked nonchalant, but on the inside, I was thinking, *Are you fucking kidding me?*

He waved his spoon at me and said, "You're a hard nut to crack."

He just called me a witch! What the hell? I wanted to say something flippant back, but instead I chose to give him a wry smile and went back to eating my ice cream. I knew that by the end of the following day, I'd be sitting on a beach, soaking up the rays. This pseudo-kindness freakshow would be a distant memory.

When we left Hesed for the beach resort, Wayne drove us to the nearest bus station and gave us $500 to help cover the rest of our expenses. God, that man was a mystery wrapped in the Christian flag and encased in hard cash. He could be so incredibly generous, but the image of blank-faced orphans wearing red tunics paying for milk that their labor produced swayed me to believe his faith was flawed.

We spent ten days at the resort sunbathing, swimming, and relaxing. At the end of our stay, we retraced our steps, spending the last few weeks saying our goodbyes to our various hosts. The day before Easter, we made our way back to Rio, where we were scheduled to fly back to Miami at ten o'clock at night on Monday, April 4.

Once again, we didn't have a clue where we'd stay in Rio, and this time, we didn't have a lot of cash. But after traveling around for three months, we were a lot savvier. We wouldn't be staying in Copa Cabana, but we'd be okay. I figured we could spend the night on the beach if we had to.

Eventually, we found a rundown hotel in a seedy part of town that cost us five dollars a night, but we had to rent the bedding and towels. With the money we saved by staying in cheap lodging, we were able to eat, and on Easter Sunday we visited Sugarloaf Mountain and Christ the Redeemer.

The view from both spots was breathtaking, but the statue of Jesus only accentuated my feelings towards the Jesus revealed to me in Brazil. The statue may be one of the wonders of the world, but it's just an inanimate, faceless redeemer looking over vast brokenness—Rio needed a living, breathing savior, not a Jesus-turned-to-stone. It wasn't until later that evening, when Maris made one last play to bring me to Jesus, that I received a true revelation. A revelation that piqued my interest in finding the real Jesus.

Back in the hotel room, I was lying on my bed, wondering if it was safe to get under the covers, when Maris said, "Hey, since it's Easter, how about I read you the Easter story?"

This would be our last night in Brazil, and I figured it wouldn't do any harm to placate her. "Sure," I said. "Why not?"

Maris dug out her Bible, found what she was looking for, and began to read the last couple of chapters of the gospel of Matthew. As she read aloud, I shut my eyes and only half listened to the words. When she was finished, she said, "I've never read that before. I didn't realize that the Jews paid the guards to lie."

I popped up and asked, "You've never read this before? Have you read the whole Bible?"

Maris looked a little uncomfortable and then became defensive. "I've studied a lot of the Bible, Laura. My parents are missionaries!"

"I guess I'm just a little surprised this is the first time you've read *that* story."

Looking down at her Bible, she said, "I guess I should read it myself. It's just usually I attend Bible studies and I study what I'm told."

Maris looked a little lost for a second, and it was the first time I saw doubt creep into her faith. Ironically, that moment marked the first time I became open to faith. It dawned on me that maybe the judgmental Jesus of Maris's faith didn't look anything like the *real* Jesus. I had worked so hard resisting Maris's beliefs that I hadn't really thought about my own understanding of Jesus. I figured the only way I would know who Jesus was would be to read the Bible for myself—the only obstacle being that, at the time, I really didn't want to find out the truth.

We spent our final day in Rio walking around different areas, spending the last little bit of money we had on knickknacks and gifts to bring back to our families. As the day came to a close, we had just enough money for bus fare to the airport. We figured we wouldn't need any cash until we reached Miami because our mothers had made arrangements for the conclusion of our trip.

Maris's mother had bought her a ticket for a connecting flight to Portland that would leave a few hours after we landed in Miami, while my mother had arranged for me to take a Greyhound bus to Atlanta. Mom had also wired me some cash that would be waiting for me at the Western Union counter at the bus station. It wasn't until we reached the Pan Am departure counter and learned of Brazil's exit tax that we realized just how short of cash we were.

We hauled our luggage up to the counter, showed the Pan Am agent our tickets and passports, and were waiting for her to print out our boarding passes when she said, "That will be ten dollars for each of you."

Maris and I looked at each other and then Maris said, "What?"

"Yes," said the agent. "Your tax is ten dollars apiece. That will be twenty dollars total."

"We don't have twenty dollars," I said.

"That's your problem," said the agent. "Next!" The person behind us pushed us out of the way.

We grabbed our bags and moved out into the terminal. "Maris, our plane leaves in two hours. What should we do?"

Maris looked around frantically, spied a bank of phones, and said, "Dad has some friends who live in Rio. I'll call around and see if they can help us out."

"I don't think we have time for that, Maris. By the time they get here, it'll be too late."

Without replying, she dug in her bag for her address book and went over to the phones. I asked, "Do we even have any change to use the phones?"

"I have a few coins. I think it'll be enough."

"I really don't think we have time for this. Let's just ask people for help. Someone'll help us out."

As I was talking, she picked up the receiver and started dialing numbers. I walked away and began approaching people to see if I could get someone to help us. Most people just shook their heads and moved on, but one gentleman stopped and asked, "Do you need some help?"

"Yes. My friend and I are trying to get to Miami, and we just found out we have to pay an exit tax to get on the plane. The problem is we don't have the money."

"Well, I'm going to Chicago through Miami. I don't mind helping you guys out. I have daughters myself."

As he was talking, Maris showed up and said, "Really? My name's Maris. This is Laura, and our parents are meeting us in Miami, and they'll pay you back at the airport."

I looked over at Maris, thinking, *Why the hell did you have to lie? He was going to help us out anyway. Jesus Christ.*

The gentleman said, "My name is Cesar, and sure I'll help you out. I still need to check in. Let's do it together and then I'll pay the tax for you."

As we made our way to the counter, I whispered to Maris, "Great. Now we have to figure out a way to ditch this guy in Miami because no one's meeting us there! Maris, he was going to help us out anyway."

"Well, I didn't know that. Trust me, it'll be all right."

At the counter, Cesar paid for our tax and accompanied us to our gate, where we discovered that we'd be sitting next to him during the flight. Brilliant!

Throughout the flight, Maris did this hair flipping and eye batting routine. As I watched her, it dawned on me that she actually enjoyed this ploy and wanted to see how far she could go with it. I had a feeling that all the flirting in the world wouldn't help us ditch this guy at the airport.

When Cesar got up to use the restroom, Maris looked over at me and said, "Listen. As soon as the seatbelt light goes off after we land, just jump out of the seat and run. If we can get off the plane before he does, we can lose him."

"Really? Then what?"

"He's going on to Chicago and has to go through immigration and customs. We do too, but we'll be in a different area. It'll be okay."

"Other than telling him the truth, I don't see what choice we have."

As we touched down in Miami, Maris nodded up to the seatbelt sign. The time it took to taxi to the gate felt like an eternity. When the seatbelt sign turned off, Maris said, "Now!" and the two of us jumped up and pushed our way to the front of the plane, leaving poor Cesar in our dust. I felt like a creep. If God had sent Cesar to save us, Maris certainly didn't pick up on it. His look of shock stayed with me for a long time.

An hour later we had made our way through immigration and customs. Maris and I walked over to the information booth and asked for directions to the shuttle to the Greyhound station so I could catch the bus to Atlanta to visit Nate.

As I picked up my bags, I said to Maris, "Well. I guess this is it."

Maris hugged me. "I realize you're still not a hugger, but thanks for coming on this trip with me."

"Thanks for asking. It was an insightful trip... I hope you get home safe. I'll see you when I get back."

With that, Maris took off down the corridor to her gate as I went to find the shuttle to the bus station. As we parted company, I thought about what an enigma Maris was. She was all about Jesus, but then she'd pull shit like she did on the plane. It was a complete mystery to me.

Nate met me at the bus station in Atlanta. When I approached him, he hit me on the shoulder and asked, "How was your trip?"

"Fucking brilliant," I said.

Nate let out a laugh. "Glad to see you still swear like a trucker."

"Some things will never change, Nate."

For the next few days, Nate and I hung out together, and I really enjoyed his company. Over the years I've come to realize that away from Willamette, and the family home, my siblings are very nice people. Visiting Nate was also a nice buffer before heading home. It allowed me time to get my bearings before walking back into Mom's house.

When it was time to fly home, Nate took me to the airport. At the gate, I tagged him in the arm and said, "Thanks for everything."

Nate gave me a wry smile. "Hey, no problem. Have a good flight and tell everyone hi for me."

"Will do," I said. Then I boarded the plane and took my seat. As I looked out the window, I said a little prayer. *Please, God, may Mom and Lindsey have a bicycle trip in the works. I can't go back to Willamette without an exit plan. Amen.*

Maybe after three months of hanging with Maris, Jesus did have an impact on my life after all?

Chapter 17

"IT'S LIKE DÉJÀ VU ALL OVER AGAIN"

I walked off the plane in Portland, thinking that either Mom or Lindsey would be picking me up at the airport. So, when everyone was waiting for me at the gate, I was flabbergasted. Mom, Flossy, Lindsey, Junior, Meg, Jake, Matt, Marc, Myrtle, and Emily were standing in the gate area with signs welcoming me home. The last time that many people surprised me, it was for an intervention.

Meg approached me first. "Damn, you have a great tan."

I replied, "I guess I achieved my primary goal!"

Jake stepped up and gave me a huge hug. "Man, I am so happy to see you."

Matt and Marc shuffled their feet and mumbled something incoherent.

Emily and Myrtle were hopping from seat to seat in the waiting area and only took a moment to say, "Welcome home!"

Mom said, "We're all going out to dinner to celebrate your safe return."

Still confused by my homecoming, I said, "Okay. Where are we going?"

"We're going to The Old Spaghetti Factory," said Flossy. "It's my treat."

Mom interjected, "Laura, how about you go with Meg and Jake and we'll meet up at the restaurant?"

"Whatever works," I replied. I was grateful that I'd be riding with Meg and Jake. They were the two people I'd missed the most.

In the car, Meg and Jake told me they'd moved to Seattle while I was gone, and that they'd driven all the way down to Portland just to see me land.

"Why?" I asked.

Jake looked over at me. "Did it ever dawn on you that people might have missed you?"

I looked back at him. "Um. Not really." I was dead serious.

Meg laughed, "Well, I missed you."

"I missed you guys too." Which was true. I'd missed Meg and Jake, but I can honestly say I hadn't missed everyone.

During dinner, I was informed that the bicycle trip was still on. We'd be flying from Seattle to Amsterdam on June 15 and returning late August. But only Lindsey, Matt, Marc, and I would be going. Mom had to back out because her mother's health was failing, and she'd be spending the summer with her.

That was the best news I heard all night. Not that my grandmother was ill (although there was no love lost between us), but that Mom wasn't going. I had loved my time in Brazil where I could just be myself. I hoped that my time in Europe would allow me to grow as an individual even more.

I had a sneaking suspicion that Mom resented having to spend the summer with her mother in Spokane and wanted me to trade places with her—a feeling that was affirmed a few weeks after my return home.

One evening after dinner Mom said, "You really had a great trip when you went to Brazil."

Here it comes.

"Yep," I replied. "It was great. I think Europe will be really great too."

"Yeah, I'll be in Spokane while you guys are off gallivanting around Europe."

And there it was.

I knew I needed to stop her in her tracks and played the only card I could. The summer when I was fifteen, Mom made me stay with her mother for six weeks. She'd sent me to Spokane with a sack of clothes and ten dollars to my name. It had been a lonely, miserable time with a woman who really didn't want me there in the first place. So, when Mom brought up Spokane, I said, "Yep, Mom. Been there. Done that. Won't be going back to Spokane anytime soon."

Her memory was conveniently selective. "Oh. I forgot you did that. I guess you won't want to switch places."

"No, Mom, I won't be switching places with you." I got up abruptly from the table.

Mom gave a small "Humph" and added, "Well, I hope you think of me while you're on your second major trip in a year."

She'd tried to guilt the wrong person. I just gave her a smile, put my dishes in the sink, and walked away, saying under my breath, "I won't be thinking of you at all."

Without Mom going on the trip, money would be a huge issue. Lindsey had enough to cover the cost of plane tickets, bicycles, and supplies, but she didn't have enough for us to live on once we were in Europe. Prior to Mom backing out of the trip, Mom and Lindsey figured that we'd need about $1,200 a month to get by. Without Mom and the little girls, Lindsey figured we'd need about $800 a month.

Mom said that she'd wire us Matt and Marc's Social Security money for the months of July and August. Their benefit checks added up to $600 a month. Her reasoning was that those funds were for the health and welfare of the boys and it was only right to allow them to use it while we were gone. That left a $200 a month deficit that we needed to cover before we left.

I found a job babysitting five days a week, and Lindsey was still working for a community organizing group in Salem. Between the two of us, we tried to make up the difference before we flew to Amsterdam.

The only downside to the buildup of the trip was that Lindsey decided to turn our adventure into a fundraiser for the American Heart Association. She was still living in the ever-present lie that Dad had died of heart disease and not from the consequences of alcoholism. To honor Dad's memory, she organized speaking engagements at various Rotary groups throughout the Willamette Valley to solicit funds.

The American Heart Association sent her literature so she could educate herself on the disease. She told me she was going to use the information in her speeches and add in how Dad's illness and death had affected us.

I really didn't want to go to Rotary luncheons and perpetuate the lie, so I tried to get out of it. One day I asked her, "So, you're giving the speech? Do Matt, Marc, and I have to be there too?"

"Laura, he was your dad too. Don't you want to help support something that will help others?"

Caught between a lie and a hard place, I said, "Of course. It's just that if you're doing all the talking, then why do we have to be there?"

"You guys need to be there because we're all going on the trip."

"Yeah, but this Heart Association thing is your idea. I didn't even know about it until a couple of weeks ago."

"The truth is, I need your support. I don't know how these speaking engagements will go and having you three there will be a big help."

Finally, a little honesty. "Okay. When you put it that way, it makes sense." And it was a good thing we were there, because our first Rotary meeting was a disaster.

The first luncheon was held on a Wednesday in West Salem. Lindsey and I picked Matt and Marc up from school and drove over to the meeting, which was held at a restaurant. On the drive over I asked her, "So, are you prepared?"

"I think so. I have a bunch of notes written down and I practiced. I just hope I can keep it together."

Matt, who was riding in the backseat with Marc, asked, "Why? Are you nervous?"

Lindsey looked behind her. "Of course I'm nervous. Plus, I just have a hard time talking about Dad. I still break down and cry sometimes."

I looked back at the boys and kind of shrugged and then said to Lindsey, "Well, I guess you just do your best."

"Yeah, that's all I can do."

Dressed in a cranberry, short-sleeved Henley shirt and casual shorts, she walked confidently up to the podium. She shuffled her papers and had a look that said, "if you challenge me, I'll take you out." However, halfway through her speech she lost her composure—breaking down in sobs and incapable of completing her prepared speech. She'd been fine until she started to talk about how Dad's death had left this huge hole in our lives. I found it hard to summon much sympathy for our father, but I did feel bad for Lindsey. She tended to shake when she got upset, and she was vibrating like the Energizer Bunny.

As she began to fall apart, Matt nudged me and whispered, "What should we do?"

"How the hell do I know? This was *her* idea."

Marc pointed out that the president of the Rotary group was getting up and said, "I think that guy is going to bail her out."

I leaned over to the boys. "Thank God."

On the way home, Lindsey said, "I obviously couldn't keep it together. Laura, I think you should do the speaking at the rest of the meetings."

And that's how I ended up standing in front of three different Rotary groups, lying my ass off about our father's death. By the time I gave my last speech, I'd convinced myself that the truth of Dad's death was irrelevant, and that maybe the funds we raised would go to good use.

By Memorial Day weekend, with Mom resigned to the fact that the four of us would be going to Europe without her, she began helping us with planning. There were still a few hurdles to jump before we departed. The biggest issue was figuring out how to get the bicycles on the plane. Lindsey, Mom, and I went back and forth between boxing them or putting them in bags. Either way, we'd have to disassemble the bikes and turn them into luggage.

In the end, Lindsey had the best idea. While the three of us were sitting around the dining room table brainstorming, she said, "How about we purchase a bunch of Gore-Tex and make bags? We'll dismantle the bikes and put them in the bags. When we get to Amsterdam, we'll use the bags to hold our sleeping bags and tent, keeping all of our supplies waterproof."

Mom's face lit up. "That's actually a really good idea. I can make the bags for you, and then Laura can take the bikes apart and put them back together when you land."

"Whoa!" I said. "Why am I always the one doing the mechanical part?"

Lindsey shot back, "Because you're the only one who knows how!"

"Don't you think it's time you learned?"

Mom slapped the table. "Oh, Laura, stop it."

"Fine," I snarled, "but don't think I'm going to fix every damn flat tire."

Lindsey snapped, "*Fine*, then I won't give you your plane ticket."

I thought about it for a second and realized that being the mechanic was a small price to pay for a ten-week trip through Europe. Besides, when Lindsey got mad, her punch hit harder than mine.

"*Fine*! I'll be the mechanic again."

In Europe, there would be no car. We'd have to carry all of our supplies on our bikes: our sleeping bags, clothes, tent, and cooking supplies. Everything we needed would have to fit either on our bike racks or in one of six panniers.

Panniers are bags that hang off of the bicycle's rear rack and are about the size of a medium backpack. We were each given one pannier to use for our clothing and toiletries. In comparison, my pillowcase from the previous trip looked like a steam trunk. In the end, my small bag could only hold a couple pairs of shorts, two t-shirts, a pair of jeans, and some socks and undies. Not a lot of clothes for the better part of ten weeks.

With limited space, we could only bring a few luxury items. I packed a couple of journals that my friend Tami had given me to document our adventures. Matt brought a Hacky Sack, Marc brought a deck of cards, and Lindsey brought a small boombox, some CDs, and a camera. It wasn't a lot of stuff, but enough to keep us entertained.

Our camping supplies consisted of a four-person tent and four sleeping bags that we'd borrowed from a neighbor. Lindsey also purchased some camping pots and pans from a local outdoor store along with some ramen noodles and tea bags. She didn't want to carry too much on the plane and figured we'd buy food once we got to the Netherlands.

On June 14, 1988, Matt and I hauled the old bicycle rack out of the garage, slid it into place on the Escort, and loaded up our bicycles and meager supplies. Mom, Myrtle, Emily, Matt, Marc, Lindsey, and I climbed into the car and headed for Meg and Jake's house in Seattle.

The four-hour car drive crammed into the Escort brought back a lot of memories. The seven of us spent the time together reminiscing and laughing about our cross-country trip. But by the time we pulled up to Meg and Jake's house, I was happy to get out. It still stank like body odor and road grime. *Yuck.*

Meg and Jake's house was a small three-bedroom bungalow, which barely held all nine of us. We'd only be there for one night, and they were gracious hosts. For a send-off dinner, Jake fired up his BBQ and they fed us all the burgers and hotdogs we could eat (which was a lot).

After dinner, Jake showed me how to take apart all the bicycles and helped me put them into our homemade Gore-Tex bags. He also gave me a few tools that would help me put the bikes back together once we landed in Amsterdam.

That night, Matt, Marc, Lindsey, and I slept on the floor of their family room in our borrowed sleeping bags. As we were getting ready to go to sleep, Marc popped up and said, "Just think, tomorrow at this time we'll be in Amsterdam."

"Where are we staying?" Matt asked.

Lindsey said, "Oh, we'll just go into the city and find a place. Don't worry about it."

"What?" Matt exclaimed. "You don't know where we're staying?"

Now I sat up. "Trust me, Matt. There's always a place to stay. It'll work out."

Marc chimed in, "How do you know?"

"Because Maris did the exact same thing to me in Rio, and I freaked out. In the end, it all worked out fine. If it worked out fine in Rio, I'm sure Amsterdam won't be any different. It's just for one night, and then we'll figure out where we're going."

"Yeah, you guys, it'll be fine," said Lindsey. "Once we get a map, we'll figure it out."

I was stunned. "We don't have a map?"

Lindsey shrugged. "Where was I going to get a map of The Netherlands?"

I looked over at Matt and Marc. "Well, I guess we're kind of back where we left off on our last trip. We don't have a clue what we're doing."

"Well that's a comfort," Matt muttered.

Lindsey's voice began to rise. She started to sound like Mom. "At least we're going. It worked out before, and it will work out now. If everything had to be perfect, we'd never go anywhere."

Matt whispered, "I'd feel better if we had a map."

"I heard that. And we don't," Lindsey snapped. "Get over it. Go to sleep, we're gonna have a long day tomorrow."

Resigned, Matt got comfortable in his sleeping bag. "We're gonna have a long summer, from the sound of it. Good night."

And just like that, in a few minutes he was asleep. Meanwhile, I lay awake thinking about the trip ahead. I really didn't care that we didn't have a plan in place. The mere fact that we'd be gone for the summer and away from home was more than comfort enough. This trip was leading me somewhere away from my past, and there was nothing in Willamette I had to return to. No senior year. No job. No nothing. This was different, and I felt excited for the journey.

Our flight left from Sea-Tac Airport on the fifteenth of June at three o'clock in the afternoon. At the counter, we checked our makeshift bicycle carriers, tent, and sleeping bags. We used our panniers as carry-on luggage. Once we were all checked in, Mom and the girls walked us to the gate and waved goodbye.

On the plane, we found our seats and buckled up. Matt turned to me and asked, "How long is this flight?"

"Don't ask me. Ask Lindsey."

Matt didn't have to ask. Lindsey offered, "It's a nine-and-a-half-hour flight. Plus, the time difference is nine hours. We're leaving at three so it's midnight there. I guess it'll be around ten in the morning before we land."

Marc held up his boarding pass. "Right here it says we land at 9:30. Duh."

Lindsey laughed, "*Okay,* Mr. Smartass."

I grabbed the airline magazine, which had a celebrity of the moment on the cover. "At least we'll have time to get our bikes together, buy a map, and find a place to sleep before it gets too late."

Matt leaned across the seats. "I just can't believe we're doing this. I thought I'd be spending my summer working at the cannery."

"Oh, God. I didn't even think about the cannery."

Marc shared, "Yeah, they changed the rules this year and they're hiring sixteen-year-old kids again. Matt and I both thought we'd be stuck there this summer."

"Don't worry," said Lindsey. "You'll get your chance at the cannery next year. This year we're doing whatever we damn well want."

The plane taxied to the runway, gained speed, and took off. From my window I could see the snowy top of Mount Rainer. Over the next few hours, we discussed the places we wanted to visit. We'd been so busy making preparations to leave that we really hadn't spent time thinking about where we wanted to travel.

Matt pulled out one of the airline's magazines from the seat pocket and opened it up to the map of Europe. "Well, we don't have a road map, but we can look at this and make some kind of a plan."

Lindsey grabbed her magazine. "That's a good idea."

Marc grabbed his copy from the seat pocket in front of him, and everyone turned to their maps. Marc was the first to speak. "I don't know about you guys, but I want to go to Italy. Milan, Florence, and Rome are the places I really want to see."

I looked up from my map and said, "No matter where we go, there are some damn big mountains that we have to cross."

Marc looked over at me with a raised eyebrow. "The Alps? Ah, they're just speed bumps."

Matt's eyes flashed. "More like the fucking 'Cliffs of Insanity' if you ask me."

"Oh, come on," said Lindsey. "We've cycled clear across the United States. We can do anything. The Alps aren't going to stop us."

Looking out the window at the sunlit clouds, I said, "Considering the fact that we're already thirty thousand feet in the air, I don't think we have a whole lot of choice at this point."

At about that time, the flight attendant asked if we wanted chicken or pasta for our dinner. We all chose the pasta dish, and when she handed us a real knife and fork, I had a horrible feeling. I looked over at Lindsey and asked, "Did you bring any silverware?"

"No. I didn't think about silverware."

Marc said, in a hint of things to come, "Don't worry about it. When they serve breakfast let's just pocket the utensils and then we'll each have our own knife and fork."

"That's a brilliant idea!" said Matt. "Also nab any condiments we may need."

I looked at my little brothers and thought, *These guys are no longer little boys. They're devious teenagers.*

By the time we landed in Amsterdam, we had silverware, salt, pepper, and a plastic cup. All things that we should have packed before we left. And all thanks to the wonderful food service of Martin Air.

Maps, utensils, food, and other supplies could all be purchased upon arrival, so I wasn't too concerned about what we forgot. The one thing that I wasn't prepared for was jet lag—it was exhaustion on another level. By the time we got our bicycles off of the luggage carousel and outside of the airport, we were pretty much zoned out, as we'd been awake for about twenty-four hours.

I was exhausted and still needed to put four bicycles together, and attach their racks and all the supplies. I looked at the four Gore-Tex bags and thought, *Fuck me, I don't think I can do this.*

Matt must have read my mind, because he tapped me on the shoulder and said, "How about Marc and I get the bikes out of the bags and you just start putting them together?"

"Okay. I guess that'll work. Will you find me the tools in one of the bags so I can get started?"

Marc started digging. "I think I have the tools, just give me a second."

While the three of us were getting organized, Lindsey approached us. "While you guys do that, I'm going back into the airport to find a map. Then we'll figure out where we're going."

I was surrounded by bike parts; travelers had to literally step over me and my piles of tools. I looked, up, wiped my bloodshot eyes, and said, "I guess that's as good a plan as any."

The problem is that when I get really tired, I get really bitchy. I could feel the ember of my bitchiness slowly growing, and there was nothing I could do to stop it. By the time I got to the third bicycle, I was beyond frustrated and pissed off.

During the flight, Matt's bicycle must have had something very heavy on top of it, because the front forks had been slightly squished together. When I couldn't get his front tire on to attach his handlebars, I threw his bike down and yelled, "Fuck this! I've had enough."

"Could you keep it down, Laura?" said Matt. "I think even in Dutch, 'Fuck this' means the same thing."

"Fine. You finish the damn bike. I've had enough."

Marc said, "Matt and I have watched you put them together. I think we can finish it off."

"Great. You do that!" I sneered, pacing along the curb.

"I was fucking trying to be helpful, Laura!" Marc snapped.

I took a deep breath, walked back to our pile of bikes, and sighed, "You're right. I'm just really tired. I didn't think I'd be this tired."

"We're all tired," said Matt. "Except maybe Lindsey, who took off over an hour ago looking for a map and hasn't come back."

I sat down on the curb. "Funny how when work needs to happen, she disappears."

Marc nodded his head and said in a low voice, "She's coming now, shut up."

Lindsey approached. "You don't have these bikes together yet? What have you been doing?"

I was about to lose my shit when Marc said, "We're almost done. What have *you* been doing?"

Lindsey held up a map triumphantly. "I got this from the train station over there." She pointed to a large building. "I bought some tickets to get us into the city. The lady that sold me the tickets told me about a bunch of youth hostels in town. It shouldn't be too hard to find a cheap place to sleep."

"When does the train leave?" asked Matt.

Lindsey glanced at her watch. "In a little over an hour."

I stared at all the bike parts strewn on the ground and glared at her. "So, it doesn't matter that the bikes aren't assembled yet? Thanks for your help, by the way."

Lindsey thought I was being sincere and said, "I just want us to have a safe place to sleep tonight."

I looked over at Matt and Marc and rolled my eyes.

It was late afternoon by the time our train pulled into Amsterdam Central Train Station, so we immediately began looking for a place to spend the night. We had no idea where we were going and finally asked a young couple sitting outside a café if they knew whether there was a youth hostel nearby. The couple looked at us and the guy said, "Well, there's Bob's Youth Hostel, but it's kind of rough. If you don't like it, there's another one near the park."

Lindsey asked which one was closer, and the guy said that Bob's Hostel was right around the corner.

Lindsey thanked them and turned to us. "Let's check out Bob's place first."

"I just want to go to sleep," said Matt. "Whatever's closer works for me."

We walked over to Bob's and instantly realized it was dodgy. We could actually smell it before we reached the door. The hostel's ragtag group of guests were standing out in front of the building sharing a joint. As we approached the front door, a young guy with dirty, long dark hair and a tie-dye shirt stepped forward and asked if we were looking for a place to stay.

"How much does it cost for the night?" asked Lindsey.

He replied, "I'm Bob, by the way, and it costs twenty dollars per person a night." He then pointed at a sign on the front of the building that listed all the rates, plus the prices for all the drugs that could be purchased at his hostel.

As I was reading the menu of how much different kinds of weed cost by the ounce, Bob said, "And you can get whatever else you want, too."

I looked over at Matt and Marc, who were taking in the scene, and kind of shook my head no.

Matt whispered to me, "I think it would be cool to stay here."

"Matt, our stuff would be gone before morning," said Marc.

At about that time Lindsey said to Bob, "We'll think about it. We have another place to check out."

Bob shrugged. "Hey, dude, whatever works for you guys. Good luck." He went back to hanging out with his guests while the four of us continued down the block. As we rounded the corner, Lindsey stopped and said, "I don't think we should stay there."

"No shit," said Marc. "Can we just ask directions to the other hostel? I'm wiped."

"It's near the park," said Lindsey. "Someone should know where it is."

Just then Matt stopped a passerby. "Do you know where the hostel is near the park?"

The guy said, "Yeah. Just follow this road for about ten blocks and then it's on the right. You can't miss it. It's a huge red brick building with a sign that says, 'International Youth Hostel.'"

"Thanks a lot," said Matt. "Is it better than Bob's?"

As the guy walked away, he said, "Depends on what you're looking for. Bob's has its uses," and then began laughing.

Within a few minutes we were all in front of the youth hostel and Lindsey went inside to see if we could get beds. As we waited for her, Matt said, "I still think Bob's would have been fun."

I turned to Matt. "Have you ever smoked weed before?"

Matt and Marc looked at me like I was nuts and Matt said, "No. But I've drunk a lot of beer and I'm sure they had more than weed there."

"Matt, really?" said Marc. "We can drink beer whenever we want. At Bob's, our stuff would've been gone. I think this place is gonna be better."

When Lindsey returned, she said, "Okay, we can lock our bikes up in a shed around the back. The sleeping arrangements are a bit weird. There's a girls' dorm and a guys' dorm. I know we're hungry and tired, so let's put our stuff away, get something to eat, and then go to bed."

As we were locking up our bikes, I looked over at my little brothers and realized they weren't so little anymore. Matt had grown about six inches over the last year and was six feet tall. Marc, who was shorter, had also filled out. Plus, they were in high school and used to calling their own shots. This wasn't going to be anything like our last trip, where Lindsey and Mom were in charge. I thought, *This trip is going to rock!*

With our bikes locked up, and our stuff secure in our dorm rooms, the four of us met in the lobby. Lindsey asked the clerk where we could find someplace to eat, and he said that the best bet was just to walk around until we found what we liked—which we tried to do and soon realized that eating at a restaurant was a little out of our price range. Instead, we found a market, purchased some bread, ham, cheese, and soda, and went back to the park to eat.

As we sat enjoying our little picnic, the food began to perk us up a bit. Marc said, "Did you notice that everyone spoke English? Like, perfect English?"

"It's kind of strange," I said. "I thought they'd speak Dutch."

"Yeah," said Matt, "but their accent is like something out of *Witness*." Then, in a perfect impression of the little boy Samuel from the movie, he said, "*Do you want to pet my kitty?*"

"*And the wire pulls the water into the house*," said Marc.

We all began laughing, punch drunk with exhaustion, and then Lindsey stopped us. "Tomorrow we take off, but what direction should we go?"

"Let's look at the map after breakfast and decide," said Marc, his mouth full of a dry ham and cheese sandwich. "Right now, I just need to go to sleep."

"Okay," said Lindsey, "but we need to get going early. I want to get a good start on our way."

Matt leaned over to me and whispered, "On our way where? We don't even know where we're going."

"Matt, we never know where we're going."

On our first day of cycling, we had a rude awakening. It'd been three years since the four of us had cycled together. Three years since we'd plotted a course using a map, set up camp, and pushed ourselves as cyclists. In those three years, we'd conveniently forgotten all the hard lessons we'd learned on that first trip.

For instance, Lindsey should never be allowed to navigate. She had control of the map and tried to lead us out of the city going south. We ended up spending the better part of two hours just trying to get out of Amsterdam.

When we finally arrived at a campground, we were shocked to learn that in Europe they charged per person and not per site. In the United States, the cost of a campsite was about six dollars a night. In Europe, the cost was around six dollars per person. The increased camping cost cut into our food budget. We'd arrived in Amsterdam with $500, but between train tickets, spending the night at a hostel, and buying food, we were down to about $300. We were quickly realizing that we wouldn't make it to the first of July on just three hundred dollars.

The situation only got worse when Marc realized he'd left his passport back at the youth hostel. The next day he and Matt had to cycle back to the city to retrieve it, meaning we'd have to spend another night at the campground, costing us another twenty bucks. While they were gone, Lindsey and I hatched a plan to get Mom to send us more money.

"I think we should tell Mom that we got ripped off and only have a few bucks left to our name," I said.

"Will she fall for it?" wondered Lindsey.

"Probably. She'll think we were stupid and left our stuff in the tent while we went sightseeing."

"I think we'll have to. I just had no idea everything would be so expensive."

"Do you want to call her, or do you want me to?" I asked.

"You do it. She's already pissed off that she's not here," Lindsey said, cringing.

"Well, I don't really give a damn. I know if we tell her it's too expensive, she'll tell us to come home," I replied.

"Let's talk to the boys when they get back here and ask them what they think," Lindsey said.

"Okay. Just know that I don't have a problem doing the talking."

That night, when the boys returned with Marc's passport, we discussed our plan to call Mom. "I think we should do it," said Matt.

"Just play it up like we're stupid," Marc chimed in.

"I don't think I'll have to play it up," I said. "I kind of feel stupid that we didn't know about the cost of things."

"How the hell were we supposed to know?" asked Matt. "It's not like we can just find this stuff out."

Lindsey added, "It's not as if the little camping icon on the map tells us how much camping cost."

"Shit, we didn't even have a map until two days ago! So, am I calling?" I asked.

They responded in unison, "Yes."

The next day, I called Mom from a campground outside of Gouda and told her our cash had been stolen out of the tent while we were sightseeing. She blew up but said she would wire us five hundred dollars to a bank in Frankfurt on Monday, June 27, which gave us eight days to get to Frankfurt, Germany. Considering the fact that the Netherlands is only one-quarter the size of Oregon, it should have been a breeze. Unfortunately, Lindsey was still in control of the map and she couldn't navigate her way out of a paper bag.

Three days later, we were still in the Netherlands, and if I never saw another windmill, I'd be just fine. Plus, it seemed as if every Dutch person traveled by bicycle. Every few minutes someone on a bike would come up behind us, ring their bell, and say, "Passing on the left." It wouldn't have been so bad if we at least knew where we were going.

When Lindsey got us lost yet again and we found ourselves pushing our bikes along a sandy path, Matt, Marc, and I staged a coup. We threw down our bikes and Marc said, "Lindsey, I'm done. Give me the damn map!"

Sweating and winded, Lindsey huffed, "What do you mean you're done? Pick up your bike. We just have to get to the other side of this trail, and then we'll be on the right road."

"Lindsey," Matt yelled. "You've no idea where we're going. Give Marc the damn map. Let Marc and Laura figure out a course."

"Fuck you guys," said Lindsey, and she continued to push her bike up the path.

"No. Fuck you," said Marc. "We have five days to get to Frankfurt and we haven't even gotten out of Holland!"

Lindsey whirled around. "Listen, everyone, when we stop for lunch, we'll all look at the map."

I picked up my bike and whispered to Marc, "When we're done looking at the map, fold it up and slide it into your bag. Tonight, we'll look at it ourselves and figure out how to get to Frankfurt."

Marc whispered back, "Deal," and picked up his bike.

An hour later, in the town of Eindhoven, there was a small grocery store where we bought some bread, cheese, and Coke. We found a small park to eat our simple lunch and to plot a course for the rest of the day. We were about three hours outside of Echt, where we planned to spend the night. The next day we'd cross over into Germany.

With the course plotted, Marc said, "I think we should get a German map now so we can see how to get to Frankfurt."

Lindsey slammed her drink down. "So, now you and Laura are calling the shots?"

"No, Lindsey," I said. "We're all trying to figure this out. We just can't spend another week going in circles."

"So this is my fault?" Lindsey whined.

The three of us looked at each other, turned towards her, and said, "*Yes.*"

Lindsey's face turned red and her green eyes shot daggers. "Fine. You guys think you can do better, then take the map." She threw it at us. "I'm *done.*"

Thank God.

That afternoon, we thought we'd solved our navigation issues. Still, we were broke. Even with the influx of Mom's money, we'd be struggling. To survive, we'd really have to think outside the box. Or in our case, outside the tent.

Chapter 18

SMILES EVERYONE, SMILES

The evening before we crossed into Germany, the four of us sat outside the tent, laid out our new map of Germany, and tried to agree on a route to Frankfurt. Marc pointed to Echt and said, "Okay. We're here. I think we should cross over into Germany at Aachen."

Matt pointed to a patch of green on the map and asked, "What are those mountains?"

Marc took a closer look. "I'm not sure, but they don't look too high. The summit says seven hundred and fifty meters, so like twenty-five hundred feet. That's not even as high as the coast range."

Lindsey, who'd changed her mind about participating, pointed out, "Well, that shouldn't be too bad. At the most, it should only take us two days to cross over, and then it looks like an easy ride to Frankfurt."

"Where should we camp tomorrow?" I asked.

Marc looked over the map. "We still have a couple hours' ride to the border at Aachen from here. So, I'd suggest camping here," he said, pointing to a place called Simmerath, which was on a lake and had a campground. "It looks like around an eighty-kilometer ride."

Matt appeared relieved. "It doesn't look like it'll be that hard of a day. Where should we try to get to the next day?"

We all looked down at the map, and I pointed. "Blankenheim? It has a campground."

Lindsey shook her head. "We need to get further than that. If we keep cycling only forty miles a day, we'll never get anywhere."

I looked up at her with frustration written all over my face. "Well, *where* do you want to get to?"

Lindsey ignored my tone of voice. "I think we need to get to at least Nürburg. It looks like that's the summit. From there, it should be all downhill to Frankfurt."

Marc folded up the map. "At least we have an idea of where we're going, and these mountains will be a good warm-up for the Alps."

As we climbed into the tent to go to sleep, Lindsey said, "It'll be great to cross into another country. The Netherlands is all right, but I'm getting a little tired of it."

As he was about to go into the tent, I whispered in Marc's ear, "Maybe if we hadn't spent days riding around in circles, we'd have been in Germany days ago."

Marc whispered back, "I know, but she'll never admit it, so drop it."

Before getting into my sleeping bag, I grabbed a journal and asked if anyone wanted to help me write an entry. Matt said, "Just write, 'We were lost, hungry, and cold. Now we're not too lost, but still hungry and cold.'"

Marc said, "That's about right."

I climbed into my sleeping bag and tried to document our day, but in the end, Matt and Marc's suggestions pretty much summed everything up. So, I wrote down their quotes, tucked my journal away, and within minutes fell fast asleep.

By eight o'clock the next morning, drill sergeant Lindsey had awakened us, and we were on the road on a clear, cool day pedaling towards Aachen. It was a fairly flat ride, and we made the border in no time. Once there, we had to have our passports checked by the border patrol. After we were cleared to continue, we found a nearby village to exchange our Dutch money—Guilders—into Deutsche Marks, and that's when we discovered that they'd only exchange paper money and not coins. Therefore, we had about fifteen dollars' worth of coins that we had to swallow. We could've crossed back over into the Netherlands and spent the coins there, but it would've put us about two hours behind schedule. In the end, we chose to keep the coins to spend when we returned to Amsterdam to fly home.

With our Deutsche Marks in hand, we found a grocery store and bought our staples for the day—bread, cheese, sliced ham, and Coke. As we rode out of town, I noticed Matt and Marc hanging back, which was strange. The boys were much stronger cyclists than Lindsey and me. Normally, they'd pull out way ahead of us and would finish the ride hours before we did.

I looked back over my shoulder at them and asked, "Why do you think they're back there?"

"I don't know. They probably just want to take it slow for a little while."

"That's weird. They hate riding slow."

"Laura, don't worry about it. Just keep moving."

I looked back over my shoulder again and noticed they'd fallen even further back, which was even weirder. But Lindsey was probably right, and they just wanted to take it slow for a bit. About ten minutes later the two of them passed us and Marc asked, "Where do you want us to stop?"

"Just follow the signs to Simmerath and we'll meet you in the town," said Lindsey. "It's about two and a half hours from here."

Matt yelled back, "Okay. We'll wait for you there. Enjoy the ride." And the two of them rode off into the distance.

I looked at Lindsey. "I'm going to pull ahead a bit too. I kind of want to cycle on my own for a while."

"Okay, keep safe. I won't be too far behind you."

During our time in Holland, we'd been so lost that we chose to stay together as a group. This was the first day we were able to break out and go at our own pace. I'd missed the solitude of cycling, spending the time daydreaming and thinking about random and abstract things. I didn't have to worry about anything, which was so different from our first bicycle trip.

When we cycled across the United States, I had a huge weight hanging over my head—the scars inflicted by my parents, coping with the hurts of my past, Mom's chaotic behaviors, the mess I'd created at school, and just living in Willamette. Throughout the whole of the last trip, I felt dread. This time around? I felt hope.

The little bit of independence that I carved out for myself in Brazil, combined with the freedom of cycling without Mom, gave me a sense of liberation. I hadn't really faced down my demons, but they weren't front and center. Eventually, I would have to confront those monsters; however, at that time I wasn't afraid of the future. Somehow, I felt that some kind of door of opportunity was opening, but I wasn't sure what it was.

About forty minutes into the ride, I became acutely aware that the road was getting steeper. The gentle climb into the forest turned into switchbacks, the trees became denser, and it began to drizzle. I looked behind me and couldn't see Lindsey, and Matt and Marc were nowhere to be seen in front of me. I stopped for a second, looked around, and thought, *There's nothing around here but forest.* I felt like a character out of a Brothers Grimm fairytale. Maybe I needed some stale breadcrumbs.

With nowhere to go but up, I pushed forward, dropped my gears, and kept moving. I figured I only had another twenty to thirty kilometers to go before I met up with my brothers, which should have taken about an hour. But because of the grade of the hill, it took me twice as long to reach Simmerath, where Matt and Marc would be waiting for me in the town square.

As I finally pulled up beside them, I panted, "That ride was a bigger bitch than I anticipated. How was it for you guys?"

"It sucked," Matt said. "I thought we'd make it in an hour, and it took us two. Plus, the cold and rain didn't help."

Marc looked around and asked, "Where's Lindsey?"

"I'm not sure. I left her a little while after you guys blew past. She should be here soon."

Lindsey was another hour behind me. When she arrived, she threw her bicycle down and began kicking the crap out of it. Perplexed, I asked, "What the fuck are you doing?"

With a wild, crazy expression, she shouted, "I didn't realize that these hills would be so steep, and I've had enough!"

"So, you're kicking your bike?!" I shouted back.

"I'll kick my bike if I want to kick my bike!"

"Well, you look like an idiot," I said, shaking my head.

Matt cut into our argument. "Lindsey, let's just go find the campground and get some rest."

Lindsey picked up her bike, which fortunately was still in one piece, and rode ahead of us. I looked over at Marc and asked, "Does she even know where she's going?"

"No. I'll go get her. We need to ask someone where the campground is. Could you go do that?"

Matt and I biked over to a shop and he went in to get directions. When he returned, he said, "We just follow this road up to the lake and we'll see signs for the campground."

Matt hopped on his bike and the two of us rode out of town, where we found Lindsey and Marc waiting for us. Lindsey said, "So, do you *know* where we're going?"

With a lot more patience than I could have mustered, Matt said, "Just keep cycling towards the lake. We'll run into the campground."

"I guess you guys know everything," Lindsey huffed, then pedaled off.

I said to Matt, "I know enough to know that kicking my bike doesn't make the ride any easier."

Matt replied, "Maybe tomorrow we should all try it because we'll be climbing all day."

"If she breaks her bike, I am not fixing it."

That night when we were all tucked into our sleeping bags, I summoned the courage to ask Lindsey why she'd thrown such a fit. She said, "Because I didn't anticipate this part of the ride being so hard. The harder I had to cycle, the more pissed off I was getting."

"Lindsey, that makes no sense. What are you gonna do in Switzerland when we have to cross the Alps?" I asked.

"Oh, that'll be fine because I know the Alps are going to be hard. I just didn't know this part was going to be so hard."

Matt looked over at her, perplexed. "What absolute bullshit."

Lindsey whined, "It's just how I feel."

As they were talking, I was writing in my journal: *Lindsey is nuts and driving me crazy. And we really didn't eat today. We paid too much for this campsite, $30. The weather sucked. The ride sucked. Probably more of the same tomorrow.*

None of us got a good night's sleep. Since it drizzled the day before, all of our clothes were damp. The Gore-Tex bags kept our sleeping bags dry, but throughout the night, the moisture creeped in and soaked our bags. By the time we crawled out of the tent, we were cold, damp, and hungry. Unfortunately, all we had for breakfast was a bit of stale bread, hard cheese, and some water. As we divided up the prison fare, I said, "We need to get some real food somewhere."

Marc pulled out the map. "I think we should stop here," he pointed to the town of Monschau. "It says there's a castle there, which would be cool to see."

"How far, do you think?" I asked.

"It doesn't look too far," Marc said. "Maybe forty minutes. An hour at the most."

"All uphill?" Lindsey asked.

I turned to her and said, "Lindsey, all of today is uphill. I think it'll be a lot like yesterday's ride. Try not to kick your bike too hard."

Lindsey glared at me. "I was pissed. Give me a break."

As I cycled off, I looked back and said, "Just don't break your bike!" She gave me the finger in reply.

An hour later, I found Matt and Marc waiting for me at the entrance of Monschau. Matt asked, "Should we wait for Lindsey or go into town?"

I looked back over my shoulder. "She has all the money, so let's wait."

A few minutes later, Lindsey arrived. She must've come to terms with the terrain, because she didn't throw her bike down and abuse it. When she pulled up to us, she asked if we wanted to spend some time looking around the town, or just eat and keep cycling.

"Let's see what the town's like and then decide," said Marc.

"Okay," said Lindsey. "Either way, we shouldn't spend too much time here because we have a long, hard ride in front of us."

"A long, hard, cold, and damp ride," I added.

"I know this weather sucks," said Lindsey. "But if we keep moving, we should be okay."

"I guess I didn't think the weather would be this miserable," I responded.

Marc said, "We just need to get out of this forest and hit the valley, where the weather should be better."

Cycling into the city center was like riding into a fairytale village. The town was built along a small river, with cobblestone streets, and all the houses and shops were half-timber buildings. A giant castle towered over the town. We circled around the center and then settled on a small shop that was both a bakery and grocery store. We locked up our bikes and went in to buy food for the day. In the store, Lindsey said, "We really can't spend that much money. We're just getting bread, ham, cheese, and water."

"We can't just live on bread, cheese, and water!" said Matt.

"Until we get the money on Monday, we're going to have to," said Lindsey. "We just don't have enough to eat and pay for camping. Something has to give."

"We're going to go look around the store. We'll meet you out by the bikes," said Marc.

The two boys took off down an aisle while Lindsey and I found a loaf of bread that was as dense as a brick, some hard cheese, and a few bottles of water. I didn't dare hope for protein. We went to the checkout, paid for our things, and found Matt and Marc by the bikes waiting for us.

"I saw a little park down by the water right under the castle," said Lindsey. "Let's go down there and eat."

We all jumped on our bikes and followed her down towards the stream, where there were a few picnic tables. Lindsey put the food on a table, dug out a Martin Air knife, and began slicing bread and cheese for us. The only difference between our breakfast and lunch was that this meal wasn't stale—yet.

While we ate, Marc took out the map. "If we want to get to Nürburg today, we'll have to push it. It's only ninety kilometers, but it's all uphill." He pointed to some zigzags on the map and said to Lindsey, "We'll be climbing switchbacks, so it'll be steep."

"Why are you looking at me?" asked Lindsey.

"I'm just saying..."

Before it could get heated, I said, "Hey, let's get a picture of you guys with the castle in the background." I had become quite skilled at deflection.

Matt jumped up. "That's a great idea. Let's stand over here on these rocks. I'll stand in the middle and Lindsey and Marc stand on each side of me."

I turned around and grabbed the camera out of Lindsey's bag, turned back, and, while I was adjusting the camera, said, "Okay, are you guys ready?" I didn't hear an answer, so I looked up. Matt was standing on top of a rock, and Lindsey was looking at him with her mouth open while Marc laughed.

Confused, I asked "What?" And then I saw it. Matt was holding a huge package of vanilla wafer cookies in his hand. I asked, "Where the hell did you get those?"

"I shoved them down my pants in the store before Marc and I left."

"We've been stealing food every time we go into a grocery store," Marc confessed.

"I knew there was something fishy going on," I pointed out. "That's why you keep hanging back, isn't it? You little thieves."

Marc shot back, "You're just pissed off that we didn't share any with you."

This was partly true. I'd been eating less food so the two growing teens could have more, and now that I knew the truth, I was mad.

"Get over it and eat some cookies," said Marc. "You'll feel better."

I sat down, grabbed a few cookies, and said, "I'll eat them, but you guys are going to get caught one of these days and then what?"

Matt smiled, with a mouthful of cookies. "Once we get Mom's money, we'll stop. I swear. Right now, we're starving!"

"Do you promise?"

"I swear..."

"Okay, give me another cookie, I'm starving too."

Lindsey grabbed a cookie. "I don't condone this, but I'm not complaining."

We spent the next seven hours ascending never-ending hills in the cold, wet drizzle. The only time we stopped was to share a few more cookies, eat a little bread, and drink some water. At six o'clock in the evening, I met up with Matt and Marc, and we still had thirty miles to go before we reached our destination. The three of us were exhausted, and Matt said, "I think we should just go in the woods and pitch our tent. I doubt if anyone will care."

"So we can do this all over again? I think we should hitch a ride," I said.

"I'm all for hitching," replied Marc. "We just need to wait for Lindsey."

"Do you think we'll find someone to pick all four of us up with our bikes and gear?" I asked.

"It's worth a try," said Matt, "and if it doesn't work, let's just camp in the forest."

About that time, Lindsey caught up with us and we told her our plan. She said, "Right about now I'm game for anything. This road sucks, I'm tired, and I'm fed up."

"At least you didn't throw your bike down and kick it," I said.

"Actually, I did a few miles back and I feel much better now."

I was too tired to react.

Marc said, "Let's try to flag down a ride."

We laid down our bikes on the shoulder of the road. As the first car approached, I said, "Too small."

"Yeah, we'll need a van or a truck," said Marc.

The next vehicle was a red van, and all four of us stood in the middle of the road and waved it down. The driver pulled over towards us, rolled down the window, and asked what was wrong.

He was a younger guy with short brown hair, and there was another young guy in the passenger seat. I walked over to the driver's side and said, "Hey, we're trying to get to Frankfurt by Monday and we're kind of stuck. Do you think you could help us out?"

"Sure," he said. "We'll take you to Frankfurt. Throw your stuff in the back and climb in. First, we have to go back to our apartment and get some things. Is that okay?"

The four of us looked at each other, and Lindsey said, "You'll take us to Frankfurt?"

The driver smiled. "Sure. Why not? We were just driving around trying to find something to do."

"Great!" said Lindsey. "We really appreciate this."

Looking back, this scene could have been the prelude to a horror story. But times were different, and these were just two nice guys trying to help us out.

The four of us took the bags off our bikes, took off the front wheels, slid everything into the back, and climbed into the back seats of the van. When we were buckled in, the driver said, "My name is Dieter, and this is Hans. We need to go back to Aachen and pick a few things up. Plus, I need to call my girlfriend and let her know what we're doing."

Lindsey introduced all of us and said, "Man, it took us two days to get from Aachen to here. How long will it take to drive?"

Dieter looked at us in the mirror. "I drive fast, so about forty minutes maybe."

Hans said, "He is a crazy driver, so more like twenty minutes."

In what felt like even less than twenty minutes we were at Dieter's apartment in Aachen, where he and Hans served us pizza while we waited for Dieter's girlfriend, Greta, to show up. Greta was a quintessential German girl, in her twenties, and she wanted to ride to Frankfurt with us and enjoy the adventure.

Soon after Greta arrived, we all got back in the van and took off. A few hours later we were at a campground outside of Frankfurt on the Rhine River. The guys helped us set up our tent, and then we went over to a tavern on the campground, where we bought them all beers as a thank you for all their help.

Everyone, even Matt and Marc, had a few beers. Because my family still believed that I was sober, I chose to just drink a Coke. For the next few hours, we chatted about where we were going on our trip. Hans and Dieter told us they were students and really wanted to visit the U.S. someday. Before they left, we exchanged addresses and told them if they were ever in Oregon to look us up. In the back of my mind, I knew that we would never see them again.

When they pulled away, I looked over at the table with the empty beer bottles and marveled at the fact that I really didn't want to drink with them. The truth was that I'd stopped drinking around them but hadn't quit drinking altogether. I knew I had to keep up the sober, happy façade around my brothers and sister, but in the back of my mind I always knew that would all change once I was back on my own. Maybe that was just as deceitful as Matt and Mark's shoplifting. But I'd been lying to my family for two years, so who was I to judge?

Between paying for three nights of camping, giving Hans and Dieter some gas money, and springing for everyone's beers, we were broke. We only had twenty Deutsche Marks to get us through three days. When I crawled out of the tent the following morning, I found Lindsey sitting in the grass, looking out over the water. I walked over to her and asked, "What should we do for breakfast?"

"We don't have much money," she said. "I think when the boys wake up, two of us need to cycle into town and buy some food."

While she was talking, I noticed all the other campers milling about, and I could smell sausages being cooked. I said, "Man, these smells are amazing. They're making me hungry."

"Just don't think about it and it won't bother you."

"How do you know?"

"Because I've been up for an hour and it's driving me crazy too."

"I'd kill for a cup of hot tea and a sausage right now."

"I know. A cup of tea would be amazing."

"Yeah it would," I sighed. "Right now, we just need some food."

A few minutes later, both Matt and Marc climbed out of the tent and joined us. I asked Matt if he wanted to ride into town and get food with me and he said, "Anything to get away from the smell of sausages. Let's go."

The two of us jumped on our bikes and pedaled out of the park. We were happy to find a bicycle path that led into the city. We weren't happy to find out that we had a ten-mile ride to get there and back.

In the city center, we discovered that the U.S. Army was hosting a huge barbecue and fair that evening. It looked kind of fun, and when we returned to the campground, we told Marc and Lindsey about it.

"How far is it into town?" asked Lindsey.

"Not too bad," said Matt. "We can walk there."

I should have said that it would be a long walk, but I wanted a break from my bike. Plus, I wanted to go and see something other than a campground, so I compounded Matt's lie. "Yeah, it's not too long of a walk."

Later that evening, when it took us two and a half hours to reach the city center, Marc and Lindsey weren't too happy with us. But when we sat down and shared two plates of barbecue chicken, corn on the cob, and apple pie, they weren't complaining anymore. But the next day, when we only had five Deutsche Marks to our name, we kind of regretted our splurging.

It seemed we would spend the rest of our time in Frankfurt playing gin rummy and snacking on stale bread. By midday, Lindsey said to Marc, "I'm going to give you our last five Marks. You and Matt go see what you can get for it."

Marc looked over at her. "Are you saying what I think you're saying?"

Lindsey replied, "I'm not saying anything. I don't know what you can get for five bucks. Just come back with something."

With that, Matt and Marc jumped on their bikes and headed off to find a grocery store. I looked over at Lindsey. "You didn't tell them to rip off food, but you know that's what they're going to do."

"Are you saying you won't eat it?"

"No. I'm just stating the obvious."

"We need to get something to eat, Laura."

"I know. I guess I'm worried that they'll get caught and then we'll be in a worse mess."

"They won't get caught."

An hour later the boys came back with Cokes, candy bars, Slim Jim's, and other junk food. "Really, this is what you get?" I asked.

"We went into a convenience store and this is all they had," said Marc.

I cracked open a soda, grabbed a pepperoni stick, and said, "This all cost five dollars, right?"

Matt raised his eyebrows. "Sure, whatever you want to believe."

On Monday morning we were to pick up Mom's money at Deutsche Bank in the center of Frankfurt. We packed up all of our gear and rode into town early so we could be there when the bank opened. While we waited outside the building, Marc pulled out the map and said, "The ride between here and Switzerland should be easy. We'll just follow the river south."

"It's flat and the weather is warmer," said Lindsey. "I think we can make some good time."

"My only problem is finding a place to sleep," I said. "I think the cost of these campgrounds is ridiculous."

" 't see another option," replied Lindsey. "If you can ᴐmething, let me know."

"I just think we need to be able to spend more on food. There has to be an alternative."

Matt chimed in, "Maybe the campgrounds will be cheaper once we're outside the city."

"I doubt it," said Marc. "It was just as expensive in Holland. I think we should figure out a different plan. Think on it and when we stop for lunch, let's decide."

Lindsey got off her bike. "I'll go get the money, then let's get some real food. Then let's take off."

She disappeared into the bank and came out about fifteen minutes later with five hundred dollars' worth of Deutsche Marks, which wasn't really all that much. At least we did have a nice breakfast of orange juice, pastries, and some yogurt. Unfortunately, no sausages. Once we were fed, we headed south on Route 3 towards the city of Mannheim.

The road cut through a lush valley of farmland, reminding me of the Willamette Valley. There were large farms with farmhouses scattered around. From time to time, we'd pass livestock in the fields and farmers on their tractors. When we stopped for lunch in Seeheim, Matt said, "I have an idea. Did you see all those farmhouses? Did you notice that some of them had kids' toys in their front yards, or swings? Well, I think we should find a house that obviously has kids and ask if we can pitch our tent on their property. That way we won't have to pay for camping."

Lindsey's eyes widened. "Do you think it'll work?"

Matt shrugged. "It's worth a try."

"Okay," Lindsey nodded. "How about we get to the other side of Mannheim and find a farm? Matt, you do the talking."

"Okay, but why me?" asked Matt.

"You're young, blond, and kind of have that all-American look. I think they'll like you right away."

A few hours later, we found a farmhouse that appeared to have young children, so we rode our bikes up their drive. As we approached the front of the house, Matt turned back towards us and said, "Smiles, everyone. Smiles!"

Matt handed Marc his bike, walked up to the front door, and rang the bell. A young boy, who looked to be about twelve years old, answered. I heard Matt ask, "Do you speak English?"

The boy said, "Ich spreche ein bischen English."

Matt asked, "Is your mom or dad home?" and the boy disappeared. A few seconds later a man who must have been the boy's father came to the door and said in broken English, "Can I help you?"

Matt pointed over at the three of us. "We're Americans and we're cycling through Europe. We're wondering if it would be okay to pitch our tent on your property."

The guy looked over at us, so we waved and smiled. He said, "Sure. That shouldn't be a problem." He pointed towards the left side of his house and said, "There's a good spot over there. Just make yourselves at home. I'll come and check on you later."

"Thanks," said Matt. "We won't be a bother, I promise."

He came back down the front stairs of the house. "I think this is our solution."

"So far, so good," said Marc.

The four of us pushed our bikes over to the area the man had indicated and pitched our tent. When we were just about finished, the little boy who'd answered the door and his sister appeared with some lemonade and cookies for us.

Lindsey whispered to the boys as she grabbed a warm cookie, "At least you guys don't have to steal these. And they're just baked."

Matt asked the boy and girl if they wanted to hang out with us for a while, and the kids plopped down on the ground and started asking us questions. A few minutes later, their mother and father showed up. Before we knew it, we were sitting around their kitchen table, enjoying a real meal. With food. Real food. Chicken. Potatoes. Vegetables. What we began to call the full meal deal.

We followed the same formula the following night at a farm outside of the town of Pforzheim. This time the family not only fed us, but allowed us to shower and do laundry. We were just blown away by the hospitality of people.

Later that night, in the tent, Matt said, "I really didn't expect people to be this nice."

Lindsey added, "I think it helps that we just ask to pitch our tent on their property and don't ask for anything else."

"Yeah," said Marc. "I doubt if we would get very far if we said, 'Hey, could we camp here, and could you feed us too? Got any warm cookies? And a laundry machine?'"

"Ya think?" I said. "It also helps that they want their kids to practice English. So, I don't feel like we're taking advantage of them too much."

Matt interjected, "I don't care why they feed us, but this is the best I've felt since we arrived in Europe."

Before I got into my sleeping bag, I pulled out my journal and wrote, *We ate today! That's two days in a row. We've met some really nice families that have taken pity on us. Hopefully, this will be a trend that continues.* Then I asked, "Does anyone want to write something?"

Lindsey said, "Write that Germany no longer sucks, and the weather is better."

"I have a feeling this journal is going to just be a series of entries that highlight our intake of food and the weather conditions," I replied.

"Aside from a few castles and a lot of farmlands, we haven't really seen much else," said Matt. I resisted adding that this was the result of Lindsey's relentless timeline.

Instead, I tucked the journal away, got into my bag, and said, "Let's just hope it stays that boring."

Mom was going to wire us another six hundred dollars to a bank in Zürich on the first of July. She didn't send all of the money to Frankfurt because she wanted to wait until Matt and Marc's Social Security checks had been deposited. The first was on a Friday, and if we didn't get there by Friday we'd have to wait until the fourth to pick up the cash. So we were trying to reach Switzerland by Thursday.

All was going great—until Wednesday, when we had a series of flat tires. First, Marc's back tire popped, and I patched it up. About ten miles later, Lindsey's front tire went, and I patched it up, too. Finally, my back tire blew near this funky, open air historical museum. I pulled into their parking lot and began to work on my tire while the others waited.

As I watched the glue drying, a young guy dressed in historical garb approached us and asked, "Are you guys Americans?"

Lindsey turned towards him. "Yeah, we are. We're just passing through on our way to Switzerland."

He said, "Where did you guys begin your trip?"

"Today, or where did we fly into?" asked Marc.

"Where did you land?" the guy clarified.

"Amsterdam," said Matt.

"That's really cool," the guy said. He then asked, "Where do you plan on camping tonight?"

"We haven't really decided yet," said Lindsey. "We were going to ask a farmer if we can pitch our tent on his property."

"You guys can camp at my house if you want," he said. "We'll have a barbecue and I'll invite some friends over."

I looked up and said, "Really? Where do you live?" I could almost smell meat sizzling on his grill.

"I just live in the next town over. I'll call my parents and tell them you guys are coming. They'll love having you stay."

He then asked if we had something to write on. I reached into my bag and gave him my journal. "Go ahead and write the address on this. Could you write some directions too since we don't know where we're going?"

"Sure," he said. "My name is Kristof, by the way. What are your names so I can tell my parents who's coming to the house?"

We told him our names, and he went back to work while I put my bike back together. Lindsey said, "We shouldn't come

"I doubt it," Matt said. "Actually, I doubt if he'll drink alcohol again...on *this* trip."

"I wouldn't blame him," I said. "I just can't believe we're in Switzerland. Zürich tomorrow, and then we hit the Alps." I turned to Matt and smiled. "Do you think we can do it?"

He grinned. "It will take a miracle."

Chapter 19

AMERICAN FRÄULEINS

The ride to Zürich should've taken us about three hours, so we all slept in the following morning. The goal was to give Marc a little extra time to sleep and recover from the pains of the previous day. It was well after nine o'clock before we'd packed up and were ready to hit the road. Before taking off, we'd agreed to stop in the town of Baden-Baden, exchange our Deutsche Marks for Swiss francs, and buy some food supplies. As we were getting ready to push off, Lindsey said to the boys, "Don't steal anything! We're getting money tomorrow and there isn't any reason to risk it."

"We didn't plan on taking anything!" Marc said with a sneer.

Matt added, "Like we would be that stupid," and they rode off.

I turned to Lindsey. "Don't you think they've put those days behind them?"

"I don't think so. I found some wrappers in the tent the other day."

"They won't do anything stupid. We'll have more than enough money tomorrow and we have enough money for food today."

"I just think a warning was needed."

"Okay, I guess I'll see you in Baden-Baden." I took off after Matt and Marc. An hour later, I found the boys standing outside a grocery store, waiting for us.

Matt pointed out, "We thought this looked like a good enough spot as any to pick up some food."

I looked over my shoulder. "Okay, Lindsey shouldn't be too far behind."

A few minutes later, Lindsey pulled up. "I already exchanged the money, so let's go in."

We took the bikes over to the side of the store, and I said, "I'll hang out here and watch the bikes while you guys go inside."

Lindsey grabbed the money out of her bag. "We'll be right back," she said, and the three of them went in.

While they were gone, I thought about how nice it would be to have a short day and maybe even take some time to walk around the city of Zürich. Just when I was wondering how expensive Swiss chocolate was, Marc came out in a panic. "Laura, follow me." He was shaking as he quickly led me behind the store.

As I followed him, I asked, "What's going on?" Which is when I realized he was pulling food out of his armpits and throwing it into a bush.

Marc looked up at me. "That dumb shit was stealing candy. What an idiot! The last thing you steal is candy. He just got caught and is in the manager's office with Lindsey."

I was still in shock at the amount of food he'd pulled out of his armpits. He was like a living Mary Poppins carpetbag. Before I could say anything, he continued, "Lindsey's losing her mind. I think you need to go in there and help. I'll stay out here with the bikes."

I glared at him in anger and disbelief. "You're both idiots," I said, and went into the store.

Once inside, I asked where the manager's office was and was directed to the back of the store, where there was a door that had a sign on it that I gathered said, "Employees Only." I knocked on the door and Lindsey opened it up. I asked her, "What's going on?"

Lindsey's angular features were sharp and rigid. She pointed to another door. "Matt's in there with the manager. He's called the police. We're screwed because the manager wants us to pay for what he took, and I already bought our food for the day. I don't have enough to cover it."

I was shocked that the police would be involved. "The manager really called the police?"

"Yeah, I tried to stop him, but the guy's a dick."

Just then, two police officers, uniformed but unarmed, came into the room and knocked on the manager's door. The manager let them in and shut the door again. While this was going on, I noticed Lindsey was grabbing a tin on top of a vending machine. Confused, I asked, "What are you doing?"

"This tin is full of Swiss francs. I'm just taking them so we can pay for Matt's stupidity."

I whispered, "Lindsey!"

She whispered back, "We need it and it's just sitting there."

Thinking we'd all end up arrested, I said, "I am out of here. Good luck," and walked back outside to find Marc.

Marc asked, "What's going on? Were those cops that went inside?"

"Yep, plus, Lindsey just stole a whole bunch of francs from the top of a vending machine. We'll be lucky to get out of this mess."

At that moment, Matt was led out of the store by the two policemen, followed by Lindsey. Lindsey came over to us. "They're taking him to the police station. It's just around the corner from here. Let's take our bikes over there and see if we can get him out."

Lindsey and I pushed our bikes while Marc pushed both his and Matt's bikes over to the police station. When we got there, I said, "I'll go in and see what's going on. Marc, watch the bikes." I ignored Lindsey, but she followed me into the station.

I stepped up to the policewoman behind the counter, who could have been straight off the Swiss Miss hot chocolate box, and asked, "Do you speak English?"

"Of course I speak English."

I wanted to say, "Of course I should just *know* that you speak English. Silly of me to ask." Instead, I said, "I believe my little brother, Matt Jacobson, is here. I would like to speak with him."

"That will not be possible," she said. "He is in with the prosecutor."

Prosecutor? What the fuck. All for a handful of candy bars? With more urgency, I demanded, "No. I need to see him now."

I must have frightened her, because she stepped away from the counter and went straight back into the station. A few minutes later a plain-clothes policeman came out and said, "Can I help you?"

I said, "I am Matt Jacobson's sister Laura, and I need to see him now."

"Right now he's being interviewed by the prosecutor, and you'll have to wait."

"Who's representing him?" I asked. "He can't just be there by himself." I pointed at

Lindsey and continued, "One of us is going back there to be with him."

The man folded his arms, more amused than frustrated. "Listen, that's not how it works here. He stole and we are considering pressing charges."

"I get that, but he is a minor and shouldn't be left in a room with no one to support him."

The guy rolled his eyes. "Let me go back there and see where they're at."

"You do that," I said.

While we were waiting, Lindsey began pacing and kicking at things. I thought, *Great, now we'll get charged with disturbing the peace.*

A few minutes later, Matt came out of the back room with one of the officers, who put his hand on his shoulder and said, "You are a very lucky young man. Next time you might not be so lucky," and he shook Matt's hand.

Matt, looking humiliated, said, "Trust me, I won't do this again."

As we were walking out the door, I said, "You better not, you idiot." Just before the door closed, I heard the policeman say, "Ach, American Fräuleins." It wasn't a compliment.

I thought, *Damn right, American Fräuleins!*

With Matt safe, the four of us hopped on our bikes and tried to get out of town as quickly as possible. About five miles past the city limits, we found a place along a river to pull over and eat lunch. It was a meal mixed with relief, and annoyance. I could have throttled all of them.

There was a silver lining to our situation. When all was said and done, we had the food Lindsey had purchased, the food Marc stole, and the francs Lindsey took from the top of the vending machine. So, I guess we came out ahead. Lindsey and the boys thought the whole situation was funny, but I felt like things were getting out of control.

I turned to Matt. "What were you thinking? You're wearing a New York Yankees hat and t-shirt. You couldn't look any more like a tourist if you tried. Plus, you stole *candy*. Dude, they had you marked as soon as you walked in the store."

Matt gave me his cheese-eating grin that always made me want to slap him. "Laura, don't be such a hypocrite. You're eating what we stole right now, and don't tell me you won't use those francs that Lindsey took."

I looked at him and shook my head, but I knew he was right. I did eat the food Marc stole and I would use the money Lindsey nabbed. The truth was I wasn't any better than them; I just wanted to feel superior.

In Zürich we found a campground in the city on the Zürich Sea, which is really a lake. We paid for two nights with the hope of getting our clothes clean and stocking up on supplies before heading up the mountains.

On Friday, the first of July, we found the bank that Mom wired our monthly stipend to and spent the afternoon checking out the sights. Zürich was the cleanest city I have ever seen, and I felt a little bit shabby walking around there. I wondered if after everyone went to sleep, the shoemaker's elves came out and tidied everything up. They'd have their work cut out with us. Our clothes were clean, but after three weeks they were beginning to look a little worn. We just looked homeless.

Back at the campground, we met some American college students, who were on a Eurail trip. They were lugging their huge backpacks around and appeared slightly more put together than I felt.

We hung out with them later that night around a small campfire. They attended Tufts University and all they wanted to talk about was German cars, their school, and their futures. The more I listened to them, the more inferior I felt. We were the same age, but their futures were all mapped out, while I didn't know *what* I was doing after August. I had a feeling everything would work out, but a feeling isn't a plan.

Later that night, in the tent, Lindsey commented, "Those guys were kind of full of themselves."

Matt agreed. "Yeah, I kind of liked Kristof, Dieter, and Hans a lot better."

While my siblings talked, I just settled into my sleeping bag and listened. Up until meeting the American students, I'd been feeling pretty good about things. Now, I was questioning my choices and doubting that things would be okay. I remembered the college students in Georgetown and questioned if I'd ever be a college student.

Just then, Marc said something that shook me out of my self-pity party. He sat up on one elbow. "You know what? I kinda like what we're doing. We meet cool people, and we aren't just going from one tourist location to the next. We're doing our own thing."

I looked over at him. "You're right. I'm glad we're doing it this way too. It's different and completely weird, but hey, that's us."

"Yeah," said Matt. "Those guys probably haven't seen the inside of a Swiss police station!"

Marc shot him a look. "I don't think that's one to be proud of, buddy."

During our stay in Zürich, the Alps loomed over us on the southern horizon. For the first day, we didn't say anything about them, or even really look at the map. I know part of my hang-up had to do with not cycling over the Rockies on our previous trip. I had doubts about our ability to climb such a massive mountain range. In a way, the Alps were more than a mountain range to me—they represented all the times I'd taken a shortcut in life. This time there'd be no shortcut—and that was scary.

On our last day in Zürich, we spent the day swimming in the cool mountain lake, in the midst of dozens of anchored sailboats, one all black like a pirate ship, reinforcing the belief that we were the goonies. Afterwards, we washed our clothes and tried to build up our courage to face "The Cliffs of Insanity."

As the shadows of the trees in the campground grew longer, the four of us were sitting on the banks of the lake, throwing pebbles into the water. Looking up at the snow-peaked mountains, Marc said, "Ah, I still think they're just speed bumps."

"Does it make you feel better when you say that?" I asked.

He stared at the jagged outline of the Alps. "Not really."

I looked at my siblings and realized just how strong we'd become. We were young, weathered, and fucking survivors. I then said, "I think we're turning this into too big of a deal. We just take it one day at a time."

"How many days do you think it will take?" asked Matt.

"I'll go get the map and we'll figure it out," said Lindsey, and she got up and went back to our campsite. While she was gone, I asked, "How many times do you think she'll throw down her bike before we reach the summit?"

Matt skipped a stone. "Ah, who cares?"

I care, because it will be me who has to fix it, I thought.

When Lindsey came back, she unfolded the map and laid it on the ground. The four of us put our heads together and tried to figure out a route.

Marc stuck his finger on the Italian border. "By the looks of things it shouldn't take us more than five days to reach Italy."

Matt pointed out a road between Zürich and Brig. "I think that's our route."

"So, we try to do the farmer thing again?" I asked.

"Yeah," said Matt. "If we can. But I don't think there'll be a lot of farmlands in the mountains. I think we'll have to figure it out as we go."

"It looks like we don't climb until here," I said, and pointed out a spot past Lake Lucerne.

Lindsey jumped in. "Let's try to get into the foothills the first day and then press on from there. At least we have a route picked out."

That night we all took turns writing in our journal. I wrote, *We are heading for the Alps tomorrow. Hopefully, it won't be too rough. Zürich has been amazing, and a much-needed break.*

Matt wrote, *Alps, schmalps, we got this.*

Marc wrote, *Speed bumps!*

Lindsey wrote, *God, help us.*

We followed our chosen route out of Zürich, which led us around the Zürich Sea and around two more lakes before we began the gentle climb up into the foothills. The freshness of the air and the beauty of our surroundings began to lull me into the belief that we'd made too big a deal about the Swiss mountains.

As I rounded the point of the last lake, I found Matt and Marc waiting for me at the city limits of a town called Littau (now part of Lucerne).

"We can go left or right here," Marc said. "Either way, we'll end up in Brig, but it's at least a two-day ride. We need to wait for Lindsey and decide together."

The three of us got off of our bikes and sat on the side of the road to wait for our sister. While we waited, I asked, "Which way do you guys think we should go?"

"It really doesn't matter at this point," said Marc. "Each way has very few towns, and I think we'll have to camp out in the woods."

"Well, let's ask Lindsey. I am sure she'll have an opinion."

Actually, when she arrived, she didn't really care which way we went. And so we chose to go right on the A8, and for the next couple of hours, we steadily climbed into the forest. From the look of things, we'd be very lucky to find a farmhouse. We were cycling along a river, and it seemed we'd entered a national forest.

I found the boys waiting for us at the entrance of a service road. "Just down this road is a great place to hang out by the river," said Matt. "I think we should eat down there."

They were standing near a sign that had a tent with a slash through it, indicating no camping allowed, so I asked, "Can we go down there?"

"It just says no camping," said Marc. "I think we can hang out down there."

When Lindsey pulled up, we told her we were headed to the river to eat, and the four of us cycled down the road. About a quarter of a mile down, we found a clearing near the river and we fixed ourselves a little picnic.

The forest was dense with fir and spruce trees, not unlike the forest of Oregon. But the rushing river appeared to be dotted with slabs of marble glistening in the sun. As we ate our lunch, we began to relax, and no one appeared to be in a hurry to get back on the road.

When we finished eating, Marc said, "I'm going to go exploring for a bit. I'll be back."

While he was gone, Matt, Lindsey, and I went down by the river and threw rocks for a while. To pass the time, we found a large slab of stone in the middle of the river and tried to see who could come closest to hitting it. As he was chucking a rock, Matt said, "I think we should just camp here. No one's going to find us."

"I don't think we should put up the tent here, though," said Lindsey. "We'll stick out like a sore thumb."

"Let's just build a shelter and camouflage it," said Matt.

I banged a rock off our target. "That would work; let's go find Marc and get going."

As the three of us walked back towards our bikes, I saw Marc moving logs and branches around in the woods. I shouted over at him, "What are you doing?"

He shouted back, "Building myself a shelter. I'm going to sleep here tonight."

"Just for you?" Matt asked.

"Yeah," shouted Marc. "You guys can do what you want."

Matt looked over at me and said, "He's such a selfish little bastard," and then he shouted to Marc, "You'd better think again because we're coming your way."

Marc shot back, "I thought you might say that."

For the next hour the four of us worked together to make one fine shelter. When we were done, we threw two of our Gore-Tex bags over the top and covered them with branches. Then we took the other two bags and laid them on the floor of the shelter. Finally, we took our bikes and hid them behind the shelter, covering them with branches too.

By the time the sun had set, we were happily tucked away in our little hideaway. Just when we were about to go to sleep, Marc popped up and said, "Hey, it's the Fourth of July!"

"Oh man, I forgot," said Matt. "We didn't even light a match as a celebration."

"We still have time!" I said.

"Let's do it now!" Lindsey grabbed a box of matches from her pannier.

We all crawled out of our shelter, struck a match, and said, "Happy Birthday, America," and then crawled back into our nest.

Matt grinned. "I feel much better now."

"As good as when we were at Mount Rushmore?" I asked.

He thought for a second. "Oddly, I kind of like this better. I feel freer."

I completely understood. I felt freer than I ever had in my life. Plus, it was the best night's sleep I'd had in weeks. The ground was soft, the night dark, the road quiet, and my mind clear. By the time I woke up the next morning, I felt like I could move mountains.

When we looked at the map in Zürich, there didn't appear to be any place to buy food until we reached Brig, so we stocked up on food supplies there. We got all the staples and even splurged on things like apples and oranges. If we could reach Brig in two days, we'd be in good shape. If it took us any longer? Well, that'd be another story. So, our goal for the day was to pass the summit and begin our descent down into the valley that lay between the two major passes of the mountain range.

Knowing that our ride would be increasingly difficult and slow, we loaded up on bread, fruit, and water. Then we divided up the remaining food between the boys and Lindsey and me so that we'd all have some food on our journey.

Before taking off that morning, Lindsey said to the boys, "I know you're stronger than Laura and me, but try not to get too far ahead."

"I'll tell you what," said Matt. "When we get tired, we'll wait for you."

"Okay," said Lindsey. "And Laura, could you not get too far ahead of me?"

I looked ahead. I couldn't see the forest through the trees, and I definitely couldn't see the mountains through the forest. "I don't think I'll be going a whole lot faster than you today. It looks like we'll be climbing about seven thousand feet. So, I won't be breaking any speed records."

When we got back up to the main road, Matt and Marc sprinted ahead and were soon out of sight. Meanwhile, I chose to ride closer to Lindsey. Within an hour, we started to feel the incline of the road, noticing the trees becoming sparse and the snow on the peaks more pronounced.

A little later in the morning, other cyclists began passing us in groups. They were all men, wearing high-tech riding gear and going faster than I ever could. As more groups blew past us, I felt increasingly ill-equipped for the challenge. At one point, I stopped to have a drink of water and take a break. Lindsey pulled up and said, "Man, where do you think all these guys came from?"

At that moment, an older Swiss man came riding up behind us, stopped, and said, "You must be Americans."

"Yeah, we are," said Lindsey. "How did you know?"

"Only American women do this ride."

I pointed at some passing cyclists and asked, "Where are all these riders coming from?"

"Zürich," he said. "They ride to the top and then back down in one day. They are crazy. Wait until you see them coming down the mountain at speed."

I asked, "They go from Zürich to the top and back down all in one day?"

"Yes," he replied. "It's a training run for serious bikers."

I shook my head. We were clearly not serious bikers. But on the other hand, we were packing all our shit, and those riders had nothing but their light-frame bikes and skin-tight outfits. "We'll be lucky to make it over to Brig in three days."

He took a drink of water and asked, "Would it be okay if I biked with you? I'm only going halfway up the mountain."

Lindsey and I looked at each other, shrugged, and then Lindsey said, "Sure. We're not in a hurry."

He told us his name was Floyd and that he just enjoyed getting out and riding. Lindsey and I introduced ourselves and explained that our brothers were riding ahead of us. For the next few hours, we rode together and chatted about Switzerland, and where we planned on going next.

When we came to a chalet along the side of the road, Floyd said, "This is where I'm turning around. Can I buy you two sporting American Fräuleins a drink?"

There it was, "American Fräuleins" again. Lindsey smiled. "Sure, why not."

So, we all parked our bikes, walked over to the chalet, and sat at a little round table on the deck of the restaurant. When our drinks came, Floyd toasted us, "To the American Fräuleins." Soon after we finished our drinks, Floyd headed back down the mountain while we continued pushing on towards the top.

As we started climbing again, Lindsey said, "That was kind of nice."

"Yeah. It's too bad Matt and Marc weren't with us, but it was also nice that it was just the two of us."

Lindsey imitated Floyd's accent, "The sporting American Fräuleins?"

I laughed, "Yeah, I guess so. I liked the way Floyd said 'American Fräulein' much better than the cop did back in Baden-Baden."

As the day grew late, the road became steeper, and eventually we were on switchbacks. It was so steep at times that Lindsey and I had to dismount and push our bikes. It seemed that every time we'd have to push, a pack of cyclists would zoom past us going downhill. I thought, *Damn, we haven't even gotten to the top and they're already on their way home.*

As we continued climbing, I noticed little waterfalls from melting snow on the side of the mountain. When we ran out of water, we used the waterfalls to fill up our bottles. At the time I didn't think too much of the snow melt and just felt grateful for the water.

Just when I'd had enough, I heard Matt's voice. He and Marc were sitting up on the side of the hill on a high wall. He waved. "Hey, we're up here! It's a campground up here. There's a path just ahead. Follow it and join us!"

Lindsey and I scampered up the hill and were surprised to see a number of tents dotting the mountainside. A free-flowing stream ran through the middle of the campsite. There were patches of snow, but also exposed grassy areas. Marc said, "I think we should camp up here. It's like being on top of the world."

Lindsey squinted. "This is a brilliant spot. Let's just find a nice, dry, grassy area and put the tent up. Then let's go exploring a bit."

Within minutes, we had our four-person, skimpy tent up on top of our Gore-Tex bags. We also had our sleeping bags rolled out, and panniers thrown inside. With all our work done, Lindsey grabbed the camera, and the four of us went walking around the mountainside, taking in the amazing view. The fact that we had a 360-degree vista should have been an indicator that we were very near the summit, but it didn't really dawn on us until later.

While we were traipsing around, Lindsey suggested that we take a picture of us spinning around in circles like Julie Andrews in *The Sound of Music*. Soon Matt, Marc, and I were spinning and singing "The Hills Are Alive." It was goofy, but how many times do you find yourself on top of the Alps?

Before long, the sun was setting, and that's when we realized just how high up we were. That nice flowing stream that ran through the campsite? Within minutes it was frozen solid, and what appeared to be a unique opportunity now didn't seem like such a good idea. We ran back to our tent, climbed in, put on our long pants and long shirts, and crawled into our bags. A few hours later we were all still freezing, and Marc said, "I think we're going to have to zip our bags together so we can stay warm. We need to share our body heat."

"Start zipping," I said, teeth chattering, and jumped out of my bag. Matt and Marc hooked the bags together and we all crawled back in and tried to get warm. It didn't work so great, but at least we didn't freeze to death.

Early the next morning, I heard Lindsey unzip the tent and crawl out. I thought, *What the hell is she doing?* But I had no desire to go find out. Instead, I fell fast asleep.

Miraculously, the tent heated up as the sun rose. Our little freezer tent became warm and toasty. Then Lindsey popped her head in the tent and said, "Get up. I want to get going."

I grumbled, "I don't care. I want to get warm. Go away."

Matt and Marc pretended not to hear her and feigned sleep. When Lindsey zipped the tent back up, Matt said, "I'm not getting out of this tent until I can feel my fingers and toes again."

Marc added, "I really thought we would freeze to death last night."

"How close to the top do you think we are?" I asked.

"No more than five miles would be my guess," said Marc. "The ride to Brig should be fast. It's all downhill."

"So, no rush then," I said.

A few minutes later, from outside the tent, Lindsey barked, "If you guys don't get up, I am just going to take down the tent with you all in it. *I* want to get going."

"Why?" I asked.

"Because," she said. "We don't know how much farther we have to go to reach the summit."

I thought, *Give it a rest. We can't be all that far from the top.* But just to shut her up I got up and rolled up my bag. As I poked my head out, I was blinded by the glare of the sun reflecting off of the snow. Once I could see again, I said to Matt and Marc, "You guys will want to see this." It was like standing on top of the world.

Matt and Marc emerged from the tent and the four of us stood there for a few minutes just blinking and taking it all in. Marc said, "Speed bumps," and we all started laughing.

It didn't take us long to figure out our altitude. As we rounded the second curve, we passed the summit sign. That night we'd slept at 10,000 feet. No wonder we were freezing our asses off!

The best part was the rest of our ride to Brig was all downhill. The grade was so steep I was scared to death most of the way. As I rode my brakes down the mountain, the fresh smell of pine trees blended with the smell of the burning rubber from my brake pads.

When the road became less winding, I began to relax and enjoy the ride. I was struck by the similarities between Switzerland and the Cascades—both have forests of fir, spruce, and hemlock on one side and pine trees on the other. Both have wet, lush forests and arid regions. I was thousands of miles away from home, but the scent in the air brought me back to Oregon.

Within two hours, we were rolling into the town of Brig in search of a grocery store. And in Brig, the discovery of Aldi grocery stores changed our trip dramatically. Not only was the food significantly cheaper there than at other grocery stores, but we also happened upon Kuchen Cake and Coco Trunk—also known as chocolate cake and Yoo-hoo. These may seem like simple things, but after weeks of eating mostly bread and cheese, they were luxuries.

We scarfed our food and then sought out a campground. We needed to shower and find someplace to wash our clothes. We also needed to figure out where we were going from Brig.

Just south of town, we found a campground, where we tidied up and plotted the rest of our course through Switzerland. By the looks of things, it would be feasible to reach Italy the next day.

"I can't believe it," said Matt. "We'll have crossed the Alps and entered Italy all in a few days' time."

"Italy," Marc said. "Now *that's* a country that has everything. I want to spend as much time there as we can."

"Well, right now it's July sixth," said Lindsey. "I think we should be able to spend more than three weeks there, which should be enough to see what we want to see."

I thought, *Three weeks in Italy in July! Three weeks of sun, and hopefully swimming in the Mediterranean Sea. Perfect!*

My excitement was shattered later that night when I got a stomach bug and spent the evening throwing up Kuchen Cake and Coco Trunk. When morning came, I said, "I don't think I can cycle."

Lindsey wasn't having any of it. "You made Marc bike with a hangover. Get over it. We're going."

I groaned, "This isn't a hangover. I've been puking all night long."

"We're not waiting another day," said Lindsey. "Get going."

I was pissed but didn't see what choice I had, so I loaded up my bike and headed out for the second pass over the Alps. About two hours into the ride I said to Lindsey, "Screw this. I'm hitching a ride. I'll meet you at the top."

"You're a fucking baby, Laura. Do what you want."

"Don't worry, I will!" I got off my bike and began hitchhiking. Soon a family in a minivan pulled over to see what I needed. I asked if they'd take me to the top of the summit, they said they would, and I threw my bike in the back. As I climbed into their van I said to Lindsey, "I'll see you at the top."

She shouted, "Just remember, *I* cycled both passes and *you* didn't."

As I shut the car door, I said, "Just remember—I. Don't. Care."

Forty minutes later, my ride dropped me off at the summit, where there was a rest area, and I waited for the others to catch up. When Matt and Marc arrived, they asked how I was feeling and I said, "Much better, thanks."

The first thing Lindsey said when she reached us was, "At least I can say I biked all of the Alps."

I couldn't figure out why she kept pushing the subject and muttered, "Not everything is a contest, Lindsey, just stop."

Matt asked me if I felt well enough to ride again, and I said, "Since it's downhill I think I'll be okay."

Lindsey started to say something, and I looked over at her with exasperation. "Lindsey, you win. You made it to the top and I didn't. Can you drop it now?"

That seemed to shut her up, and Marc said, "I think we should get into Italy and then decide how much farther we can go."

"How far from here to the border?" I asked.

Marc looked at the map. "From here to the border, about forty-five minutes max."

I said, "Really? We're that close?"

"Really!" he replied.

"I can do it. Let's go," I said.

As we descended the Simplon Pass towards the Italian border, it became increasingly obvious that we were entering terrain that was foreign to us. Up until this point we'd been cycling within the same latitude as the Pacific Northwest, with landscapes similar to Oregon's. That day, as we cruised south, the air became humid, and the landscape almost tropical.

The ride was all downhill, and the road ran along the Diveria River, with waterfalls flowing down the side of the hill and the road cutting through numerous tunnels. By the time we crossed over into Italy at Iselle, I felt transformed. The days being lost in Holland, the dreary mountains in Germany, the snafu with the police, and the struggle to cross the Alps now all seemed worth it.

The four of us met up at the border crossing, where we got our passports stamped and changed our Swiss money into Italian lire. We also decided to end our day in the town of Domodossola. Our hope was that we'd find either a farmhouse or a campground near the city to spend the night. But we needed to get some food and drinks first, and Lindsey told Matt and Marc to wait for us at the city limits.

In what felt like no time, we were in Domodossola, where we went into a small convenience store to buy some sodas. The owner of the store asked us where we were headed and Marc said, "We're stopping here for the night. Do you know where there's a campground nearby?"

The guy said, "Hey, you can camp out back if you want. I have a bit of space back there that you can pitch your tent on. Just one question. Who are you supporting in the American presidential election?"

It was 1988, Reagan's two terms were up, and it appeared as if Michael Dukakis and George H.W. Bush would be vying for the presidency. It was an awkward question, and we had a 50/50 chance of getting it right. Lindsey looked at us and then said, "We're Democrats. So, whoever gets the Democratic nomination."

The shop owner smiled. "Good answer. You can pitch your tent out back."

"Thanks," Lindsey said, and we pushed our bikes behind his store to find a nice shady patch of grass and a small table with chairs.

As we were pitching the tent, Marc said to me, "That was strange. He was the first person to ask us about politics."

"I'm just glad you didn't steal anything from his store," I said.

"I thought about it," he grinned, glancing back at the store. "And then he offered us a place to sleep."

"Marc, you didn't learn anything from Matt?" I asked.

"Of course I learned something from Matt. You don't hang out around the candy. If you're going to steal something, make it cheese and meat. No one expects a kid to steal cheese and meat."

I handed him a tent peg. "How about you don't steal anything?"

"Actually," he said, "I haven't taken anything since Matt got caught."

"Let's continue that trend, okay?"

That night in the tent, as we wrote in our journal, Marc exclaimed, "Dudes, we're in Italy!"

It was just so ridiculous that we'd made it over the mountains and were actually in a place that we really wanted to be. As the night wore on, we talked about where we wanted to go next. The general consensus was we really wanted to see Florence and Rome.

We'd not purchased a map yet and had no idea how to reach our destinations. But the thrill of reaching the other side of the Alps filled us with optimism, and at one point Matt said, "I just feel like ANYTHING'S possible."

I felt the same way and struggled to fall asleep. I lay awake, listening to the night noises, long after my siblings drifted off. Left alone with my thoughts, I began to realize how lucky I was to be traveling with Matt, Marc, and even Lindsey. They were the only people I knew who were crazy enough to take this trip.

With Lindsey's bizarre notions about our father and the whole Heart Association nonsense, I'd been a little worried that she'd talk about Dad a lot. But that hadn't been the case. No one talked about Dad *or* Mom. We were so busy enjoying each day that we weren't thinking about the past. We were learning how to get along with one another, and, in the process, I was discovering that at least these three siblings were pretty great people. A good thing—because things were about to get crazy.

Chapter 20

MY ITALIAN RENAISSANCE

Before we left Domodossola, Lindsey and I went into the store to buy some food and a map. While we were at the counter, the owner, a small man with a moustache, asked us where we were headed, and Lindsey told him we wanted to see Florence and Rome.

With disgust in his voice, he said, "Everyone wants to see Firenze and Roma and Venice. That's not Italy. You are up here in the north; you need to see the lake."

"What lake?" I asked.

"What lake?" he repeated in mock indignation. "Let me see your map."

We unfolded the map and laid it on the counter. He pointed out Domodossola and then placed his finger slightly southeast on what appeared to be a series of lakes. "Here. You need to go here. This is Lake Como. It is the most beautiful area of Italy. Go there first and you won't be disappointed."

Lindsey looked down at the map. "I guess we can go there and then head south through Milan."

"Yes, now you're talking. That is a beautiful region. Go that way. Experience Italy. Don't just see the tourist places."

I looked over to Lindsey. "We can take all the time we want in Italy. I think we should do it."

The shop owner smiled. "You must do it. Now go."

So, we folded up the map, found Matt and Marc, and told them we were going to Lake Como because the shop owner said so.

"Which way do we go?" asked Matt.

Lindsey pointed southeast. "We go east. It looks like it'll take all day to get there, but the guy said it was beautiful."

"Well, if the guy said so, we might as well check it out," said Marc.

It took us seven hours to reach Lake Como. Seven hours of cycling in and out of little villages and across rolling hills with a view of the Italian Alps to our north. By the time we reached our destination, I realized a couple of things. First, after climbing the Alps, cycling had become much easier. Second, I was very glad we'd taken the shopkeeper's advice. He was right— the area was like nothing I'd ever seen in my life. The Alps encircled the lake, and small villages with gorgeous parks overflowing with flowers dotted the shores. I felt like I was cycling through an impressionist painting.

We didn't know where to camp that night and began riding around the lake looking for a campground. We didn't have to go very far before we came across one outside the small town of Lenno. When we went into the office to pay for a campsite, we were pleased to discover that the price was a fraction of what it had been in Germany and Switzerland. Before paying, Lindsey turned to us and asked, "Should we stay here more than one night?"

I looked over at my brothers and shrugged. "We're not in a rush. We can take all the time we want. I think we should stay a couple of nights and enjoy ourselves." Matt and Marc agreed, and we ended up spending three restful, glorious days camping on the lake.

During that time, the boys met a couple of guys who were about their age. They were from around Bologna and were camping with their families. Over time, we all began to hang out together, playing cards and talking about movies, music, and our countries.

By the time we left Lake Como, I'd fallen in love with Italy. The weather was perfect, the people were friendly, the food delicious, and best of all, it was affordable.

The only aspect of Italy I didn't like was its drivers. They drove fast on what seemed to be invented lanes. We'd been cycling for weeks along back roads with very little traffic, and our next destination was Milan, which worried me. We'd have to navigate a huge city and dodge crazy drivers. I soon discovered that I was okay with the navigation part, but not very good at dodging cars.

The first part of our ride from Lake Como to Milan went smoothly since the road wound through countryside. As we passed through the villages, each one grew larger and they seemed to get closer together. By the time we reached the outskirts of Milan, the traffic was insane. We chose to ride together and were trying to cycle on the shoulder of the road. However, the drivers kept turning the shoulder into another lane. Towards the end of the day, one determined driver tried to squeeze between me and another car and bumped my pannier, which sent me skidding into a ditch.

When the driver realized what had happened, he pulled his car over and jumped out. The guy was a middle-aged doctor and wanted to make sure I was okay. Initially, I was more worried about my bike than I was about my body. It wasn't until I got my bearings that it dawned on me that I had been hit and needed to sit down.

The driver led me away from traffic and began checking my legs and arms. He apologized for hitting me and then chastised me for not wearing a helmet. I was just beginning to tell him that I don't like bicycle helmets when Lindsey arrived.

I told the driver she was my sister and I'd be okay. He told us that we probably needed to find a place to stop for the night and try to get out of the city after the morning rush hour. Then he got back in his car and drove off.

Lindsey asked me what had happened, and I said, "I really don't know. I was going along and the next thing I knew I was on the ground. I think he bumped me."

"I think the guy's right, we need to find a place for the night. Matt and Marc said they'd wait for us at the first exit into the city. They'd better have stopped."

I was more rattled than injured. I got back on my bike and rode the rest of the way, as far away from the cars as I could. As the shock wore off, I began to feel a bit battered. By the time we found a campground for the night, I was pretty shaken up and had a huge desire to talk to my mom. I had been hit by a car and thrown from my bike, and I just wanted to hear a reassuring word. So, after we set up camp, Lindsey and I went to the campground office to see if we could use their phone to make a collect call home.

The campground manager, a guy named Julio, was short and dark with a wiry build. He took us to his office to use the phone. When he was leaving, he said, "When you're done, just come back out here. I want to talk to you guys."

I should have known better about talking to Mom. She'd never been a very compassionate parent, so I don't know why I thought she'd be a comfort that day. I just felt so vulnerable and hoped she'd be different.

When I told Mom what had happened, she said, "Well, you're all right. Do me a favor, don't call home collect every time you have an accident. These phone calls cost a lot of money."

I was hurt but resigned to the fact that she would never be the parent I needed. "I know they do. I hope you're doing okay. We'll speak to you later maybe." I hung up the phone.

As I walked out of the office, Lindsey asked, "What did she say?"

"Not to call her every time I fall off my bike."

Lindsey shook her head. "Well, that sucks," she said, and we walked out of the office to speak to Julio.

When he saw us, he said, "Now, you guys look like you've had a rough day. How about you and your brothers join me in my cabin for a spaghetti dinner? We'll have some wine, and some conversation. My groundskeeper, Tony, is going to be there too."

"Where's your cabin?" asked Lindsey.

He pointed behind him. "Right behind this building. Come around ten o'clock. Just knock."

We said we'd see him then and went back to the campsite to tell Matt and Marc we'd been invited to dinner. Between the office and our tent, I came to the realization that I needed to quit expecting my mother to be the mom I wanted her to be. The impact of this reality hurt worse than being hit by a car.

Spending the evening with Julio and Tony was just what I needed to boost my spirits. Julio was Persian and went to great lengths to clarify that he was *not* Iranian. His family had fled Iran in the '70s during the revolution. Tony was from Egypt and had left after the Yom Kippur War in '73. They were both refugees of sorts, and I enjoyed hearing their stories about how they came to live in Milan.

But they were more interested in hearing about our travels. Julio turned to Marc and said, "You're Italian. Why aren't you translating for them?"

Marc replied, "I'm their brother. I'm not Italian."

Julio shook his head in surprise. "Man, you look Italian. I bet you get that a lot."

Then Matt told them about how Marc had been run off the road in West Virginia just because he looked Mexican.

Tony pointed at Marc. "That one would blend in here very well."

Later on, the topic of Matt's arrest in Baden-Baden came up and Tony said to Matt, "You should never shoplift. You will get caught every time."

I thought he was just telling Matt not to steal, but then he turned to Marc and said, "Now that one. He'll get away with it every time because he's quiet and blends in."

I thought, *Oh great, that's like giving Marc permission to be a thief*, and quickly said, "I don't think he needs any encouragement."

Marc said, "I've promised to quit stealing," and then, when he thought no one was looking, I saw him give Tony a wink.

It was close to one o'clock in the morning before we returned to our tent. By the time I crawled into my sleeping bag, I'd put the car bump and Mom out of my mind. With a belly full of home-cooked spaghetti, and an evening full of laughter, I was ready to get back on the road.

We'd set a course from Milan that ran through Parma to Bologna and then on to Florence. Each day's ride was seventy-five miles of beautiful scenery as the road cut through plains and wound around villages. In Parma, we camped at a campground outside of the city, where we were introduced to *bocce*. We spent the late afternoon getting our butts kicked by other campers.

The following day in Bologna, we discovered a free campground within their city park where Lindsey and I spent the afternoon sitting in the shade, listening to music, and resting. Matt and Marc found a group of guys playing basketball and joined in. Everything was going smoothly—almost too smoothly.

We had enough money to purchase good food, the camping was inexpensive, the cycling was easy, and we were meeting interesting people. Matt and Marc seemed to be keeping their hands to themselves in grocery stores, and we were all getting along.

Actually, everything was perfect, even the three days we spent in Florence. We found a reasonably priced campground just a few miles outside of the city. This one had a place where we could lock up our bikes, and we walked into town each day. We spent our time touring the Uffizi Museum, seeing the statue of David, visiting cathedrals, and eating gelato. It was wonderful—until it all went to hell.

The day we left Florence, we got off to a late start. Our goal for the day had been to reach the city of Livorno on the Mediterranean Sea. But by five o'clock in the afternoon, it was obvious we wouldn't make it before dark. We stopped in the town of Cascina to have a bite to eat and take a look at the map. We couldn't see any markings for a campground and decided to look for a farmhouse instead.

About a mile out of the city, we came across a gorgeous farm that sat back from the road. "I think this is a good spot," said Matt. "Should I go see if they'll let us pitch our tent?"

"Go do your thing, Matt," said Lindsey. "We'll be right behind you."

The four of us rode up their drive, where we found four older women sitting on kitchen chairs, cutting vegetables and talking to each other. Matt said, "Excuse me. Do any of you speak English?"

They all said "No," but one shouted out, "Marsha!" A few seconds later a teenage girl came around the corner and said something to the women. The woman who had called her said something, and then the girl, in English, asked, "Can I help you?"

"Um, yeah," said Matt. "We were just wondering if we could pitch our tent on your property?"

Marsha spoke to the women, the women nodded their heads, and then Marsha said, "They said that won't be a problem. I'll show you where you should pitch your tent. Follow me."

Marsha led us to the back of the farmhouse, where there was a huge garden, a vineyard, and a barn. I said, "This place is amazing."

Marsha pointed out, "There are five homes here. My parents, my aunts and uncles, and my cousins all live here. My dad is a dentist, and my uncles are engineers, but the family farms all of this."

Marsha hung out with us while we set up our camp. She said she was studying English and asked if she could practice it with us.

"You can hang out as long as you want," said Lindsey. "We don't really have anything to do."

During our visit with Marsha, we discovered that where we were staying was more than a family farm—it was a commune, and her family members were all communists. This was a new one for me. My only concept of communism was China and the USSR, so I asked, "Like Russia?"

"No, we are not like Russia. That is totalitarianism. My parents can explain it better." And that night when her family invited us to dinner, her father tried to explain the difference. In the end, I gathered there must be a huge difference but couldn't really grasp the concept.

Before we left to go back to our tent, they served us some chocolate and a small espresso. The following morning, Marsha's mother brought us fresh bread, jam, and warm milk before we departed. I don't know what kind of communists they were; I just gathered they were the generous kind.

That morning we headed for Cecina, where we planned on purchasing some supplies before we continued south towards Grosseto. As we left the commune, Lindsey told Matt and Marc to wait for us at the first entrance to the town. Matt and Marc stayed with us for a bit and then sped off into the distance. Little did we know that we wouldn't see Matt again for two days.

Only Marc was waiting for me at the first entrance into Cecina. When I reached him, I asked, "Where's Matt?"

Marc waved his hand around. "I don't know. He got way ahead of me and I thought he'd be here. When he wasn't here, I went to the next exit and he wasn't there either. There're only two entrances, so I rode through town looking for him and didn't see him."

"He can't have just disappeared. He has to be somewhere nearby."

Soon Lindsey caught up with us and blew a gasket when we told her Matt was missing. "That fucking moron!" she said. "How hard is it to just stop? Where do you think he went?"

In order to distract her, I suggested, "I think we should go into the center and see if he's waiting there." But he wasn't there either.

We spent the next few hours looking for Matt. The three of us split up and went in different directions, confident that one of us would find him. When we met back up later in the town center, still without Matt, we decided to go to the police station and report him missing.

We went over to the station, an ancient three-story stone building, and tried to explain our situation. The officer at the front desk found someone who spoke English to help. We told the English-speaking officer the problem, and he took down Matt's description. We told him Matt was tall and blond, wearing shorts and a New York Yankees shirt. With the description in hand, he told us to go to a campground just outside of town and that he would contact us there once they found Matt.

By this time, it was seven o'clock in the evening and we hadn't eaten anything since we'd left the commune. We went into a small grocery store to buy some food. When the three of us walked into the store, the clerk pointed at Marc's New York Yankees ball cap and in perfect English said, "That's the second time I've seen a New York thing today."

We stopped dead in our tracks and Marc asked, "When was the first time?"

The guy said, "A kid came in here looking for his brother and two sisters earlier. Hey, that's you guys, isn't it?"

Lindsey slapped the counter. "What a fucking idiot. Why couldn't he have just stayed in one place? We would have found him."

"Look at it this way," I said. "We know he's all right."

"He won't be once I wring his fucking neck," said Marc.

It was dark by the time we reached the campground. Marc and I put up the tent while Lindsey kicked her bike, our bags, rocks, and anything else that wasn't screwed to the ground. Each kick came with an expletive. I did my best to ignore her, but damn, it was hard.

No one slept well that night. I kept wondering where Matt was and if he was okay. I had a feeling he was fine, but then I'd begin to wonder if he'd been hit or was lying in a ditch somewhere. I had flashbacks to the night Mom decided to scatter Dad's ashes without telling anyone. Just thinking about that feeling of limbo, caught between fear and hope, brings about an anxiety attack to this day.

The next day, we tried to keep ourselves occupied. The three of us played gin rummy, and when we tired of that, I wrote in our journal. About every twenty minutes, Lindsey would kick and throw things. There was no talking to her, and at one point, I journaled about just how annoying I found her behavior.

I left the journal where she could see it, and when she read it, she blew up at me. In response I said, "You're a fucking embarrassment, Lindsey. Your tantrums are not helping. Personally, I don't blame Matt for taking off just to get a break from you!"

Lindsey got up in my face. "I'm sick of you and the huge chip on your shoulder. Get a life."

Just when I was ready to say something snide back, I heard my name called over the campground intercom. Hearing my name stopped the both of us. "Maybe they've found him," I said, and ran to the office.

In the office, I was handed the phone. I thought it would be a policeman on the other end, but it was Mom. In a very whiny voice, she said, "Laura, the Consulate called me. Where is your brother?"

I had to think quick, and came up with, "Um, he can't come to the phone right now, Mom."

With a more exaggerated whine, she said, "I know he's lost. Once he's found I think you guys need to come home."

"Nope," I snapped back. "Not gonna happen, Mom. I'm sure Matt's fine. I'll call you when we know something," and then before she could say anything else, I hung up. On my way back to our campsite, I wondered why Mom asked to speak to me and not Lindsey. Did she think I'd cave and say, "No, you're right, Mom, we should come home"? Because if that was the case, she didn't know me very well at all.

Back at the campsite, I told Marc and Lindsey that the Consulate had informed Mom that Matt was missing and that she thought we should come home.

"No way!" said Marc. "Matt's fine. He's just an idiot."

"Do you really believe that, or are you just saying that to make yourself feel better?" I asked.

"A little of both. I just hope he tries to steal a candy bar and gets caught. I think that's our best hope of finding him right now."

At about ten o'clock that night, I was called back to the campground office for a phone call. Thinking it was Mom again, I braced myself. But this time it was the police officer, and he told me Matt had been found sixty miles to the south in Grosseto. The police put him on a bus to Florence, and then he'd be put on a train to Livorno. I don't know why they didn't just send him directly to us, but I wasn't in a position to ask.

I was filled with relief, but also frustration. He was safe and sound, but I wanted to kill him. Back at the campsite, I told Marc and Lindsey that Matt was in Grosseto, and that he'd be in Livorno the following day.

"I told you he was okay," said Marc.

I wondered if Marc still wanted to *wring his neck*. I knew how I felt. I could've killed him.

The next morning, Marc, Lindsey, and I rode to Livorno to meet up with Matt at the train station. His train was due to arrive at one in the afternoon. We reached Livorno before noon, which gave us some time to walk around the city center and make some necessary purchases. I needed to replenish my tire kit and found a bicycle shop to load up on supplies.

The bicycle shop owner was an older gentleman who asked us about our journey. We told him what had happened with Matt, which he thought was kind of funny. I had yet to find the humor in Matt's misadventure.

The shop owner asked, "Where are you going to next?"

"We plan on going south to Rome," said Lindsey. "We're just waiting for Matt's train and then we're taking off."

He sighed, "That'll be a beautiful ride. I envy you guys."

We bought our supplies and then went back to the train station, where we met Matt as he got off the train. Just seconds before he arrived, I was ready to lay into him. But once I actually saw him, any thoughts of retribution for days of worry vanished. He sheepishly approached us and said, "I blew it. I am so sorry."

We're not a demonstrative family and hugging isn't really our thing, but that day was different. We all hugged, and then Marc said, "You're still a fucking idiot. Why didn't you just stay in Cecina?"

"I waited around forever, and then I thought you must've continued on," said Matt.

While he was talking, the train departed, and I realized Matt didn't have his bike. "Matt, where's your bike?"

"Oh, I had to leave it at the Consulate in Florence. Some guy is bringing it to Livorno on Tuesday."

It was Friday afternoon, which meant that Matt would be without his bike for four days, and we wouldn't be able to travel. Lindsey began kicking things again, saying, "I can't believe this! What are we supposed to do now?"

Marc pointed at a train. "Let's take the train to Rome and hang out there until we need to be back here."

"What?" said Lindsey. "And take our bikes on the train?"

"How about we ask the guy at the bicycle shop if he'll hold our bikes for us?" said Marc. "He seemed like a nice guy. It's worth a shot."

Lindsey calmed down. "I guess we could ask. I mean, it wouldn't hurt."

The four of us took our bikes and gear back to the bicycle shop, where the owner said he would be happy to watch our stuff for us and that it would be there when we returned on Tuesday.

As we walked to the train station, Marc said to me, "I hope our stuff's still there when we get back."

I looked back at the shop. "I think he's a decent guy, Marc. Our stuff will be there."

Looking back at the shop too, he said, "Let's hope so."

All we took with us to Rome was a pannier filled with a change of clothes for each of us, our passports, cash, camera, and our boombox. We didn't know what we'd do once we reached the Eternal City. Just the idea of four free days in Rome was compelling enough for us. We couldn't just sit around Livorno waiting for Matt's bike to arrive.

The train to Rome left at eight o'clock that night and arrived close to midnight. During the journey, we traveled with a number of Eurorail tourists in our compartment. They were all guys from England who let us know there wasn't a campground near Rome, and not many youth hostels either.

I asked one of the guys where they were staying, and he said, "Tonight we're just staying outside the train station. Then tomorrow we're going to a cheap hotel."

I asked, "Hey, would it be okay if we hung out with you guys tonight? We don't know where we're going either."

"Sure," he said. "That shouldn't be a problem. There's safety in numbers."

When we pulled into the station in Rome, all of us grabbed our stuff and headed for the exit. Once outside, we found other backpackers who were forced to spend the night there. They were all lined up against the wall in a dirty little courtyard.

The first thing that struck me about Rome, aside from the heat, was the stink. The whole area smelled like perspiration and urine. It was gross, and the idea of sleeping in those conditions wasn't very appealing.

Our little ragtag group found a spot in the dirty square and we put our stuff down, forming a circle. I took in our surroundings. The area was busy with backpackers and tourists. There were also actual gypsies, who fascinated me, weaving around the tourists. I spent most of the evening watching them work the area.

From what I could gather, they worked in groups. A woman would carry her small child who feigned sickness, and she would ask people for money. Most people brushed her off and continued walking. But while she was talking, another child would rifle the tourist's pockets. At which point a police officer would throw them out of the station. Once out of the station, the young child, who was supposed to be sick, would begin running around the square. The whole process was amazing to watch.

No one slept well that night. Between the noise, heat, and stink, it was hard to get comfortable. By the time the sun rose up in the east, the four of us were ready to get away from the station and walk around the city. We had no idea where we were going or what we would find. We didn't have a map of the city, so we just walked around aimlessly.

The Coliseum rose up before us as we walked down the street. The sun shone behind it, so we stopped to take in the surreal sight. It was hard to believe we were actually standing in front of one of the most famous buildings in the world. I took a picture of Lindsey and the boys with it in the background. Then we walked around the building and took a tour.

By midday, we were all exhausted. We'd not really slept in over thirty-six hours and needed to find a place to rest. Eventually, we found a park with a shady spot under a tree and slept for a few hours.

When we awoke, Matt said, "The train station reeks. Do we have to sleep there again tonight?"

Lindsey wrinkled her nose. "I don't think we have an option. We don't have any money for a hotel room, and camping's out of the question."

"How much money do we have?" asked Marc.

Lindsey responded, "Let's put it this way. We'll have to hitchhike back to Livorno if we want to eat."

"I guess we should have thought about that before we came here," I said. "Do we have enough money to get food?"

"Just," said Lindsey. "I want to see the Vatican, and that's gonna cost us money. Then we'll see what we have left over."

"Why don't we just skip the Vatican and eat instead?" said Marc.

Lindsey looked at him as if he was crazy. "We can't skip the Vatican. What about the Sistine Chapel?"

"What about not starving?" countered Matt.

Lindsey insisted, "We're seeing the Vatican," and that seemed to be the end of the conversation.

I was kind of conflicted. I really wanted to see the Sistine Chapel, but damn, I was hungry. From the time Matt had gotten lost, we'd been living on bread, water, and cheese again. I could have devoured a pizza, but I really wanted to see the Vatican, too.

We spent another filthy night at the train station, but this time we slept better. However, we woke up to discover that our boombox had been stolen. I figured one of the gypsies had taken it while we were sleeping. Fortunately, they didn't get our passports, which were in a bag serving as my pillow that night.

Our plan for the day was to get something to eat, visit the Vatican, and then figure out how to get back to Livorno. On the way to the Vatican, we found a little shop, bought some yogurt, bread, jam, and water, and then found a little plaza to eat in. We were a smelly, dingy mess. We hadn't bathed in days, and the gray tinge of our clothes was permanent. As we sat and ate, we could hear the honking horns of Rome's legendary traffic.

Between bites of yogurt, Matt asked, "When and how should we try to get back to Livorno?"

"I think we should take the train out of the city and then hitchhike from there," I said.

"Why?" Lindsey asked. "Wouldn't it be easier to catch a ride here?"

"I don't think so," I replied. "I think we'll have better luck if we get on the right road going in the right direction."

We talked it over a little more, and then decided that my idea was probably the best option. When we were done with breakfast, we walked over to the Vatican, where we were informed that we weren't allowed to wear shorts inside the Sistine Chapel. Luckily, we'd packed a couple pairs of Levi's in our bag, but that meant only two of us could go at a time.

Lindsey and I went into a back alley and changed into the jeans. Before going in, Lindsey said to the boys, "Try to stick around here and don't get lost."

Lindsey and I climbed the stairs to Saint Peter's Basilica and walked into the rotunda. It was dark and cool inside, and we spent a few minutes checking out the stained-glass windows and statues. I was looking up in awe as I walked around a pillar and was greeted by pure beauty. Michelangelo's statue of Jesus lying across Mary's lap, the Pietà, was right in front of me. I literally gasped. It was so beautiful, and yet so painful.

At that precise moment, God gave me faith.

Seeing the masterpiece revealed to me more about Jesus, love, and compassion than all the worship services Maris had dragged me to in Brazil. In the image of a martyred Jesus, I saw all my pain. I saw a little girl being screamed at in a bathroom. A young child left alone in an old woman's house. A daughter being dehumanized. Young orphans in red tunics, and the slums of Rio. In a flash, I grasped the magnitude of Jesus's sacrifice. As I stood there, a sense of peace came over me and a small voice said, "Everything will be okay, Laura."

Lindsey pulled me away from the moment when she tapped me on my shoulder to tell me that the tour was about to begin. I looked over at her and said, "Have you ever seen anything quite so beautiful?"

Without really looking, she said, "Wait until you see the Sistine Chapel. Now *that* will be beautiful."

The chapel was pretty, but it didn't have the same impact as the Pietà, because nothing would. That moment in front of Michelangelo's statue began my faith journey. A journey of differentiating between feeling shame and being shamed. It's a journey that would lead me to Jesus, but at *that* time I was more worried about surviving the rest of our trip and couldn't fully grasp what had happened to me that day.

When we were done with our tour, we found Matt and Marc waiting for us and changed back into our shorts while they put on our Levi's. At the time we thought they'd gone on the tour too, but later that night they confessed the truth—they'd walked around the back of the Vatican, found a pizza place, and bought a few slices.

I understood why they did it. They were starving, and pizza outweighed culture at that point in their lives. I'm just glad that I chose to do the tour. My experience seeing the Pietà revealed to me what I would come to view as the true Jesus: a savior who embodied human suffering and pain. The Pietà changed my life forever. The seed of faith that was planted that day empowered me to live life to the fullest. I didn't realize that I'd still have to face the ghosts of the past; I just felt free to take every opportunity that presented itself. There was a little voice in my head urging me on.

That night, we took a train to a town just north of Rome and hitchhiked our way back to Livorno. It took us a day and a half to get there, but we made it with a day to spare before Matt's bicycle would arrive. We spent the night outside of town, sleeping under the stars near a Roman aqueduct. As we drifted off to sleep, I heard the voice again, this time even more clearly: *Everything's going to be okay.*

Chapter 21

AS YOU WISH

The following morning, we called the U.S. Consulate from Livorno to see when Matt's bike would be arriving. We were told that at ten o'clock, a member of their staff would meet us with the bike at the train station in Livorno. But collecting Matt's bike would only solve our transportation problem. The bigger problem was that we were broke. By that point, I think we had the equivalent of twenty dollars to our name, and it would be a week before Mom would wire our last six hundred dollars.

As we hung out at the train station waiting for Matt's bike, we discussed our options. Matt suggested calling Mom and asking her to send us the money early.

I asked, "Do you want to make that call? Because I sure don't. The last time I talked to her, I hung up on her."

Matt thought about it for a second. "You're right. She'll just tell us to come home."

"I think we should go back to the commune," said Marc. "They were really nice people, and if we explain what happened, they might let us stay there for a week."

Matt added, "We could offer to work there. I mean, we don't have to be beggars."

We talked about it some more, and by the time Matt's bicycle arrived, we all agreed that the commune was our best option. So, we headed back to Cascina.

It was late afternoon when we cycled up to the home of our communist friends. Nothing had really changed. The four older women were sitting in a circle on kitchen chairs, prepping dinner. When they saw us, they all laughed, and one of the ladies yelled, "Marsha!"

As Marsha came out of the house, she saw us and smiled. "Let me guess," she said. "You need a place to stay tonight?"

"Well, we need a little more than that," said Lindsey. "You won't believe what happened after we left here," and she proceeded to tell Marsha about our misadventures over the past week. When Lindsey was done talking, Marsha relayed the story to the women.

Marsha then asked, "How long do you need to stay?"

"Six days at the most," said Lindsey. "Our mom is sending money to the U.S. Consulate in Florence and then we'll be okay. We can give you guys the money we have to help pay for a site, or you can put us to work."

Marsha and the women talked some more, and when they were done talking Marsha said to us, "You guys can stay as long as you need. Plus, keep your money. You guys need it more than we do. Just go pitch your tent where you did last time and then I'll come and get you for dinner later."

Lindsey breathed a sigh of relief. "Really? Man, you guys just saved our lives! Thank you so much."

The women all laughed and said, "Partire."

I asked Marsha, "What are they saying?"

"They are telling you to go and set up your camp."

"Okay, then," I said. "I guess they're really okay with us staying."

The next six days felt like being at a retreat. Every day, one of the ladies would bring us a new bottle of wine from their vineyard. Throughout the day, different ladies fed us. One would bring us breakfast. Another would serve us spaghetti for lunch, and different families would host us for dinner. They even paid our fare to take the bus to the beach, where we'd spend the day with Marsha. The night before we left, they took us to the Italian Communist Party festival in town, where we danced and partied until one in the morning.

The morning we said our goodbyes, we wrote down their address and names in our journal. We asked them if there was anything they wanted from the States, and all the guys said Levi's. So, we wrote down their sizes and promised to send them a thank you package when we returned home—a promise that we kept. We sent them Levi's, Oregon State University sweatshirts, and jars of Oregon blackberry jam.

By the time we left for Florence, we felt refreshed and re-juvenated. Ironically, we owed it all to Matt. It was Matt who had found the farm in the first place. Plus, if Matt hadn't gotten lost, we wouldn't have gone back there. We would've missed out on one of the best parts of our trip thus far. So, I guess Matt's blunders did have their uses.

Our first stop in Florence was the Consulate to pick up our cash. All four of us went into the building, but Mom sent the money in my name, so I had to go back to an office and sign for it. While I was doing that, the others waited for me in the cool lobby.

When I came back out, Lindsey and the boys were talking to a young woman who appeared to be in distress. When I walked up to them, Lindsey said, "Hey, we need to help this girl out."

"Okay. Why?" I asked.

The woman said, "My name's Jennifer. I've been traveling around the world for the past year. Well, to make a long story short, I got really sick and passed out in the train station here. Three days later, I woke up in the hospital. I had to max out my credit card before I could be discharged. My mom's paying my bill, but I won't be able to use my card for a day and I don't have any cash."

"I told her she could camp with us tonight," said Lindsey.

"I think that's the least we can do after all the help we've gotten," I said.

"Oh, my God. Thank you," she said. "All I have is my back-pack. I won't take up much space."

"It'll be nice to have some company," I replied.

Outside of the Consulate, we were unlocking our bikes when we heard a window open and a man call out, "Which one of you is Matt?"

I looked up and saw three people looking out the window.

Matt stepped forward. "I am Matt."

The guy said, "We just wanted to meet the kid that had us looking all over the country for him. I have a few words of ad-vice. Stay. With. Your. Family!"

Matt gave a wry smile. "I'll try, but they're slow."

"Then bike slower," the guy said, laughing, and then he added, "Just be safe, you guys."

We said we'd do our best and then waved goodbye.

"What was that all about?" Jennifer asked.

On the way to the campground, we shared our story with her. By the time we reached our destination, she said, "I'm so glad you guys found me. I feel like you understand my situa-tion."

"Dude, you just got sick," I said. "Our issues are because of stupidity. Plus, after everything people have done for us during our trip, the least we can do is help someone out."

That night, Jennifer told us she'd made a small fortune in Silicon Valley and was taking time off to travel around the world. Listening to her talk made me realize that unpredict-able situations while traveling happened to everyone.

The next day, Jennifer was able to use her credit card again, and she took a train to Paris.

We had to stay in Florence another day because France required Americans to have a visa to enter the country, so we had to wait in line at the French Consulate to get our passports stamped.

Once our documents were in order, we took off for the Mediterranean Sea. By this time, we knew the area between Florence and the sea like the back of our hands. In what felt like no time, we were in Pisa. That night, we slept out in a field on the outskirts of the city, where we had a gorgeous view of the leaning tower. The four of us sat outside of our tent and watched the sun go down in the west. "This all feels really surreal," said Matt.

"What's amazing is that it's real," I said. "We are so damn lucky to be here."

Lying in our tent that night, we figured out the remainder of our trip. We had three weeks before our flight left Amsterdam. We decided to cycle along the Mediterranean past Cannes, turn north for Paris, and then on to Holland. It all sounded so simple.

If I could go back and relive one day, it would be the day before we entered France. We were cycling along the Mediterranean, on a road that hugged the cliffs above the sea. Between the view of the water and the beauty of the area, I felt like Cary Grant in *To Catch a Thief.*

Our first stop that morning was just east of Genoa in the town of Savona. We stopped to eat breakfast and decide how far we wanted to go that day. Lindsey said, "I think we should try to reach France and then enjoy the French Riviera while we can."

"I think that'll be difficult," said Marc. "It's about sixty miles from here—I think we should just see how far we can make it before it gets too late."

"We can cycle sixty miles in no time," replied Lindsey.

Lindsey was pretty adamant, and to mollify her, we said we'd give it our best shot. Once we finished eating, we continued west, hoping that we might cross into France by the end of the day. I'd resigned myself to the idea that I was in for a long day of riding. But two hours later, I found the boys waiting for me on the shoulder of the road outside of the seaside town of Andora.

I thought maybe one of them had a flat tire and asked if that was the case. Matt pointed to a path and said, "We saw some people going down this path with towels and coolers, so we went to check it out. There's an awesome swimming hole down there. People are jumping off a pedestrian bridge into this huge pool of water that looks like a reservoir."

"I don't care what Lindsey wants," said Marc. "I think we should hang out here today. I mean, how many times will we have a chance to do something like this?"

I totally agreed with them, and when Lindsey arrived, Matt and Marc led us down the path, where I learned that Matt's description of the area was spot on. There were about twenty people dotted around the swimming hole. They were swimming, jumping, sunbathing, and picnicking. In no time, we'd locked up our bikes and jumped off the bridge into the glistening water. As the four of us plunged into the water, I felt like

Butch Cassidy and the Sundance Kid. However, we weren't running from the Pinkertons; we were incredibly free. We spent the next few hours enjoying the swimming hole. It was pushing six in the evening before we got back on the road with no idea where to camp that night.

An hour later, Matt found us a place on the top of a hill between Sanremo and Monte Carlo. It was really just a pull-in along the side of the road, but there was a path that led down to a plateau, which was a perfect spot to camp.

It was so warm out that we didn't bother to pitch our tent, choosing to just roll out our bags and sleep on top of them. The night sky was clear, and even with the haze of city lights in the distance, the stars were incredible. Marc said, "I think today was the most fun I've had this whole trip. I can't believe we just found that place."

"Swimming in that place kind of made me miss home," said Matt. "I miss *our* swimming hole."

I thought, *I'd take today's find over a million trips to our swimming hole*, which was where Dad's ashes had been scattered. There were too many bad memories there, whereas today's adventure was all ours. It wasn't tainted by the past, and I wanted to keep it that way. To change the subject, I asked, "Aren't the stars amazing?"

"The whole day's been amazing," said Marc, and then the four of us drifted off to sleep.

Three days later, when we reached Cannes, the buoyancy we felt after swimming and sleeping under the stars had waned. The ride along the sea was beautiful, but we were hot and tired—so hot and tired that Matt was ready to go home. Unfortunately for him, we still had more than two weeks to go.

In Cannes, we found a campground that had a swimming pool, and we spent the afternoon lounging by its edge. At one point Matt said, "I know this'll sound really bad, but I kind of wish our bikes would get stolen, or maybe someone would get hurt so we could go home early."

I laughed and told Matt that, earlier in the day, I'd thought the same thing. We still had a long way to bike before reaching Amsterdam, and I was exhausted. Out of curiosity, I asked him, "So, who should get hurt?"

"I don't know," Matt said. "I don't want someone to get really hurt. Just maybe *one* of our bikes could get totaled. That would do the trick."

"Just as long as it's not me," I said.

"How about *no one* gets hurt?" said Lindsey. "We're almost done!"

We left Cannes early in the morning and headed towards the town of Fréjus. The plan was to meet in Fréjus, have a small lunch, and then turn north into the hills of Provence, hoping to find either a campground or a farm to spend the night.

I was tired of the traffic along the coastline and ready for a change of scenery. I was excited about riding along the Rhone River and working our way towards Paris. During the ride I was wondering what the rest of Provence looked like, and how many days it would take to reach the City of Lights. Then, from across the road, I heard someone shout, "Laura, stop!" It was Marc, and he was near a service station.

I stopped and yelled back, "What's wrong?"

"My pannier broke. Can you help me fix it?" he shouted.

"I'll be over in a second."

We'd just crested a hill, and to my left I could see a motorcycle approaching. There was nothing on my right. I figured that I had enough time to cross the road and began cycling towards Marc.

The next thing I remember is lying in the middle of the road looking up at the sky and Marc leaning over me saying, "Jesus. Laura, are you okay?"

I looked up at Marc and asked, "What happened?"

Before he could answer, a man leaned down and, in a French accent, said, "You've been hit. You're in shock, so just stay down." He said something in French to someone and then said, "An ambulance is coming. Let me check you out."

While he was checking my arms and legs, I could see Matt, Marc, and Lindsey standing nearby. I looked at the guy who was helping me and heard myself asking again, "What *happened*?"

The man answered, "A motorcyclist hit you while you were crossing the road."

I was bewildered. "How? He was a long way off."

He pointed behind him. "That guy. He tried to pass the other motorbike on the hill. There's no way you could've seen him. My friend is checking him out right now." He then said, "You have a hole in your leg that will need stitches, but I don't think you broke anything."

I looked down at my leg, which was bleeding profusely, and realized my shoes were missing. I'd been knocked right out of my shoes! I must've still been in shock because I didn't feel any pain.

The ambulance took me to the hospital, where I was stitched up and x-rayed. I had a few broken ribs and a lot of bruises and abrasions, but otherwise I was okay. When I was discharged, I found Lindsey and the boys in the waiting room. Matt was the first one to approach. "Damn. I didn't really want you to get hurt."

"You did a bit," I said. "But it's not your fault. I didn't see the guy."

Marc then told me exactly what happened. "You didn't see him because he passed on a hill. The first motorcyclist slowed down, but the guy behind him sped up to pass and didn't see you. When he hit you, you went flying straight up in the air. It was crazy."

Lindsey handed me my shoes and asked, "How do you feel?"

By this time my ribs had begun to hurt. "My ribs are killing me, and I feel shaken up. Kind of like I got hit by a motorcycle. Where's my bike?"

"Matt got his other wish too," Marc said. "Your bike's destroyed. We took all your stuff off of it, and then threw your bike away."

I looked at Matt. "You really did get your wish."

Lindsey took charge. "You need to take a taxi to a nearby campground. We'll meet you there later."

I stood there, all bandaged up. "Okay. I guess." I struggled to get my shoes on, so Matt helped me. Then the four of us went to find a taxi. The taxi driver told Lindsey and the boys where he was taking me and then we split up. A few minutes later, I was sitting alone at our campsite, waiting for the others. I was sore but felt very alive.

I'd been hit hard, but I was still going. Looking out over the sea, I came to the realization that the world is a really big place, that life is beautiful, and that it can be gone in an instant. I told myself that I needed to quit wasting my life pissed off about the past and embrace the future. That voice I heard in the Vatican had been true. I was okay, and I would continue to be okay.

When the others arrived, we sat around and talked about our options. Lindsey had called Mom from the hospital and told her what had happened. We still had two weeks left, and between the two of them, they'd decided to change our flights. Mom made the arrangements, and we'd be flying home in a week. In the meantime, we needed to figure out how to get back to Amsterdam.

Bicycling was out of the question for me, so later that night we decided to sell our bikes and gear to raise some money. Lindsey and the boys would find a bicycle shop to try to sell them while I stayed back at the campground. It was a good idea—except for the fact that Lindsey was doing the selling.

They left the next morning with about six hundred dollars' worth of equipment and came back with the equivalent of a hundred dollars. Marc said, "We tried to tell her it wasn't enough and to walk away from the shop, but before we knew what had happened, she agreed to the price."

Pissed, I turned towards Lindsey. "Jesus, Lindsey, did he throw in some magic beans too?"

Lindsey exclaimed, "He ripped me off!"

"Bullshit!" Matt shouted. "You didn't even try to get a better price. You didn't even think about going to a different bicycle shop. You took the first offer at the first place, and now we're screwed."

Lindsey snapped, "Next time you do the selling!"

"There won't be a next time! You moron!" shouted Matt. "Because we don't have anything to sell!" and then he stormed off in one direction while Lindsey stormed off in the other. With our bikes gone, we were left wondering what she was going to go kick.

I looked at Marc. "Was she really that bad?"

"It was pathetic. She just wouldn't listen to us."

"Do you know how much money we have?"

"I think we have a few hundred dollars. It should be enough to get by until we reach Amsterdam. It just depends on how we spend the next week."

When Lindsey returned, she asked if I felt well enough to hitchhike. I felt like crap and was shocked she would suggest it. "I really don't want to do that. My ribs are killing me, and I kind of just want to stay in one place for a bit."

Lindsey kicked the ground. "You're being a baby. You're not *that* hurt."

I shot back, "I guess I'd have to be flattened by a car for you to realize I was in pain."

She shook her head and stormed off again.

Maybe I was well enough to hitchhike, but my whole body was sore. I could barely get in and out of the tent; the idea of climbing in and out of cars, not knowing where we were going or where we were staying, didn't appeal to me at that moment. All I wanted to do was stop and heal. But my comfort was not on Lindsey's agenda.

While the four of us spent the day arguing, our mother had contacted a friend whose sister lived in France. Later that evening, when Lindsey called home, Mom gave her the name and phone number of the woman, who lived in Lille. She said that the woman would let us stay with her for a while. We just needed to get from Fréjus to Lille.

When Lindsey came back, she asked, "Would you be willing to hitchhike if you knew where we were going?"

I couldn't believe she was still pushing this. "What is up with hitchhiking?"

"Mom found us a place to stay in a town called Lille," she said. "If we go straight there by train, we can't afford to go to

Paris, and I really want to go to Paris. If we hitchhike, we'll save money."

There it was. Out of pure stubbornness, I emphatically stated, "I am not hitchhiking to Lille or to Paris. If we have a place to stay, I say let's go there, and then go home."

"Oh, come on. You can do this," Lindsey begged.

The more she wanted me to hitchhike, the more I dug in my heels. In the end, the next day we took a train to Lille. We never did make it to Paris. Years later, Lindsey got there via her daughter's high school choir. But over three decades later, she was still holding a grudge. Some families never get over their resentments. In hindsight, I should've relented. Our time in Lille was a bit tense.

In Lille, we were greeted at the train station by a small, frail woman accompanied by two boys, who appeared to be about ten and twelve years old. The woman was American and told us her name was Wendy. She then introduced us to her sons, Alexander and Paul, led us to her Volvo station wagon, and drove us to her home, which was in a small village on the outskirts of Lille.

Even before we reached her house, I had a feeling things were not quite right. She barely spoke to us and only conversed with her boys. When we arrived at her house, she showed us in and said, "I think it would be best if you all went sightseeing while I get things ready. Maybe come back in a few hours."

We kind of had an idea of how to get back to town and headed that way. I was still sore but had to grin and bear it. As we walked along, Matt said, "I don't think she really wants us to stay."

Lindsey looked back at the house. "Yeah, but what can we do now? We spent most of our money on the train," she glared at me pointedly, "to get up here, and we don't have a lot left over."

I knew I was to blame for the hitch in our circumstances and kept my mouth shut. Looking back, I would have been sore for a few days, but I could've sucked it up and hitchhiked. But Lindsey had sold our bikes for next to nothing, and she never owned her role in our predicament. If she'd gotten anything close to the value of the bikes, we would have had enough money to rest up *and* see Paris. Now it was clear that anything would've been better than the situation we found ourselves in.

Marc pointed out, "It wouldn't be so bad if we weren't in the middle of nowhere. I mean, there is nothing but farmland around here."

It was a desolate area. We were surrounded by flat fields, soaked in drizzle accentuated by howling wind. The bright homes of the Mediterranean were replaced by houses built of gray stone.

We returned to Wendy's house a few hours later and were greeted by her husband, Jacques, who was not happy to see us. During dinner, he didn't speak at all. The following morning, Wendy told us that we were no longer welcome at her home and needed to leave. So much for staying for a week.

She said, "I have contacted some friends of mine who live in Lille. They have a foreign exchange student from Oregon staying with them, and they said you could stay there until you're ready to go back to Amsterdam."

Lindsey asked, "Are they going to pick us up or should we figure out how to get there on our own?"

"I'll drive you over there in about an hour," said Wendy, and then she left the room to speak to her husband. I gathered that she was telling him we'd be gone soon.

After staying with so many gracious and hospitable people along the way, we'd come to believe everyone would want to host us. We were young and fun to be around—weren't we? I looked over at Matt. "I guess our dumb *lost American* act doesn't work all of the time."

Wendy was on her own when she drove us to her friends' house. Along the way, she opened up about her situation. Her husband was abusive, and she wanted out of the marriage. The only thing keeping her there was her boys. Lindsey, who was sitting in the front with her, talked to her the most. Meanwhile, the boys and I just listened. By the time we reached our destination, I would've been more than happy to sleep in a ditch rather than spend another night in Wendy's home.

Wendy pulled up to a beautiful, white, four-story house across the street from a park. She looked over at us and said, "This is where my friends live. Their names are Peter and Audrey.

Their daughter's name is Clair." She couldn't remember their exchange student's name. She went on to say, "They are very nice people and I think you'll enjoy your time here much better than at our house."

Wendy led us up to the door and rang the bell. As I stood on their porch, I wondered what kind of people could afford a house like this. When a man with a mop of curly hair and jovial face opened the door, I thought, *Someone like this.*

The man introduced himself as Peter and then waved us all into the front room, where his wife, daughter, and the exchange student waited for us. Peter had us introduce ourselves, and then offered us some coffee and cake.

From Wendy's Volvo to Peter's front room, everything had changed. We were welcomed with open arms. As we drank coffee and ate our cake, the foreign exchange student, Emma, a high school student from Salem, Oregon, leaned over and said to Matt, "These people are wonderful. Crazy, but wonderful."

Matt smiled. "I can do crazy."

For the next week, we hung out with Peter and his family. They fed us fresh fruit and rolls for breakfast, and dinners were everything from savory pies to roast beef. Every night after dinner, Peter pushed the furniture to one side, put on a Beatles LP, and said, "Now we dance to the Beatles."

For the next couple hours, all of us would dance, even Matt and Marc. Emma was right: they were wonderful people. Maybe a little eccentric, but wonderful. By the time we left for Amsterdam, the memory of being battered by a motorcycle and rejected by Wendy's family had faded. France would forever be dancing to the Beatles with the fab four: Peter, Audrey, Clair, and Emma.

The day before our plane was to depart, we took the train from Lille to the Amsterdam airport, where we spent the night in the main concourse with other travelers. We'd come full circle, and in fewer than twenty-four hours, we'd be landing in Seattle.

Without bicycles, we were traveling much lighter than when we arrived, but we looked pretty ragged. During our week at Peter and Audrey's we were able to get showers and do laundry, but there's only so much a washing machine can do. We'd been wearing the same three outfits for months. Between the dirt, sweat, road grime, and the usual wear and tear, our clean clothes were basically rags.

We were all rail thin, too. Peter and Audrey's delicious food put a little more meat on our bones, but it would take much more than a week of eating well before we'd regain a healthy weight. And we all had mad crazy hair. My short, curly hair had grown out into a huge bush. Lindsey's hair was long and straggly, and the boys both looked like Jeff Spicoli, the stoner from *Fast Times at Ridgemont High*.

As we boarded the plane for the flight back to Seattle, Marc said, "At least this time we won't have to steal any silverware!"

I looked over at him and asked, "Did you quit stealing when you said you did?"

Marc grinned. "What do you think?"

"Well, I want to think you quit, but I doubt it."

"I may have stolen the odd cola here and there. What really matters is that I didn't get caught."

I smiled. "You're an idiot."

He smiled back. "So are you."

Which is the closest we'd ever come to saying, "I love you."

Mom, the little girls, Meg, and Jake were all waiting for us at the gate as we got off the airplane. When they saw us, they all began laughing. As we approached them, Lindsey asked, "What's so funny?"

"You guys should see yourselves," said Mom. "All the other passengers looked so sophisticated, and then you four came out. You guys look like you're homeless."

I looked at the four of us. "Well...we're really glad to be home."

"Hey, let's get you guys back to our house, cleaned up, and then I'll take you out on my sailboat," said Jake.

"You got a sailboat?" I asked.

"Yeah, it's not very big, but it's big enough for all of us. While we're sailing, you can tell us all about your trip."

Jake's boat was docked at a wharf in Tacoma. It was indeed small but bigger than our four-person tent or two-door Escort, and in no time, we were sailing around Puget Sound, sharing all of our adventures. Sometimes we'd start laughing so hard we couldn't finish our sentences. Mom and the others just looked at us like we were nuts.

By the time Jake turned back for the wharf, the sun was beginning to set. It had been close to twenty-four hours since the sunrise in Amsterdam. As I watched the same day slowly come to a close behind the Olympic Mountains, I looked at Lindsey, Matt, and Marc and realized how much I loved them. I also knew I had to leave them.

Between my time in Brazil and Europe, I'd also realized that the world was an enormous, beautiful place, and that Willamette, Oregon was just a tiny, insignificant spot on the map. Hell, if it weren't a county seat, it wouldn't even be a spot on a map. To be truly free, I needed to find a way out of Willamette and out of Mom's house. I just needed an opportunity.

TIME TO GET GOING, TIME TO MOVE ON

My return to Willamette felt anti-climactic. For the better part of two years, I'd been working, saving, and planning for those two amazing trips, but now that they were over. I was back to square one—Willamette and my childhood home.

For a few weeks, it was nice to be around familiar people and places. A number of high school friends contacted me, and we began hanging out. I easily reverted back to my old habits of drinking and partying all night. However, I was uncomfortable with the choices I was making.

While I was in Brazil and Europe, I had no desire for alcohol. I hadn't quit drinking—hell, I was just twenty years old and wanted to enjoy life. I'd never really embraced recovery, or AA, but I was learning that alcohol just left me feeling blah.

During this time, I drank because everyone else was and I wanted to fit in. The combination of drinking again and lying to my family took a toll. Not a big enough toll to make me quit

(because I was still young and dumb). I had no intention of truly giving up drinking, but I did have every intention of getting
the hell out of Willamette. Then, one night, Macy took me to
go visit our high school friend, Angel, and I knew I needed to
leave for good.

I hadn't seen Angel since she'd dropped out of high school
our junior year. Macy had stayed in touch with her and told me
that Angel was now married, had a baby, and wanted to see me.

Before Macy took me to see her, she said, "I have to warn
you. Angel's not in a good place."

"Do you mean in her life, or where she's living?"

Macy hesitated. "Both, so brace yourself," she said, and then
she pulled up in front of Angel's apartment building.

Right away, I knew things were bad. The apartment was a
shitty complex near the city park that housed the town's drug-
gies. "She lives here?"

"I warned you," said Macy. She led me up to the second level of the building and into a unit with a front door that was
already propped open. In the darkened front room, Angel sat
smoking a cigarette next to a baby in a small cot. The whole
situation felt depressing, and icky. I wanted to get out of there
as soon as possible.

Before I could leave, Angel turned and said, "Laura, come
and meet my little boy."

With nowhere to run, I said, "You have a boy? That's
amazing," and went in and sat down.

This was late August, and the night was stifling hot, so the
apartment stank. I asked how she was doing, and she told me

how great everything was. Just from where she was living and how she looked, I knew she was lying. Her hair was stringy, and her teeth were rotting—all signs of meth use.

In Macy's car, after we left Angel's apartment, I said, "I don't think I can go back there."

"It's rough, but she needs friends right now," said Macy.

Before Macy pulled away from the curb, I looked up at Angel's apartment and said, "She needs more than that."

Seeing Angel only reaffirmed my desire to leave Willamette for good. I knew that if I stayed, there was a good possibility that I'd end up like her. I wasn't going to let that happen.

On Labor Day, Mom sat me down and told me I had two choices if I wanted to continue living in her house: I could either get a job or go back to school. I explained to her that I felt incapable of attending school, and that I'd begin looking for a job that week. My thought at the time was that I'd return to the fruit cannery.

Tami and Macy planned on getting an apartment in Salem and had invited me to move in with them. The three of us were figuring out how we could make it work when another opportunity knocked—and I answered.

It was the first day of the new school year. Matt and Marc were back in high school. Myrtle and Emily were still in elementary school, and Mom was back at work. Lindsey, who'd returned to working for the local political action group, was employed too, so I found myself alone in the house with not a lot to do. I made myself a cup of tea and sat down to read *The Oregonian*.

Out of curiosity, I turned to the Help Wanted ads to see if I qualified for anything. I really didn't think I'd find a job, but I was curious about what kind of jobs were out there. All of a sudden, an ad for a live-in nanny caught my eye.

The advertisement read: *Young Washington, D.C. couple looking for a nanny for their energetic four-year-old son. Two years childcare experience required.* At the bottom of the ad was a telephone number. I thought about the position for a couple of seconds, then made the call. I didn't know who or where I was calling, but something inside of me said, *Go for it.*

The phone was answered by a woman named Lillian, who told me her daughter had placed the ad. Lillian explained that she lived in Portland and was conducting the initial interviews. She asked me a few questions and then invited me to meet her in Portland for a formal interview. I said that I'd love to sit down and talk with her at her convenience. We chose to meet the next Monday at 10 a.m. at the Burger King right off of Terwilliger Boulevard in Portland. When I got off the phone, I looked at the cigarette scars on the countertop and realized that I may have just punched my ticket out of Willamette.

Later that afternoon, when Mom got home from work, I told her about the ad and that I felt this was a real opportunity. I knew Mom wanted me out of the house, and that I wouldn't get any pushback from her. Flossy, though, was a whole other story.

Flossy told Mom that she didn't want me to be a "domestic servant" and didn't think I should pursue the position. I thought that was rich. I'd been my mother's domestic servant for years. At least as a nanny I'd actually get paid.

The following Monday, Macy drove me up to Portland to meet with Lillian. I didn't really have any appropriate clothes for an interview, so I just wore Levi's, an oxford shirt, and Stan Smith Adidas. I looked like a preppy college student, and not the community college flunky that I was.

Macy and I arrived early and went into the Burger King, ordered a cup of coffee, and sat down. "How will you know who she is?" Macy asked.

As she was talking, a sleek silver Jaguar convertible pulled into the lot and a sophisticated older woman got out of the car. I pointed out the window and said, "I have a feeling that's her."

Lillian oozed wealth but seemed comfortable being in a Burger King. The two of us found a booth together and Macy went to wait for me in the car. Lillian asked me about my background, and I shared with her that I was the middle of nine children, that I had years of childcare experience, and that I loved adventure.

When Lillian was done asking questions, she invited me and Macy to follow her up to her house, where she wanted to phone her daughter in D.C. and have her speak to me. I went out to the car and told Macy the plan.

Lillian led us around the West Hills of Portland and into the wealthiest section of the city. As Macy kept pace with the Jag, she asked, "Where the hell are we going?"

"Like I fucking know?" I answered. "It's the West Hills, they're obviously loaded."

Lillian pulled into the driveway of a single-story home with tasteful landscaping. As we walked into the house, it became apparent that Lillian had great taste. The walls were painted a fresh cream, the carpet was plush, and there was an inground pool glistening in the sun out back. Lillian led us into the living room, offered us a drink, and then went to call her daughter, Lorena. A few minutes later, she returned with a phone and said that Lorena wanted to speak to me.

It was difficult to get much of an impression of Lorena over the phone, but from what I gathered, she was in her thirties and trying hard to sound young and hip. She explained that she and her husband both worked and that they needed childcare for their young son, David. She described David as a bright, energetic child who needed a lot of attention.

I immediately assumed that David was a little bit of a pill and explained that I was used to working with kids and had handled many challenges. She then told me they were Jewish and wanted to make sure that wouldn't be a problem.

I found this statement odd. I'd never really thought about Jews. Religious diversity in Willamette consisted of Protestants and Catholics, so I didn't have an opinion about Jews. After spending three months in Brazil with charismatic Christians and then visiting the Pope's house, I thought hanging out with Jewish people would be interesting.

I told Lorena that her family's faith practices really were of no concern to me. With that, she asked if I'd give the phone back to her mother, which I did. Lillian and Lorena talked for a few minutes and then Lillian told me that she'd get back to me after she checked my references.

By that Friday afternoon, Lorena offered me the job. She'd purchased me a plane ticket from Portland to D.C. that would depart in ten days' time. It was at this point that I learned that Lorena was married to Ken, who was a U.S. Congressman for Oregon.

Lorena explained that I'd be living in the heart of D.C. with an inside view of national politics. I couldn't believe this was all happening. I was really leaving Willamette and going to the city that spoke to me so profoundly at the end of our bicycle trip across the country. I was beyond giddy.

When I said yes to being David's nanny, I was saying yes to a new life. I had no idea what life in D.C. would look like, and I didn't know how I'd get along with complete strangers. I knew very little about the situation I was walking into.

Still, I knew what I was leaving behind. I was walking away from a self-image manufactured by my family, as well as the belief that Willamette was the center of the universe. I was finally seizing the opportunity that I'd been sensing would somehow come my way.

The night before I left for D.C., I sat on my window ledge, the same one where I'd spent so many hours looking for answers. The evening was warm and the air sweet. In the distance I heard the sounds of the mill and a radio playing down the street. I looked down at the streetlights, thinking of all the balls Matt, Marc, and I had thrown to each other over the years. I'd miss my little brothers and sisters, but I wouldn't miss my home. This house had too many ghosts and too many bad memories.

I told myself that once I got on that plane for D.C., I'd be taking my first step on a new journey. I needed to make the most of this opportunity and enjoy every moment.

And you know what? I did.

Three years before, when I'd read Martin Luther King's speech on the Lincoln Memorial, I wondered if I could dream, too. Everything I hoped for that night came to fruition. After I'd been working for Lorena and Ken for two years, they convinced me to go to college. Ken helped me get into George Washington University, and I became one of those college students I'd seen waiting in line in Georgetown.

I discovered that alcohol would never solve my problems and eventually quit drinking altogether. It wasn't easy, because I enjoyed hanging out in the Georgetown pubs with friends, but over time I learned how to accept life on life's terms.

A few years later I discovered the root of the world's beauty that I had glimpsed in Michelangelo's Pietà. My senior year at G.W., I took a class on the life and thought of Jesus, where I discovered it was Jesus all along. Not the Jesus Maris tried to pound into me. The Jesus who greeted me was the historical Jesus, and he changed my life.

How did this happen? Well, that's a much longer story for another book. In the end, this community college flunky received
her master's in divinity and became a Lutheran minister. Today
I am a pastor, wife, and mother of one beautiful little girl.

When Dad died that dark morning of February 21, 1984, I
felt hope for the first time. It took two crazy bicycle trips, with a
Brazilian adventure wedged in between, to discover what that
hope looked like. That little spark of hope that morning kept
me going through some pretty rough times. That same hope
spurs me on today. Hope is what allows me to dream, and over
time I have learned that dreams do come true.